£17-50

KT-165-158

Praise for the UK edition of

*Accomodating Brocolli in the Cemetary*

"Cook serves up a pleasantly diverting mishmash of word lists, puzzles, historical digressions and *Private Eye*–style howlers . . . as a browsable treat for self or others, it will fit that stocking-shaped gap in the gift market very neatly."

—Boyd Tonkin, *Independent*

"A serious study of orthography in the trendy form of a book of lists."

—*Times Literary Supplement*

"I started laughing as soon as I opened the book."

—Barry Cryer

"First-rate bedtime browsing . . . will surely find a place in many cultivated loos."

—Richard Jenkyns, *Prospect*

# Accomodating Brocolli in the Cemetary

*or why can't anybody spell?*

VIVIAN COOK

A TOUCHSTONE BOOK

PUBLISHED BY SIMON & SCHUSTER

NEW YORK   LONDON   TORONTO   SYDNEY

TOUCHSTONE
Rockefeller Center
1230 Avenue of the Americas
New York, NY 10020

First Touchstone Edition 2005

Originally published in Great Britain in 2004 by Profile Books Ltd

Published by arrangement with Profile Books Ltd

TOUCHSTONE and colophon are registered trademarks of Simon & Schuster, Inc.

For information regarding special discounts for bulk purchases,
please contact Simon & Schuster Special Sales at 1-800-456-6798
or business@simonandschuster.com

Designed by Nicky Barneby

Manufactured in the United States of America

10 9 8 7 6 5 4 3 2 1

Library of Congress Cataloging-in-Publication Data
Cook, V. J. (Vivian James).
[Why can't anybody spell]
    Accomodating brocolli in the cemetary, or, Why can't anybody spell? /
Vivian Cook.—1st Touchstone ed.
        p.   cm.
    "A Touchstone book."
    1. English language—Orthography and spelling—Problems, exercises, etc.
I. Title.
PE1145.2.C65   2005
421'.52—dc22                            2005041891

ISBN-13: 978-0-7432-7099-1
ISBN-10:    0-7432-7099-1

# INTRODUCTION
*Should We Worry About Spelling?*

\* \* \*

Many people argue that English spelling is terrible. George Bernard Shaw reckoned that the English "spell it so abominably that no man can teach himself what it sounds like." It is easy to find words like *their/there/they're* with the same sounds but different spellings. Some words have unique spellings all of their own, such as *colonel* and *yacht*. Fifteen-year-olds can't write ten lines without making at least one spelling mistake, and adults struggle with words such as *accommodate* and *broccoli* all their lives.

By contrast, Noam Chomsky, the greatest linguist of our time, claims the current spelling of English is "a near optimal system." He feels that spelling that departs from the pronunciation sometimes helps us to understand what we are reading. Silent letters like the "g" in *sign* connect one word to other words in which the letters are not silent, like *signature*; the fact that the past tense ending "-ed" is said in three different ways, "t" (*liked*), "d" (*played*), "id" (*waited*) but written only as "-ed,"makes clear their common meaning.

The difference between Shaw and Chomsky comes down to how they think spelling works. One of its functions is indeed to show the sounds of words. The word *dog* links the letters to the sounds one by one—"d," "o" and "g." Italian and Finnish use such links virtually all the time. But in English the correspondence between letters and sounds is usually far less straightforward. Sometimes one letter corresponds to several sounds; the letter "a," for instance, has three different sounds in *brat*, *bravo* and *brave*. Sometimes two letters link to one sound—the "th" in *thin* or the "ng" in *wrong*. The sequence of letters can be out of step with the sequence of sounds; the "u" in *guess* shows the pronunciation of the letter "g," which occurs *before* it. Our problems with spelling are often due to not knowing the rules, say the doubling of "c" and "m" in *accommodation* or the consonants that go before particular vowels—*cemetery* ("c" is pronounced "s" before "e") versus *camel* ("c" is pronounced "k" before "a").

With some written symbols, you either know what they mean or you don't, say "$," "#" or "%." You can't use the spelling to work out how they are said. The second function of spelling is, then, to show what words mean. Common words like *the* and *of* connect directly to their meanings in our minds, rather than being converted into sounds letter by letter. Unique words have to be remembered as one-off spellings, such as *sapphire* or *chamois* (shammy leather). Some systems of writing, like Chinese, work primarily by linking whole symbols to meanings in this way. To use English spelling, you have not only to connect letters and sounds but also to remember a host of individual words, whether frequent ones like *an* or unusual ones like *supersede*. In other words, English uses spelling both for sounds, as assumed by Shaw, and for meaning, as believed by Chomsky.

English spelling is far more systematic than most people suspect. The best-known rule, "I before e except after c," applies to only eleven out of the 10,000 most common words of English—eight forms of *receive*, plus *ceiling*, *receipt* and *perceive*. Other less familiar rules work far better, for instance the rule that a surname with the same pronunciation as an ordinary word can take a double consonant, *Pitt* and *Carr* rather than *pit* and *car*, or have an extra "e," *Greene* and *Wilde* instead of *green* and *wild*.

The great asset of English has always been its flexibility. Starting with a stock of letters borrowed from the Romans, the Irish and German tribes, it has evolved with the English language for 1,500 years. In the Old English spoken by the Anglo-Saxons every letter corresponded to a sound in words such as *fæder* (father) and *riht* (right). After 1066 the system had to cope with a deluge of words derived from French and Latin, such as *tricherie* (treachery) and *nice*. Over the centuries it has adapted words from many other languages, including *coffee* from Arabic and Turkish, *broccoli* from Italian and *sushi* from Japanese. Whatever the language a word comes from, English spelling can handle it.

At the same time, the pronunciation of English has been

changing. Some Old English sounds died out: the "h" (pronounced like Scottish "loch") in *riht* became the silent "gh" in *right*. Long vowels changed their pronunciation between Chaucer and Shakespeare: *wine* was once said as *wean*, *stone* as *stan*. Punctuation marks were introduced and their use gradually stabilized, the apostrophe last and most eccentric of all. Because of the changing pronunciation, the rules linking letters and sounds became more complicated and the number of eccentric individual words people had to remember increased. The sound-based spelling of the past tense in *barkt*, *changd* and *parted* gave way to the uniform meaning-based spelling "ed" in *barked*, *changed* and *parted*.

All this change and outside influence has meant that English spelling now presents a rich set of possibilities for our use and entertainment. Pop musicians call themselves *The Beatles*, *Eminem* and *Sugababes*. Novelists hint at dialects, *ax* (ask) and *tole* (told), and think up unusual book titles—*Pet Semetary* (Stephen King). Owners invent names for drugs like *Zyrtec* and for racehorses like *Sale the Atlantic*.

It is indeed important for the international use of English that it is *not* too closely tied to speech. People from Houston, Glasgow, Hong Kong or Bristol understand each other's writing but might well not understand each other's speech. Much world business uses written English although the writers are not native speakers. Over three quarters of research papers in biology are written in English, and more than half of all Web pages. Spelling and punctuation seldom betray whether an English-language newspaper comes from Santiago, Kuala Lumpur or Jerusalem, apart from the choice between American and British styles of spelling in words like *labor/labour*.

So do we need to get excited about the mistakes that people make with spelling? Mistakes don't necessarily prevent our understanding the message. We still know what *extasy*, *Mens Toilets* or *england* mean. Spell checkers can now handle most of these mistakes without any trouble. A mistake that interferes with the meaning of the message is more serious. The writer may need help or the spelling system itself may need modifying. Yet we hardly notice similar problems in speech: people are not sent to speech therapy for mispronouncing odd words. No one suggests that *spoken* English should be reformed because some people find it hard to say "th" sounds. The most talented writers make spelling mistakes. Keats once spelled *fruit* as *furuit*, Walt Whitman wrote *depressed* as *deprest* and Hemingway wrote *professional* as *proffessional*. Does this detract in any way from their achievements?

Our discussions of spelling often suggest that there is an ideal of perfect spelling that people should strive for. Correct spelling and punctuation are seen as injunctions carved on tablets of stone: to break them is to transgress the tacit commandments for civilized behavior. Spelling and punctuation can become an emotional rather than rational area of dispute. No individual or institution has ever had the right to lay down the rules of English spelling. Nor are public discussions usually based on accounts of how modern spelling actually works, but on the traditional rules handed down from the grammarians of the eighteenth century. Attempts to meddle with the spelling without this kind of factual basis have often been disastrous in the past, landing us with the "b" of *debt* and the "c" of *scissors*.

The English writing system is the rich and fertile creation of those who use English. Its rules are the ongoing living response to how people express their ideas in writing in an ever-developing and changing world. Rather than continually carping about the decline of the English language, as people have been doing since at least the sixteenth century, we should try to understand and develop the amazing resource that is available to us.

This book, then, celebrates the richness and resourcefulness of English spelling, taking examples from real-life use. Its contents are not set out in any particular sequence. There are tests on various aspects of spelling with answers at the back. Also at the back is a thematic guide for those who want to follow particular themes such as novel spellings, spelling mistakes or the history of spelling.

# THE ROUTE OF THE ENGLISH ALPHABET

\* \* \*

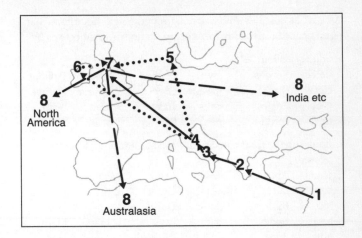

1. Phoenician (22 letters, no vowels), 8th to 1st centuries B.C.
2. Early Greek (24), 8th century B.C.
3. Etruscan (26), 6th century B.C.
4. Roman (26), A.D. 114
5. Germanic Runes (24), 4th to 7th centuries A.D.
6. Irish (25), 7th century A.D.
7. Old English (c. 24), 10th century A.D.
8. Modern English

The word *alphabet* itself comes from the Phoenician *aleph* ㄍ (ox—rotate 90° to see the horns) and *beth* 𐎤 (house).

# FLATTS AND SHARPES
*Spelling Surnames*

\*   \*   \*

As well as starting with a capital letter, English surnames are often spelled differently from ordinary nouns or adjectives by:

- **adding a silent "e"**

| | | | | | |
|---|---|---|---|---|---|
| bowls | Bowles | fry | Frye | trollop | Trollope |
| clerk | Clarke | green | Greene | young | Younge |
| coats | Coates | oaks | Oakes | wait | Waite |
| ford | Forde | penny | Penney | wild | Wilde |

- **doubling the final consonant** (and sometimes adding an "e" as well)

| | | | | | |
|---|---|---|---|---|---|
| angel | Angell | crib | Cribb | leg | Legge |
| bar | Barr | cuts | Cutts | lily | Lilley |
| bib | Bibb | done | Donne | lug | Lugg |
| bud | Budd | fag | Fagg | man | Mann |
| bun | Bunn | faithful | Faithfull | nun | Nunn |
| but | Butt | fat | Fatt | pot | Potts |
| car | Carr | fin | Finn | star | Starr |
| chapel | Chappell | flat | Flatt | tab | Tabb |
| club | Clubb | fur | Furr | war | Warr |
| cop | Copp | hog | Hogg | web | Webb |
| crab | Crabbe | kid | Kidd | wren | Wrenn |

- **using "y" instead of "i"**

| | | | | | |
|---|---|---|---|---|---|
| blithe | Blythe | miles | Myles | tie | Tye |
| crier | Cryer | pie | Pye | tiler | Tyler |
| kid | Kydd | smith | Smythe | wild | Wylde |
| kite | Kyte | tailor | Taylor | win | Wyn |

## Movie stars that fit the pattern

| | | |
|---|---|---|
| Randall Cobb | Leslie Mann | Brad Pitt |
| Johnny Depp | Demi Moore | Anthony Quinn |
| Sherilyn Fenn | Julie Parrish | Tim Robbins |
| Jack Lemmon | Sean Penn | Winona Ryder |

# GOURM KIT WITH HKPS:
*Classified Real Estate Ads*

\* \* \*

Before you buy property from a classified ad you need a training course in the abbreviations in American newspapers.

**Size**

| | | |
|---|---|---|
| 4br/den/2.5ba | 2.5 ba 2 gr | 2BR twnhme |
| 1,800 sf | 3bd | 2,380 s.f. |

**Rms**

| | | |
|---|---|---|
| bonus rms | Liv rm | mstr suite w/gas fp |
| formal din rm | weight rm | full warr. Bedrm |

**Kits**

| | | |
|---|---|---|
| gourmet kitch | gourm kit | huge kit |
| new kitc | new kitch | |

**Gars**

| | | |
|---|---|---|
| att gar | hkups | dbl gar |
| Carpt | RV prkng | |

**Special features**

| | | |
|---|---|---|
| 14 ft clgs frpl | Wood wraped | secluded PUD |
| Compl. updtd | windows | Excellent cond. |
| blt-in bkcases | Orig wd wk | Secure bld. |
| hrdwd flrs | appls stay | |

**Amenities**

| | | |
|---|---|---|
| golf crse | PvtLndspdGrounds | lge wooded lot |
| pvt bch | IngrdPoolw/spa | cent. air |
| shy 3 Acres | great nghbrhd | big bkyd |
| 24-hour drmn service | Prvt setting | perfect lndscp. |

**Prices**

| | |
|---|---|
| $900 dwn | 30 yr fixed mt |

# DIFFICULT WORDS SPELLING TEST

\* \* \*

Circle whichever one is right. Answers on page 151. Note in some cases *Webster's Unabridged* gives more than one possibility as a variant.

| | | | |
|---|---|---|---|
| 1. | dessicate | desiccate | desicate |
| 2. | ecstasy | exstacy | ecstacy |
| 3. | milenium | millenium | millennium |
| 4. | dumbel | dumbbell | dumbell |
| 5. | seperate | separate | seperete |
| 6. | necesary | neccesary | necessary |
| 7. | peddler | pedler | pedlar |
| 8. | minuscule | miniscule | minniscule |
| 9. | adress | adres | address |
| 10. | accomodate | accommodate | acommodate |
| 11. | iresistible | irresistable | irresistible |
| 12. | liaison | liaision | liason |
| 13. | harras | harrass | harass |
| 14. | definitely | definately | difinately |
| 15. | ocurence | occurrence | occurence |
| 16. | embarass | embaras | embarrass |
| 17. | pronounciation | pronounceation | pronunciation |
| 18. | independant | independent | indipendent |
| 19. | questionnaire | questionairre | questionaire |
| 20. | wiered | weird | wierd |
| 21. | brocolli | broccolli | broccoli |
| 22. | refering | referring | refferring |
| 23. | recommend | recomend | reccommend |
| 24. | cemetery | semetary | cemetary |

# NOAH WEBSTER
*On Spelling (1828)*

\* \* \*

From the period of the first Saxon writings, our language has been suffering changes in orthography. The first writers, having no guide but the ear, followed each his own judgment or fancy; and hence a great portion of Saxon words are written with different letters, by different authors; most of them are written two or three different ways, and some of them, fifteen or twenty. To this day, the orthography of some classes of words is not entirely settled; and in others, it is settled in a manner to confound the learner and mislead him into a false pronunciation. Nothing can be more disreputable to the literary character of a nation, than the history of English orthography. . . .

In regard to the acquisition of our language by foreigners, the evil of our irregular orthography is extensive, beyond what is generally known or conceived. . . . the English language, clothed in a barbarous orthography, is never learned by a foreigner but from necessity; and the most copious language in Europe, embodying an uncommon mass of science and erudition, is thus very limited in its usefulness. . . .

As our language has been derived from many sources, and little or no systematic effort has been made to reduce the orthography to any regularity, the pronunciation of the language is subject to numerous anomalies. Each of our vowels has several different sounds; and some of the consonants represent very different articulations of the organs. That part of the language which we have received from the Latin, is easily subjected to a few general rules of pronunciation. The same is the fact with most of the derivatives from the Greek. Many words of French retain their French orthography, which leads to a very erroneous pronunciation in English; and a large portion of our monosyllabic words of Saxon origin are extremely irregular. . . .

# THE SKIRT WITH THE SHIRT
*Words with Two Faces*

\*    \*    \*

English often incorporated the same word from two languages with slightly different spellings. Sometimes the meanings differ so much that no one would notice their common source. Sometimes they still bear some resemblance of meaning.

### Scandinavian
Words from the Viking settlements in England (about 850–1066 A.D.) came in alongside the Old English equivalent. Often the difference is between an English "sh" pronunciation and a Scandinavian "k":

    shirt/skirt, ditch/dyke, child/kid, bench/bank, shatter/scatter, shriek/screech

### Anglo-Norman
The French spoken in England after the Norman Conquest (1066) came from Normandy rather than Paris. Hence English often has pairs of words from both sources, for example the Anglo-Norman "w" versus the Parisian "g":

    ward/guard, wage/gauge, warden/guardian, wile/guile,
    war/guerrilla (possibly Spanish), warranty/guarantee

Others:

    catch/chase, cattle/chattel

**Which of these pairs originally from the same word do you still think of as having similar meanings?**

| | | |
|---|---|---|
| differ/defer | canvas/canvass | whole/hale |
| metal/mettle | person/parson | of/off |
| plait/pleat | price/prize | broach/brooch |
| temper/tamper | calibre/caliper | plain/plane |
| course/coarse | discreet/discrete | flower/flour |
| artist/artiste | blond/blonde | draught/draft |
| feint/faint | human/humane | lightening/lightning |
| troop/troupe | arch/arc | |

# SPELLING AND MEANING

\* \* \*

While most people see English spelling as connecting speech sounds with written letters, Noam and Carol Chomsky claim that it is a system for connecting symbols with meaning, rather like Chinese. It is the meaning that is shown directly in "$," "%," "&," "-ed" and "+," not the pronunciation. The advantages of this are:

- **silent letters show connections between words with related meanings in which the silent letter *is* pronounced**

| | | | |
|---|---|---|---|
| "g" | sign/signature | "b" | bomb/bombard |
| "k" | know/acknowledge | "n" | autumn/autumnal |
| "t" | soften/soft | "c" | muscle/muscular |
| "d" | handkerchief/hand | "w" | two/twin |

- **keeping spelling the same connects word families despite different pronunciations**

| | | | |
|---|---|---|---|
| "c" | critic/criticize | "i" | decide/decision |
| "e" | extreme/extremity | "a" | nation/national/ |
| "c" | medicate/medicine | | nationalist |
| "a" | telegraph/telegraphic/ | "o" | photograph/photographer |
| | telegraphy | "g" | sagacity/sage |
| "o" | one/only | "i" | child/children |
| "ea" | meaning/meant | "a" | image/imagine |
| "e" | college/collegiate | "s" | revise/revision |

- **keeping word endings the same, despite different pronunciations, preserves the common meaning**

"ed" past tense   said "d":   opened, uttered, wagged, lodged . . .
                 said "t":   liked, rushed, watched . . .
                 said "id":  waited, parted, insisted . . .
"s" plural       said "s":   cups, units, packs . . .
                 said "z":   miles, pounds, times . . .
                 said "iz":  wages, matches . . .

- **some exceptions where spelling changes, not meaning:**

| | | |
|---|---|---|
| four/forty | high/height | jelly/gelid |
| fire/fiery | speak/speech | strategy/stratagem |

# LITTERARY SUSTINENCE
*Poets' and Writers' Mistakes*

\* \* \*

These spelling mistakes (and some punctuation mistakes) by famous poets and writers are mostly taken from editions showing the original manuscripts of their writings.

*Emily Dickinson*
**words:** extasy, extatic, boquet, Febuary, nescessity, nescessary, unannointed, teazing, bretheren, independant, boddice, shily, witheld
**apostrophes:** does'nt, did'nt, it's solemn abbeys, it's dripping feet

*Ezra Pound*
**words:** tarrif, diarhoa, damd, supercedes, indespensible, sustinence, devines (verb), assylum, wierd, assininities
**apostrophes:** cant, dont, isnt, wouldnt, thats, wont

*William Wordsworth*
**words:** eughtrees, questined, craggs, vullgar, untill, lillies, pennyless, impressd, fellt, receved, anixious, plungd, th (the), whith (with), strage (strange)
**apostrophes:** your's

*W. B. Yeats*
**words:** proffesrship, origonol, descreetly, a complementary allusion, devided, immitation, peculearitys, beleive, sattelites, salid (salad), ceifly, seperate, litterary
**apostrophes:** 'till, Unwins reader, Mathers letter

*Walt Whitman*
**words:** staid (stayed), opprest, propt, almanack, deprest
**apostrophes:** dont, surpass'd, havn't

*Virginia Woolf*
**words:** pannelled, naiv
**apostrophes:** cant, shant, wont, dont, wouldnt, isnt, thats, your a woman of genius, I feel sure your worse, Prima Donna's, a childs highchair, a donkeys head, fathers state, the Fabians discourse

*Ernest Hemingway*
**words:** archiologist, condences, mirricle, proffessional, ungry, mistyque, useing, Hawaia, loseing
**apostrophes:** didnt, dont, couldnt, in ones life time

Many of these mistakes are essentially the same as those on today's Web pages. Some may have been a spelling variant at the time the person was writing or may, indeed, have been deliberately chosen for various reasons. The four mistakes in the first ten lines of "Ode to Autumn" compare with the 1.6 found on average in every ten lines of fifteen-year-old children's essays.

*John Keats*

### ODE TO AUTUMN *(manuscript)*

Season of Mists and mellow fruitfulness
Close bosom friend of the maturing sun
Conspiring with him how to load and bless
The Vines with fruit that round the thatch eves run
To bend with apples the moss'd cottage trees
And fill all furuits with sweeness to the core
To swell the gourd, and plump the hazle shells
With a white kernel; to set budding more
And still more later flowers for the bees
Until they think wam days with never cease
For Summer has o'erbrimm'd their clammy cells

# THE THREE-LETTER RULE

\* \* \*

Many short English words have the same pronunciation but different spellings.

| | | | | | |
|---|---|---|---|---|---|
| oh | owe | an | Ann | we | wee |
| by | bye, buy | in | inn | be | bee |
| to | two, too | no | know | I | eye, aye |
| or | ore, oar, awe | so | sew, sow | | |

## THE RULE

Words that are closely tied into the sentence, like "to" and "so"—called "structure" words—have fewer than three letters. Ordinary "content" words, like nouns and verbs, etc., can be any length from three letters upward ("bee" and "sew"), but must *not* have fewer than three letters:

| One- or two-letter structure words | More-than-two-letter content words |
|---|---|
| They went *by* boat. | They went to *buy* a boat. |
| She flew *to* Paris. | They had *two* children. |
| Gold *or* brown dirt. | Gold *ore*, brown dirt. |
| *Oh* dear. | What do I *owe*? |
| *No*, yourself. | *Know* yourself. |
| I think *so*. | I think: *sew*. |
| *We* men must stand tall. | *Wee* men must stand tall. |
| *Be* safe. | *Bee*-safe. |
| *I* drop. | *eye*-drop. |

## EXCEPTIONS

**content words with two letters:** go, ax, ox, hi; spelling of musical notes (do, re, mi, etc.) (but compare doh ray fah soh lah), pi, id; letter names (a, b, c . . . ); acronyms, AA, UN, etc.; printer's terms en, em.

**Scrabble players' exceptions (unusual two-letter words):** aa, ai, ba, bo, bu, jo, ka, ky, od, om, oo, qi, ri, xi, ut . . .

**Some words have an "extra" letter to show they are content words:** add, egg, ell, odd, ebb, err, ill, owe.

# STAGES IN CHILDREN'S
# DEVELOPMENT OF SPELLING

\*   \*   \*

1. **Prewriting.** Many children start by making marks that look like letters but do not form words.

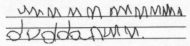

2. **Sound-based writing.** Children relate letters to sounds.
   - **letter names:** The names of the letters are useful in the early stages.
     soge soggy · seds seeds · ran rain · bik bike · nit night
     bot boat · flu flew · tha they · He did in his sleep died
   - **letters and sounds** (phonemes): Children try to make spelling fit the pronunciation of words.
     strabree yorgoat
     He dropted his samwisch
     she had a wobily tooth
     a little girl colde Lucy
   - **missing "n"s:** Children persistently leave out "n"s, perhaps because they do not "hear" them until they start to read.
     figz fingers      lad land      feheg fishing
   - **accents.** Children have problems in relating a non-standard accent to spelling "l," "th," etc. The following are from children who speak the Hoosier dialect of southern Indiana (source Treiman, 1993):
     pritty · min men · thim them · fit feet · nels nails · keng king · rilee really · pen pin · beg big
3. **Pattern-based writing:** Finally, children have to learn the patterns of English spelling that are *not* to do with the sounds of the word, such as:
   - **correct spelling of past tense "ed."** Children take some time to realize that the spelling of the past tense "ed" stays the same whether it is pronounced "t" as in "washed," "d," "played" or "id," "sorted." Even by eight years of age they are still getting this ending only 57 percent right.

# FROM CWEN TO QUEEN
*How Spelling Changed*

* * *

The spelling of individual words has changed considerably over the past thousand years, as this sample shows. Dates come from citations in the *Oxford English Dictionary*.

| | |
|---|---|
| **magic** | 1386 magyk, 1390 magique, 1490 magyque, 1590 magicke, 1642 magick, 1776 magic |
| **doubt** | 1225 dute, 1300 doute, 1483 dowte, 1559 doubt |
| **yacht** | 1557 yeaghe, 1616 yaught, 1630 yaugh, 1645 yought, 1660 Jacht, 1666 yaucht, 1673 yacht |
| **asparagus** | 1000 sparagi, 1558 asparagus, 1580 sparage, 1601 asparagi, 1711 sparrowgrass |
| **island** | 888 iland, 900 ealond, 1275 illond, 1320 yland, 1546 islelandes, 1585 iland, 1598 island |
| **hiccough** | 1580 hickop, 1581 hikup, 1621 hick-hop, 1626 hiccough, 1635 hecup, 1671 hiccup |
| **subtle** | 1050 sotyle, 1400 sutill, 1422 sutil, 1566 subtle |
| **queen** | 893 cwen, 1205 quene, 1290 quyene, 1400 qwhene, 1591 queene, 1622 queen |
| **knight** | 893 cniht, 1250 knicht, kniȝt, 1369 knyght, 1400 knight, 1411 knythes |
| **perfect** | 1290 parfit, 1387 parfiȝt, 1477 parfight, 1552 parfecte, 1580 perfect |
| **cemetery** | 1387 cimitorium, 1460 cymytery, 1480 cimiteri, 1601 cemitory, 1644 cemetery |
| **scissors** | 1384 sisoures, 1400 sisours, 1530 sycers, 1440 sysowe, 1568 scissoures, 1809 scissors |
| **whale** | 893 hwæl, 1220 qual, 1330 whal, 1386 whale |

**REASONS FOR CHANGE**
- French influence after the Norman Conquest: queen, island
- deliberate Latin-based spelling: subtle, perfect, doubt
- loss of sounds: "gh," knight; "h," whale
- odd ideas about words: sparrowgrass, shamefaced (<fast)

# TYPES OF WRITING SYSTEMS

* * *

**CHARACTER-BASED** *(symbols link directly to the meaning)*
**Chinese** 中文      中国 (China) 一 (1) 二 (2) 三 (3)
                     星 期 一 (Monday)
**MINOR ENGLISH USE** & @ # ☺ + 1 % 27 = π $ ✔ ✗
**SYLLABLE-BASED** *(each symbol links to a whole syllable)*
**Japanese kana**      にほん (Japan) い ち (1) に (2) さ ん (3)
                     げつようび (Monday)
**CONSONANT-BASED** *(letters link to consonants only) (right to left)*
**Arabic** العربية      الجزائر (Algeria) ١ (1) ٢ (2) ٣ (3)
                     يوم الاثنين (Monday)
**Hebrew** עברית      ישראל (Israel) א (1) ב (2) ג (3)
                     יום שני (Monday)
**MINOR ENGLISH USE:** no 1 had n e brsl sprts (texts)
**ALPHABET-BASED** *(letters link to all sounds [phonemes], both consonants and vowels)*
**Italian** Italiano      Italia (Italy) uno (1) due (2) tre (3)
                     lunedì (Monday)
**Greek** Ελληνικά      Ελλάδα (Greece) ένα (1) δύο (2) τρία (3)
                     Δευτέρα (Monday
**Finnish** suomi      Suomi (Finland) yksi (1) kaksi (2) kolme (3)
                     maanantai (Monday)

**APPROXIMATE NUMBER OF USERS OF DIFFERENT TYPES OF WRITING SYSTEMS IN THE WORLD (MILLIONS)**

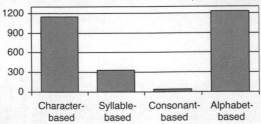

# KRUSTY'S KUSTOM KOLORS
*Spellings with "k"*

\* \* \*

At the beginning of a word, a "k" sound corresponds either to the letter "c" (before "o/a/u/r/l") or to the letter "k" (before "e/i") or to "q" (in words sounding "kw"). Many businesses have used "k" for "c" in product names, etc., since at least the 1920s, when Louise Pound said, "All in all, there is no mistaking the kall of "k" over our kountry, our kurious kontemporary kraving for it, and its konspicuous use in the klever koinages of kommerce."

**Krazy businesses**

Krazy Korner

Kid Krazy

Krazy Cool Kustomz

R-U-Krazy Inc.

Krazy Koyote Bar & Grill

Krazy Kapers

**Krusty businesses**

Krustys Power Wash

Krustee's Pizza

Golden Krust

Krusty's Bar

Tropical Krust

Krustys Bakery

**Kar firms**

Konsigned Kar Korner

Kar Krafters Inc.

Kut Rate Kar Rental

Klassy KARZ

Danca's Kar Korral Inc.

Kar Kolors

Kar Konnection

Kwality KARS

**Kwick businesses**

Kwick Kopy

Kar Kwik

Kwik Ticket Bellaire

PIK Kwick

Kwik Cash Check Cashing

Kwik Kill Exterminators

Kwik-Kopy Inc.

Kwik-Wash Laundries LP

**Houston, Texas**

Keyboard Kastle
Kay's Kurios
Culinary Kreations
Gotcha Kovered
Hair Korral

Allie Kat Candles
Aqua Kare Inc.
Hartz Krispy Chicken
Breakfast Klub
Kustom KutPG

# TEST
## *American or British Style of Spelling?*

\*   \*   \*

|  | American | British | Both |
|---|:---:|:---:|:---:|
| 1. honour | ☐ | ☐ | ☐ |
| 2. meter | ☐ | ☐ | ☐ |
| 3. mediaeval | ☐ | ☐ | ☐ |
| 4. catalyze | ☐ | ☐ | ☐ |
| 5. labor | ☐ | ☐ | ☐ |
| 6. waggon | ☐ | ☐ | ☐ |
| 7. favour | ☐ | ☐ | ☐ |
| 8. neighbor | ☐ | ☐ | ☐ |
| 9. travelling | ☐ | ☐ | ☐ |
| 10. encyclopedia | ☐ | ☐ | ☐ |
| 11. moustache | ☐ | ☐ | ☐ |
| 12. color | ☐ | ☐ | ☐ |
| 13. paralyse | ☐ | ☐ | ☐ |
| 14. extol | ☐ | ☐ | ☐ |
| 15. center | ☐ | ☐ | ☐ |
| 16. dialogue | ☐ | ☐ | ☐ |
| 17. molt | ☐ | ☐ | ☐ |
| 18. analyse | ☐ | ☐ | ☐ |
| 19. plow | ☐ | ☐ | ☐ |
| 20. sulphur | ☐ | ☐ | ☐ |
| 21. vigour | ☐ | ☐ | ☐ |
| 22. skeptic | ☐ | ☐ | ☐ |
| 23. catalog | ☐ | ☐ | ☐ |
| 24. enrol | ☐ | ☐ | ☐ |
| 25. archaeologist | ☐ | ☐ | ☐ |
| 26. fulfil | ☐ | ☐ | ☐ |
| 27. glamour | ☐ | ☐ | ☐ |
| 28. theatre | ☐ | ☐ | ☐ |
| 29. saviour | ☐ | ☐ | ☐ |
| 30. distill | ☐ | ☐ | ☐ |
| 31. litre | ☐ | ☐ | ☐ |

*Answers on page 152.*

# POSSITIVE ENTHOUSIASM
*Why Can't Students Learn to Spell?*

\*   \*   \*

College students still make mistakes with spelling. Typical problems are:

- not knowing when to double consonants: usefull, accomodate, refering, fueled, finnished
- confusing vowels: independant, relevent, compulsary
- confusing words with the same spelling: knew/new; or that sound similar: quite/quiet
- making unusual spellings regular: well-payed, senario

accomodate
acheive
affect ("effect")
ammount
appendicies
aproved
asses
   ("assess")
avocets
   ("advocates")
bare ("bear")
beginers
catagories
choosen
compulsary
concieve
confidantly
controlls
corect
correspondance
definately
dictionarys

discrepency
dissappear
eazily
effect ("affect")
elabourate
embarassing
enthousiasm
forsee
grater ("greater")
hinderance
illicit ("elicit")
independant
intergrated
intermidiate
knew ("new")
layed out
lerners
minites
occassion
occurance
percieved
possitive

principle
   ("principal")
profficiency
pronounciation
pyschology
questionaires
quite ("quiet")
refering
relevent
senario
sence ("sense")
seperate
sited ("cited")
their ("there")
to ("too")
tradditional
universitys
usefull
vocabularly
well-payed
where ("were")

# OBJECTS USED AS LETTERS IN SHOP SIGNS

\* \* \*

# THE RITE NITE LITE
*Spellings in "ite"*

\*   \*   \*

For some time a small group of words spelled with "ght" has had alternative novel spellings in "ite"—"nite," "rite" and "lite" and so on. These are used more in informal writing in notices, etc., than in books or newspapers. However, they are also found in the names of many businesses and organizations, some-times suggesting cool modernity: "Nite Hawks," sometimes old-fashioned solid virtues: "Done-Rite." They seem to have been on the margins of spelling reform for many years. Isaac Asimov and Melville Dewey (Dewey Decimal System Classifica-tion) were both supporters of "nite."

**Nite**

| | |
|---|---|
| Nite Hawks | Video Nite |
| Good Nite Inns | *Late Nite Catechism* (play) |
| Nite Iceboat Racing | *Boyz Nite Out* (disk) |
| Skule Nite | Nite Rider |
| Friday Nite Improvs | good nite irene (pop group) |
| Phantasy Nite Club | Karaoke Nite |

**Rite**

| | | |
|---|---|---|
| ShopRite | ValuRite | Load Rite |
| Rite Spot Cafe | Flow-Rite | Maid-Rite |
| Kleen-Rite | Kut-Rite | Thermo-Rite |
| Sta-Rite | Pik Rite | Rite Rhythm |
| Done-Rite | Dun-Rite Kitchens | |

**Fite**

| | | |
|---|---|---|
| Fite Club | food fite | Fitehouse |
| Fite Bite | | |

**Combinations**

| | |
|---|---|
| Rite Aid Nite Time Cold Formula | All Nite Party Rite |
| Spell—Rite—Nite | Rite Lite Rounds |
| Lite-Rite Light Controller | No Bull Fite Nite |
| NITE-IZE LITE LOK | We Roll-Rite Through the Nite! |

# A JOB FOR JOB
*Homographs*

\*   \*   \*

Words with the same spelling but different pronunciations and meanings are homographs. Some involve changing to a capital letter, for example "Polish/polish." Obviously, some may not be homographs in all accents of English.

bass (fish/instrument)
sow (pig/to sow seed)
tier (one who ties/level)
wind (air/turn around)
reading (to read/
   Massachusetts city)
furrier (more furry/fur shop)
degas (let gas out/French
   painter)
axes (tools/dimensions)
do (verb/musical note)
row (line/argue)
hare (animal/religion)
tear (liquid from eye/rip)
invalid (chronically sick/
   not valid)
dove (past of "dive"/bird)

job (occupation/biblical
   character)
pasty (pie/pale-faced)
does (carries out/female deer)
lead (go in front/metal)
minute (small/time unit)
putting (golf stroke/placing)
wound (injury/turned around)
polish (make shiny/from
   Poland)
sewer (person who
   sews/waste pipe)
buffet (food/push about)
sake (drink/for the sake of)
bow (bend/weapon)
mobile (movable/city)
moped (past of "mope"/vehicle)

*Now try to read these sentences aloud without hesitating.*

1. Playing the bass with a furrier sound, the furrier fancied eating a bass.
2. The pasty-faced man took a pasty from the buffet.
3. Putting on his jacket, he putted for the green.
4. Reading in Reading, mobile in Mobile, he drank a sake for the sake of old times.
5. Sewing in the sewer, the sewer tears tears from his eye.
6. The minute numbers made him number and number by the minute.
7. Job's job was as a jobbing gardener.

# AMERICAN VIEWS OF SPELLING

*   *   *

"It is a damn poor mind that can think of only one way to spell a word." *Andrew Jackson, U.S. president*

"Nothing you can't spell will ever work." *Will Rogers*

"Correct spelling, indeed, is one of the arts that are far more esteemed by schoolma'ams than by practical men, neck-deep in the heat and agony of the world." *H. L. Mencken*

"Don't write naughty words on walls if you can't spell." *Tom Lehrer, "Be Prepared"*

"Take care that you never spell a word wrong. Always before you write a word, consider how it is spelled, and, if you do not remember, turn to a dictionary. It produces great praise to a lady to spell well." *Thomas Jefferson to his daughter*

"Many writers profess great exactness in punctuation, who never yet made a point." *George Prentice*

"Spelling counts. Spelling is not merely a tedious exercise in a fourth-grade classroom. Spelling is one of the outward and visible marks of a disciplined mind." *James J. Kilpatrick*

"You're not a star until they can spell your name in Karachi." *Humphrey Bogart*

"Add one little bit on the end. . . . Think of 'potatoe,' how's it spelled? You're right phonetically, but what else . . . ? There ya go . . . all right!" *Vice President Dan Quayle, correcting the spelling of "potato"*

"English orthography . . . is archaic, cumbrous and ineffective; its acquisition consumes much time and effort; failure to acquire it is easy of detection." *Thorstein Veblen*

"They spell it Vinci and pronounce it Vinchy; foreigners always spell better than they write." *Mark Twain*

"You teach a child to read, and he or her will be able to pass a literacy test." *George W. Bush*

# KURUPT PLAYAZ
*Pop Group Names*

\*  \*  \*

All of the following groups have been in the U.S. Top 40 (apart from the Be Sharps).

*Ways of inventing names for pop groups*

**letter names for syllables** (a device often found in children's spelling): Eminem, X-wife, Qfx, V-male, Pay As U Go, L8r

**number names for words:** 2 Sweet, 4clubbers, 2Pac, 6 Teens, 2gether

**informal spoken form of "and" as " 'n'"** (a frequent form in ordinary speech): Red 'n' White Machines, Paps 'n' Skar, Bald 'n Spikey

**"k" for "c"** (a traditional novel spelling in English, often found in business names, see p. 14): Outkast, Uniklubi, Kaskade, Kontakt, Uncle Kracker, Krossfade, Kurupt, Boomkat

**"c" for "ck":** Roc Project

**"k" for "ch":** K-os

**"z" for "s"** ("z" is an alternative for "s" in a limited number of English words but not for plural "s"): Jay-z, 4 Girlz, Airheadz, Az Yet Feturing Peter Cetera, Ralph Myerz, Rascalz, Sporty Thievz Featuring Mr.woods, Youngbloodz, Def Rhymz, Young Gunz, Outlawz, Beginerz

**consonant doubling:** G-spott, Gang Starr, Puddle of Mudd, Caramell, Dizzy Lizzard

**"y" for "i":** Zyx, Sylver, Sylk-e, Fyne, Kevin Lyttle, Silkk The

Shocker Featuring Mystikal, Tymes 4, Profyle, Prymary Colorz, Big Tymers, Cyn, Def Rhymz

**"i" for "y" and vice versa:** Kandi, Cyndi Lauper

**puns or sound-alikes:** Raymzter, Reelists

**"a" for "ar"/"er"/"our"** (apparently associated with "rebellious" tough speech): Rhythmkillaz, Floorfilla, Twista, Platinum Bound Playaz, Gorillaz

**actual spelling "mistakes"** (fairly rare, as this might suggest ignorance): Poloroid

**"lil' " for "little":** Lil' Kim, Lil' J., Lil' Mo, Lil' Flip

**"x" for "ex"/"cs"/"cks":** Xploding Plastix, Rednex, Xscape, X-ecutioners, Xtraordinary, Trance Jax

**odd punctuation** (using apostrophes, capitals, etc): @junkmail, &g, S.h.e., 'n Sync, W-inds, Fu:el, D!-nation, Di-rect, B'z4

**"da" for "the":** Da Hool, Da Mob, Da Muttz

**lack of word spaces:** Wiseguys, Americathebeautiful, Amillionsons, Goodshirt

**"f"/"gh"/"ph":** Ruff Endz, Phreeworld, Phixx, Phish

**extra letters:** Skandaali

**others:** Afro-dite, Absoluuttinen, Nollapiste, Hoobastank, Fab For, Floetry, Dis L'heure, 2 Zouk, Plusch, Salt5, Tiktak, Tenacious D, Tatoo, Zed, UGK, Jemini, Eye Q, Ginuwine, Be Sharps (the Simpsons)

*Make Up Your Own Pop Group*

Choose one word from each column; the second column is optional.

| | | |
|---|---|---|
| He!!o! | 2 | Ph8 |
| Phiting | 'n | Koldz |
| Kreetchas | 8 | Karavan |
| Screemin' | of | Cheez |
| Hunnee | II | Kriminalz |
| Muthaz | Woz | Xit |
| Dirti | 4 | Peece |
| Ir8 | R | Sistaz |
| Phantastik | LikZ | Kryin' |
| Medsyn | B | B-trayaz |
| &U | C | Krusade |

# FROM "HWY" TO "WHY"
## Old English Spelling
\* \* \*

Differences in spelling between Old English (circa 5th to 11th centuries A.D.) and modern English

- Old English "þ/ð"(thorn and eth) = modern "th," "þing" (thing)
- Old English "æ" often = modern "a," "wæter" (water)
- Old English "sc" = modern "sh," "scield" (shield)
- Old English "cg" = modern "dg," "ecg" (edge)
- Old English "h" sometimes = modern "gh," "miht" (might); sometimes lost, "hring" (ring)
- Old English "hw" often = modern "wh," "hwȳ" (why)
- Old English "c" often = modern "ch," "stenc" (stench), or "k," "folc" (folk), or "q," "cwēn" (queen)
- Old English "g" often = modern "y," "gēar" (year)
- Old English "f" often = modern "v," "heofone" (heaven)

Here are some words of Old English, as typically spelled before the Norman Conquest in 1066. Which words do they correspond to today?

| | | | |
|---|---|---|---|
| 1. æsc | 13. gēar | 25. niht | 37. tōþ |
| 2. bedd | 14. hecge | 26. ofen | 38. þe |
| 3. cīese | 15. heofone | 27. riht | 39. þicce |
| 4. cild | 16. hlāford | 28. sǣ | 40. þing |
| 5. circe | 17. hors | 29. sceaft | 41. þrī |
| 6. clǣne | 18. hring | 30. scēap | 42. þurh |
| 7. cwēn | 19. hwæl | 31. scield | 43. tunge |
| 8. dēofol | 20. hwȳ | 32. scilling | 44. wæter |
| 9. ecg | 21. lēoht | 33. scip | 45. weg |
| 10. fisc | 22. miht | 34. seofon | 46. weorþ |
| 11. flǣsc | 23. mōnaþ | 35. siextig | 47. woruld |
| 12. folc | 24. nacod | 36. stenc | 48. wrītan |

*Answers on page 153.*

# DE DOCTAH'S AMBEETIONS
*Accents of New York*

\*   \*   \*

Showing accents by adapting the spelling is less common in modern American novels than in British ones (see p. 116 for London). Here are some depictions of speech in New York, mostly showing ethnicity rather than a New York accent itself.

**O. Henry, *The Four Million*, 1906**

De agent what represents it pussented me with a dollar, sah, to
distribute a few of his cards along with de doctah's. May I
offer you one of de doctah's cards, sah?

Where, now, will ye be drivin' to? . . . 'Tis drivin' for pleasure
she is. . . . I want to see four dollars before goin' any further
on th' thrip.

If yer don't know de guy, and he's tryin' to do de Johnny act, say
de word, and I'll call a cop in t'ree minutes. If yer does know
him, and he's on de square, w'y I'll spiel yer de bunch of hot
air he sent yer.

**Jonathan Lethem, *The Fortress of Solitude*, 2003**

I tole you. . . . Now we gotta fight. . . . Think Gus be gonna
proteck you forever?

**John Dos Passos, *Manhattan Transfer*, 1925**

A man vat is ambeetious must take chances. Ambeetions is vat
I came here from Frankfort mit at the age of tvelf years, und
now that I haf son to vork for.

Oh I'm afwaid I was indiscweet to say that . . . I'm dweedfully
indiscweet.

You kin juss come an git it. . . . Soivice at this toime o night.
. . . If my husband was aloive he wouldn't have the noive.

# OPINIONS ON AMERICAN VERSUS BRITISH STYLES OF SPELLING

\* \* \*

"The differences between American and, say, British English spelling are quite modest." *Donald Cummings, 1988*

"England and America are two countries divided by a common language." *Attributed to George Bernard Shaw*

"Although American customs in spelling have never differed widely from British, such differences as have existed have nevertheless been treated as though they were matters of some moment, as though the Americans had really done something startling to spelling." *George Krapp, 1960*

"All that can be safely asserted of the contemporary conventions of standard Canadian English spelling, when there is a British/American choice, is that the norm is not yet to choose either indifferently for the same word in the same text." *T. Pratt, 1993*

The Australian Government Style Manual "arbitrates on many of the currently variable points of English spelling, generally adhering to what is often thought of as British rather than American practice." *P. Peters and A. Delbridge, 1989*

"In spelling as in vocabulary the tendency to innovation and playfulness is noticeably stronger in American than in British English." *Peter Strevens, 1972*

"A somewhat lengthy list of words that are spelled differently in the United States and Britain can be generated from published discussions on this topic. . . . What is most noticeable about this list is not its length but its shortness relative to the full vocabulary of the English language." *Richard Venezky, 1999*

# OPEN 8:30 TIL 11:00
*Uses of "Till," " 'Til," "Til" and "Until"*

\* \* \*

"Till" was a separate word from "until" throughout the history of English and was mostly spelled "till" since 1200 A.D. Sometimes it is treated as an abbreviation for "until" and so spelled with an apostrophe, " 'til," and/or a single "l" "til." *Webster's* gives "til" as a variant.

"I LAUGHED 'TIL I CRIED"

Shop 'til your Personal Shopper drops

Extra 10% OFF WITH THIS VOUCHER Valid 'til 8th JUNE 2003

Lunch from 12 untill 5

"Scissor sharp script will have you laughing til' your short back and sides split" TOTAL FILM

WE'LL BEAT ANY COMPETITOR'S PRICE 'TIL IT HURTS! so call us last!

*Frequency of Forms of "Till" in Google*

|                    | Google      |
| ------------------ | ----------- |
| Until              | 93.0%       |
| Untill             | 0.6%        |
| Till               | 3.8%        |
| Til/'til           | 3.7%        |
| Number of examples | 57,730,000  |

It is almost impossible to eliminate the Scandinavian word "til" from the Google scores, hence overestimating it considerably. Similarly, the British noun "shop till" distorts the figures for "till."

27

One of the decisions in printed text is how to divide words that are too long with hyphens.

*Eccentric Hyphens*

| | | |
|---|---|---|
| mans-laughter | male-volence | rear-ranged |
| fin-ding | pos-twar | ever-yone |
| unself-conscious | fru-ity | da-ily |
| rein-stall | berib-boned | se-arched |
| ch-anges | spi-noff | bre-akfast |
| the-rapist | pain-staking | af-ternoon |

## RULES FOR HYPHENATION

British style tends to divide words up into meaningful parts: American style tends to divide words up into syllables. However, dictionaries vary considerably, many British ones using "American' style."

| American | British | American | British |
|---|---|---|---|
| struc-ture | struct-ure | mys-tery | myst-ery |
| trium-phant | triumph-ant | rec-tangle | rect-angle |
| knowl-edge | know-ledge | impor-tant | import-ant |
| geog-raphy | geo-graphy | infor-mation | inform-ation |
| inspira-tion | inspir-ation | commu-nity | commun-ity |
| desensi-tize | desens-itise | | |

**Some syllable divisions in American business names**
Bayou Ka-Nex-Shun Home Cooking
Ar'Ke-Tek-Cher Inc.

*Awkward Divisions*

**MAN SHOT IN TIT
FOR TAT KILLING**

*Irish Newspaper headline*

# DISCRETE HANDYCAP FACILITIES
*Foreign Hotels*

\*   \*   \*

While these come from hotels in Italy, Greece and Spain, similar facilities are doubtless available in other countries.

*Your Hotel*

nize, cozy and elegant three stars hotel · Would you like a discrete, warm and friendly welcome? · handycap facilities · fantasically placed for access to all the major attractions · modern and confortable hotel renued in 2001 · very clen and comfortable · All ages wellcome · spectacular panoramic views over the three famous golf course's · Italian garden with statues and secolar trees · important lobby in the low plant · nise environment · a managment that loves the ways of an ancient tradition of ospitality · Smiles and kidness are waiting for you · it rappresents an experience born to estabilish a direct contact between guests and the hotels · Emersed in Nature · Prices qouted are per night · Confortable rooms toghether with its renowned cuisine make the hotel an ideal residence in a unique place · Familiar cooking · Our fine cuisine, wich uses products from the region, toghether with our attentive service, meets the exacting standardts of our guests · a reserved and particular house, located directly on his own sandy beach · on leaving we'll refound you the cost of the 1 day ticket

*Your Room*

shared bathroom, for baoys or girls · insonorized windows · rooms With matrimonial beds · Closed captioned tv · hydromassage tube in suites · wasin in rooms · with luxury en-suits bathrooms · Bathtub At Bathroom · The accomodation has all the comforts and high quality implants · furnished with antique mobiles · Recently painted a-fresh by the owner · Brite new · In exclnt cond · Hi ceils · Children's' Bed Available · All Rooms Have Central Air · and a lot of beautiful things as accesorys · Littered with details · Thelephone · Tv-colors · The mini bar is adeguately substituted

## Some of the Facilities
espectacular garden · landcaped lawns · bay sitting · Lit grass tennis court · Peddle-boats, canoes, houseboats · snorking · Escursions · 18 holes golf gruond, riding school, clay pingeon shooting · Bycicles at your disposal from the Hotel for your pleasur · the quiteness you need · indipendent entrance · adjacent to the principle structure · In the immediate nearby guests can find tennis courts · Start the day in a positive mood with our sel service buffet · Make a gift with venetian artesany · Campings, Bed and breakfast, Rent Houses, Hostels · busparking places

## The Whole Package
In the next pages you will find three localities, where for only characteristics in their kind, for confort, tranquillity and landscaped harmony, they are between beautifulst of Italy. You will find apartments in rent, furnishes to you with taste, complete of every type of confort, every the most exasperated requirement, can be satisfied. The property puts highly to disposition of local referenziate persons qualitati to you, where a vacation is one mrs vacation and the satisfaction staff is better the provisions for a journey for one optimal working resumption. We wait for you for a visit without engagement, in order to show the fabulous places to you and the apartments that we propose to you
YOU RESERVE YOURSELVES ENDURED HERE

An indespensable leg of a journey for those who want to know the "Magna Grecia," a necessary stop off for pilgrims of eastern spirit, a votive place dear to phylosophers who went looking for knowledge even within the volcanos. Agrigento was a meeting point for all the civilizations that have influenced the scene both externally and internally of Sicily and its proud inhabitans.

# LIL' SPYDER
*American Show Dogs*

\*   \*   \*

These dogs have all competed in recent U.S. dog shows.

**lack of word spaces**
   Mistymoor, Gonewiththewind, ShengCheeRightOnTarget,
   Meadowsbrookspatrioticbanner
**letter and number names**
   Y Not Simon, C. Clearly, Xtreme Hero, For-U-To-N-V,
   IT HAD 2 BE YOU, Bells R Ringing, B MY VALENTINE
**"'n" for "and"**
   Cheese-N-Crackers, Step N'Style, Up N'Adam, Lucy N Sky
   Diamonds, Up-N' Atem, Buttons 'N Bows, Top Hat N'Tails
**"n" for "ing"**
   Dancin Desparado, Hunka Burnin' Love, Gettin' Jiggy with it,
   I'm Just Chillin', Travelin' Man, Sumthin To Talkabout, Dig
   N' The Dream
**conventional "novel" forms**
   Hi Caliber Bullet, Mr. Saturday Nite, Brite Bernice,
   Nite Autumn, Hi Sierra, Sno Storm, Midnite Magic
**"lil'"**
   Rockin' Lil' Rascal, Lil Sassy Kassy
**various puns**
   Turn the Paige, Oh Oh Seven, Son Also Rises, Knot-A-Yacht,
   Bear Necessities, Steel the Show, Love Bytes, Boy Named
   Sioux, Blow Ye Aweigh, Speckle & Hyde, Look's Like Reign
**others**
   Bumble Brie Blue, Whimsical Winafred, One Formy Master,
   Ice Krusher, One Tuff Cookie, Megnificent, The Wiz Kid,
   Chicklett, Time To Rocon Roll, Mys Tory, Razaldasal Dolli,
   Xelena, Khlassic Hicliff, Kwontum Leap, Bar Nun,
   Khan-Frontation, Lotsa Spots, Shakn Not Stirrd, Spyder

# SILENT LETTERS

\*   \*   \*

Silent letters may indicate: different words: "whole/hole," "plum/plumb"; "long" vowels: "rid/ride," or "hard" consonants: "guest/gesture"; different forms of the same word: "resign/ resignation." In English, only "j," "o" ("colonel"?), "v" and "y" cannot be silent.

**A** artistically, dramatically, stoically, musically, romantically · **B** climb, numb, comb, thumb, crumb, debt, doubt, subtle · **C** acquit, czar, indict, Connecticut, muscle, scissors, Tucson · **D** grandson, handkerchief, sandwich, handsome, Wednesday · **E** rite, fame, enclose, bridge, careful, cemetery, hope, corpse · **F** halfpenny · **G** though, light, reign, champagne, diaphragm, high, gnaw · **H** hour, hurrah, khaki, Gandhi, heir, exhaust, Thames, ghost · **I** business · **K** know, knot, knife, knickers, knell, knight, blackguard, knock · **L** salmon, psalm, almond, calf, folk, yolk, calm, talk, Lincoln · **M** mnemonic · **N** autumn, solemn, damn, hymn, monsieur, column, chimney · **P** corps, pneumonia, pseudo, ptomaine, receipt, Thompson · **R** myrrh, diarrhoea, February · **S** island, viscount, Illinois, aisle, debris, bourgeois, fracas · **T** ballet, Christmas, gourmet, rapport, asthma, listen, castle · **U** guest, guitar, catalogue, tongue, dialogue · **W** sword, whore, answer, Norwich, two, wrist · **X** faux pas, Sioux · **Z** rendezvous, laissez-faire, chez

### CAUSES OF "SILENT" LETTERS

*historical change:* the sound has dropped out over time but the spelling has not changed: light, hope, knot · *addition of letters:* the letter was added to make the spelling more like French or Latin: debt, victual, island · *difficult sound combinations:* handkerchief, sandwich · *word borrowing:* the word was originally taken from another language: champagne, khaki, myrrh

# SPELLING GAMES
*Set 1*

* * *

## Hangman

1. One player thinks of a word and writes it as a series of dashes instead of letters, for example: _ _ _ _
2. The other player(s) have to guess what the word is by suggesting letters—"Does it have any 'c's?"
3. If the guess is correct, the first player substitutes the letter for the appropriate dashes. _ _ c _
4. If the guess is wrong, the first player adds one element of the hangman drawing, starting with the pole.
5. The game finishes either when the word is complete or the hangman drawing is finished and all the other players have been hanged.
For the squeamish, the drawing can be the Stop Sign, completed in eight steps.

## Guggenheim

1. Players choose (a) a set of five different categories, say, places, first names, vegetables, cars and sports, and (b) a word five or six letters long, say, "praise."
2. Each player has to provide a word for each category starting with each letter of the target word, i.e.:

|  | P | R | A | I | S | E |
|---|---|---|---|---|---|---|
| **place** | Poland | Rio | Aden | Ireland | Santiago | Essex |
| **first-name** | Paula | Rita | Arthur | Ian | Sam | Edith |
| **vegetable** | potato | radish | avocado | — | spinach | — |
| **car** | Porsche | Renault | Alfa Romeo | — | Saab | E-type |
| **sport** | polo | riding | archery | — | swimming | — |

3. Scoring is either 1 point for each word supplied or 1 point for each word no one else supplies, each blank counting 1 minus point.

GEORGE BERNARD SHAW
*Preface to R. A. Wilson,* The Miraculous Birth of
Language, *1941 (extracts)*

\* \* \*

Professor Wilson has shewn that it was as a reading and writing animal that Man achieved his human eminence above those who are called beasts. Well, it is I and my like who have to do the writing. I have done it professionally for the last sixty years as well as it can be done with a hopelessly inadequate alphabet devised centuries before the English language existed to record another and very different language. Even this alphabet is reduced to absurdity by a foolish orthography based on the notion that the business of spelling is to represent the origin and history of a word instead of its sound and meaning. Thus an intelligent child who is bidden to spell *debt*, and very properly spells it d-e-t, is caned for not spelling it with a b because Julius Caesar spelt the Latin word for it with a b. . . .

. . . the waste does not come home to the layman. For example, take the two words *tough* and *cough*. He may not have to write them for years, if at all. Anyhow he now has *tough* and *cough* so thoroughly fixed in his head and everybody else's that he would be set down as illiterate if he wrote *tuf* and *cof*; consequently a reform would mean for him simply a lot of trouble not worth taking. Consequently the layman, always in a huge majority, will fight spelling reform tooth and nail. As he cannot be convinced, his opposition must be steam-rollered by the overworked writers and printers who feel the urgency of the reform.

Though I am an author, I also am left cold by *tough* and *cough*; for I, too, seldom write them. But take the words *though* and *should* and *enough*: containing eighteen letters. Heaven knows how many hundred thousand times I have had to write these constantly recurring words. With a new English alphabet replacing the old Semitic one with its added Latin vowels I should be able to spell t-h-o-u-g-h with two letters, s-h-o-u-l-d with three, and e-n-o-u-g-h with four: nine letters instead of eighteen: a saving of a hundred per cent of my time and my typist's time and the printer's time, to say nothing of the saving in paper and wear and tear of machinery. . . .

I could fill pages with instances; but my present point is not to make lists of anomalies, but to show that (a) the English language cannot be spelt with five Latin vowels, and (b) that though the vowels used by English people are as various as their faces yet they understand one another's speech well enough for all practical purposes, just as whilst Smith's face differs from Jones's so much that the one could not possibly be mistaken for the other yet they are so alike that they are instantly recognizable as man and man, not as cat and dog. In the same way it is found that though the number of different vowel sounds we utter is practically infinite yet a vowel alphabet of eighteen letters can indicate a speech sufficiently unisonal to be understood generally, and to preserve the language from the continual change which goes on at present because the written word teaches nothing as to the pronunciation, and frequently belies it. . . .

My concern here, however, is not with pronunciation but with the saving of time wasted. We try to extend our alphabet by writing two letters instead of one; but we make a mess of this device. With reckless inconsistency we write *sweat* and *sweet*, and then write *whet* and *wheat*, just the contrary. Consistency is not always a virtue; but spelling becomes a will-o'-the wisp without it. . . .

If the introduction of an English alphabet for the English language costs a civil war, or even, as the introduction of summer time did, a world war, I shall not grudge it. The waste of war is negligible in comparison to the daily waste of trying to communicate with one another in English through an alphabet with sixteen letters missing. That must be remedied, come what may.

# A THORO PROGRAM
*Did U.S. Spelling Change Work?*

\*   \*   \*

In 1898 the National Education Association (NEA) listed twelve words whose spelling should be reformed. Have they succeeded more than a hundred years later?

*Percentage of NEA Spellings on the Web*
This includes sites with British spelling, which seldom use these spellings (apart from "program" in the computer sense). It also fails to show the common use of these spellings in informal street notices, etc.

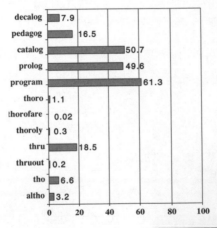

# FNOMNL 4EN JUNK
## American License Plates

\* \* \*

Unusual spelling is often used to personalize car license plates.

### Numbers for Letters or Words

| | |
|---|---|
| CYNICL1 | 1NTSTND |
| SEEUL8ER | 22 NICE |
| EZ4ME | 2BENVD |
| 2HOT4U | 4EN JUNK |
| PD4BYEX | 4GETIT |
| O2BINLA | 2FAST4U |
| 10SPRO | CD8D |
| 1BUG2C | W84ME |
| 81TCH | |

### Leaving Out Letters

| | |
|---|---|
| HIP CHC | CHZHED |
| FNOMNL | QUIKNSS |
| XPIRED | WNDW95 |

### Letters for Words or Syllables

| | |
|---|---|
| XTAZ | IFLUBYU |
| CRZY 4U | ETBLVR |
| O2BNLA | 1BLU BYU |
| 9WONWON | CYCOPTH |

### Others

| | |
|---|---|
| YA HOO | YESLORD |
| 88 KEYS (Liberace) | |

# K'YARDS AND SICH THINGS
*Southern Accents*

\* \* \*

In *Huckleberry Finn*, Mark Twain claims to use "the Missouri negro dialect; the extremest form of the backwoods Southwestern dialect; the ordinary 'Pike County' dialect; and four modified varieties of this last." Which of these four groups do you think the following characters belong to?

*Jim:* I didn' know dey was so many un um. I hain't hearn 'bout none un um, skasely, but ole King Sollermun, onless you counts dem kings dat's in a pack er k'yards. How much do a king git?

*Huck Finn's Pap:* I says look at my hat—if you call it a hat—but the lid raises up and the rest of it goes down till it's below my chin, and then it ain't rightly a hat at all, but more like my head was shoved up through a jint o' stove-pipe.

*Jake Packard:* What I say is this: it ain't good sense to go court'n around after a halter if you can git at what you're up to in some way that's jist as good and at the same time don't bring you into no resks. Ain't that so?

*Old man:* I've done considerble in the doctoring way in my time. Layin' on o' hands is my best holt—for cancer and paralysis, and sich things; and I k'n tell a fortune pretty good when I've got somebody along to find out the facts for me.

*Tom Sawyer:* I hain't ever done you no harm. You know that. So, then, what you want to come back and ha'nt ME for?

*Mrs. Hotchkiss:* You all hearn me: he's crazy, s'I; everything shows it, s'I. Look at that-air grindstone, s'I; want to tell me't any cretur 't's in his right mind 's a goin' to scrabble all them crazy things onto a grindstone, s'I?

Nowadays it is felt that the more accurately such spelling reflects an accent, the more it biases the reader towards thinking the character illiterate and uneducated. In Jonathan Lethem's portrait of Brooklyn, *The Fortress of Solitude*, for example, about the only examples of accent spelling seem to be "ax" for "ask," "tole" for "told" and "proteck" for "protect."

# GENES FOR JEANS
*English Homophones*

\* \* \*

As several speech sounds can correspond to each letter in English, many words have the same pronunciation but different spelling (homophones), the source of many puns and rhymes. Of course many homophones depend on the word being said with a particular accent.

allowed/aloud
banned/band
beer/bier
boarder/border
boos/booze
brews/bruise
ceiling/sealing
cent/scent/sent
chews/choose
cite/site/sight
colonel/kernel
cops/copse
days/daze
dear/deer
die/dye
doe/dough
earn/urn
ewe/yew/you
father/farther
fisher/fissure
great/grate
grosser/grocer
hair/hare

hear/here
idle/idol
jeans/genes
key/quay
knot/not
knows/nose/noes
liar/lyre
lode/load
meatier/meteor
mussel/muscle
one/won
ore/or
owed/ode
pail/pale
pair/pare/pear
paw/pore
paws/pause
pedal/peddle
plum/plumb
rains/reins/
    reigns
rapped/wrapped/
    rapt

rite/right/write/
    wright
roes/rows/rose
sell/cell
sighs/size
soul/sole
stake/steak
stalk/stork
suite/sweet
swayed/suede
tacks/tax
taught/taut
tea/tee
throne/thrown
toe/tow
vein/vain/vane
weak/week
whales/wails/
    Wales
which/witch
whole/hole
wrap/rap
yoke/yolk

# THE E-CANCELLATION TEST

* * *

Some letters can be all but invisible in normal reading. Cross out all the letter "e"s in these short passages. Go straight through the passages; do not have second thoughts; do not go back or check your answers.

A. At the beginning of the twentieth century, there was a large farm near Los Angeles called the Hollywood Ranch. A few decades later, it was one of the most famous places in the world. The first movies were made in New York on the East Coast. But, as they used the light of the sun, the advantages of Los Angeles soon became apparent, where there were at least three hundred and fifty days of sun every year as well as picturesque natural scenery such as mountains, beaches and desert. After its heyday in the nineteen-thirties and nineteen-forties, Hollywood had to turn to television films before getting back to the blockbusters that dominate movie houses today. However, its position as the place that produces most films has been overtaken by Bollywood in India.

B. Grace Paine lived in an isolated cottage for most of her life. In middle age she came to London and was astonished at city life. Best of all she loved her cooker with its row of controls. One day she told me about her amazing cooker. She had left her whole evening meal in the oven; at five o'clock the electric clock would switch it on and by seven a three-course meal would be ready to welcome her home. I almost envied her. But when we next met she related what had actually occurred: however automatic your cooker, you still have to remember to turn it on.

*Answers and explanation are on page 154.*

# AMERICAN AND BRITISH STYLES OF SPELLING

* * *

In many cases American style has one spelling for a word, while British style has two (often with different meanings—"meter"/"metre"). Many countries vary between the two styles, for example Australia and Canada.

| American -or | British -our | Exceptions |
|---|---|---|
| color, favorite | colour, favourite | Am: glamour |
| **American -old** | **British -ould** | |
| mold, smolder | mould, smoulder | Am: shoulder |
| **American -er** | **British -re** | |
| center, theater | centre, theatre | Am: acre, ogre |
| **American -ize** | **British -ise** | |
| analyze, apologize | analyse, apologise | Brit: capsize, seize |
| **American -se** | **British -ce** | |
| defense, offense | defence, offence | Brit: advice/advise |
| **American -og** | **British -ogue** | |
| catalog, dialog | catalogue, dialogue | |
| **American -ll** | **British -l** | |
| fulfill, counsellor | fulfil, councillor | |
| **American -e** | **British -ae** | |
| feces, anemia | faeces, anaemia | |

**Inconsistent American and British spellings**

LONDON CENTER COLLEGE

*"Center" in London, England*

University Square 4 Theatres
1 STARSK YAND HUTCH

*"Theatres" in Madison, WI*

**American -l**
jeweler, woolen

**British -ll**
jeweller, woollen

## ONE-OFF DIFFERENCES BETWEEN WORDS

| American | British | American | British |
|----------|---------|----------|---------|
| pajamas | pyjamas | karat | carat |
| skeptic | sceptic | sulfur | sulphur |
| tire | tyre/tire | jail | jail/gaol |
| check | cheque/check | ax | axe |
| disk | disc/disk | plow | plough |
| story | story/storey | whiskey | whisky (Scotch)/ whiskey (Irish) |
| mustache | moustache | | |
| aluminum | aluminium | | |
| z "zee" | z "zed" | | |
| | | draft | draught/draft |
| | | curb | curb/kerb |

## LO-COST GLAMO-NIT
### Businesses and Products
\* \* \*

**Number-name spellings**
> Turn 4 Pizza, 2 Hot 4 Ice, 4 Ever Nails, 4 Runners Only,
> Nails & Tan 4 U

**Letter-name spellings**
> B-secure Locksmiths, The Four Cs, Esso, Xpert Stationers,
> EXS, Just FX, Pow-R-Jac, Fax-U-Back Services

**Initials**
> Jaycee Fruits, Essanelle Hair, Emangee Clothing, Teecee
> Cleaners, Gee Jay's Pet Marts

**Letter substitutions**
> *"n" for "ng"*: Stormin Records, Talkin' Loud
> *"n" for "and"*: This 'N' That, Heads 'N' Extras, Plain n Fancy,
>    Snip 'N' Shape, Chris 'N' Alice, Roots N Fruits
> *"ite" for "ight"*: Northern Lite Scentsations, Nite-Cap Tavern,
>    Hi-Lite Candles, Cut-Rite Barber Shop, Kleen Rite, Plumb
>    Rite, Dee Lite Bakery, Girlz Nite Out
> *"hi" for "high"*: Toyota Hi Lux, Hi-Power, Hi-Style, Hi Tec
>    Autos, Hi-Spec Opticians
> *"lo" for "low"*: Lo Cost Foodstores, Hilo Offset, Lospred
> *"flo" for "flow"*: Flo-Rite, Crossflo, Doorflo, Freflo
> *"nu" for "new"*: Nuchem, Nuvox Electronics, Nu Twist
> *"a" for "er/ar"*: Betaware, ComputaTune, Mastascrew, Supa
>    Shop, Supadriv, Supatravel, Solaglas Windscreens
> *"o" for "of"*: Wood-O-Cork, Cleen-O-Pine, Rentokil
> *"o" for "or" or "our"*: Flav-o-Lok, Glamo-Nit
> *"k" for "k/ck"*: Krooklok, Hotpak, Bloc-Kote

**1920s American examples (Louise Pound)**
> Pret-O-Lite, Ra-dee-O, U All Kno After Dinner Mints,
> Uneeda Biscuit, Phiteezi Shoes, Rinkelaid, U-Rub-It-In

# SERIOUS AND FRIVOLOUS
# SPELLING REFORM

\*   \*   \*

### Classic Satire, Doubtfully Attributed to Mark Twain
In Year 1 that useless letter "c" would be dropped to be replased
either by "k" or "s," and likewise "x" would no longer be part of
the alphabet, apart from the kase of "ch," which will be dealt
with later. Year 2 might reform "w" spelling, so that "which"
and "one" would take the same konsonant, wile Year 3 might
well abolish "y" replasing it with "i" and Iear 4 might fiks the
"g/j" anomali wonse and for all.

Jenerally, then, the improvement would kontinue iear bai
iear with iear 5 doing awai with useless double konsonants,
and Iears 6–12 or so modifaiing vowlz and the rimeining voist
and unvoist konsonants. Bai Iear 15 or sou, it wud fainali bi
posibl tu meik ius ov thi ridandant letez "c," "y" and "x"—bai
now jast a memori in the maindz ov ould doderez—tu riplais
"ch," "sh," and "th" rispektivli.

Fainali, xen, aafte sam 20 iers ov orxogrefkl riform, wi wud
hev a lojikl, speling in ius xrewawt xe Ingliy-spiking werld.

### Cut Spelling (CS) 1998
Som peple fear spelng reform wud mean spelng caos (as if
english spelng wer not alredy caotic). Th flexbility of th CS concept minmizes that danjer. CS is not a rijid systm, but a
synpost pointng to th omission of redundnt letrs as th most
practicl and advntajus way of modrnizing english spelng.

### Regularized Inglish, Axel Wijk, 1969
By the adoption ov such a system of spelling az Regulaized Inglish it wood be possible to lay down definit rules ov pronunciation for the Inglish language, which wood make it considerably
eazier for children to lern to read and write. In aul probability it
wood lead to a saving ov at least wun year's wurk for aul
scoolechildren.

# THE "I" BEFORE "E" RULE

\* \* \*

| **THE USUAL RULE:** *"i" before "e" except after "c"*

Test it out on this sample.

1. recieve/receive
2. niece/neice
3. grief/greif
4. believe/beleive
5. wiegh/weigh

6. ceiling/cieling
7. sieze/seize
8. biege/beige
9. percieve/perceive
10. field/feild

*Answers:* "ie" words; 2 niece, 3 grief, 4 believe, 10 field; the rest are "ei" words.

The rule applies only when "ei" goes with long "ee" ("eel") not with the "ay" ("pay") sound of "beige" or with "ay" plus silent "g": "eight."

**THE EXTENDED RULE:** *"i" before "e" except after "c" when "ei" is said with a long "ee" sound*

However, there are still exceptions:
- some words have "ei" rather than "ie" despite having the long "ee" sound: seize, caffeine
- plural "-ies": currencies, policies; diphthongs: society, science; when "c" is said as "sh": sufficient, ancient

---

**PERCENTAGE OF MISTAKES ON WEB PAGES**

| | | | | | |
|---|---|---|---|---|---|
| niece | 8.7% | perceive | 1.9% | caffeine | 2.9% |
| deceive | 2.5% | receive | 1.8% | receipt | 0.6% |
| conceive | 2.3% | seize | 1.7% | ceiling | 0.3% |

The only words with "cei" in their spelling in the top 5,000 for American English in the Brown corpus are: received, receive, receiving, ceiling, conceived, receives. Get these six right, and you won't need the rule very often.

# OMG ur cooooool
## Chat Rooms
\* \* \*

**Mistakes**
suside, castore oil, mimick, dissapointed, attrack, masker-
ade, potiential, meen to, saty awake, condeming, expecdency,
sypathize, refering, removeing, carryoke

**Initialese** (see p. 95)
lmnsbbo, OMG, brb, lol, bbl, gtg, rotk, nlol, thx, lmao, pm,
ty, im, bf, alc, nyc, wtc, wtf

**Leaving Out Vowels**
pls, ppl, mayb

**Short Forms Common in Computer**
**Mediated Communication (CMC)**
u, ur, c, n, r, y, k, p

**Expressing Extra Emotion**
hahahahah, sooooooooooo complicated, awwwwww, hhehehe,
hellllooo, haiiiiiiiii, naaahhh, grrrr shhhhhhhhhhh,
heyyyyyyyyyy, Pwoooohoooo, who is
gayyyyyyyyyyyyyyyyyyyyyyyyyyy?????????????????????????????,
soooooooooooooooo cooooool, woohoo, excuuuuuuse me
plzzzzzz, backkkkkkkkkkkkkkkkkkkkk, lalalala, hugssssss

**Others**
wat is ya problem, lotsa, l8r, hai (hi), wafor, wots up, gawd,
wassup, wat's up?, dat

**Sample**
A: i like soundtracks more than real music.
B: evil isnt always a bad thing
C: how can evil not be bad lol
C: that's why it's evil
C: heheheh
B: trust me . . .

# A 2 B IN A KLASSY KAB
*Taxicab Names*

\* \* \*

**Letter names and number names**

| | | |
|---|---|---|
| Y-Drive Taxis | E Z Taxi | Tony Xpress |
| L O Taxis | Go2 Cars | AirportLimo 2 Go |
| Xpressair | R-Cars | U-wana Taxi |
| Uneed | A2b Taxis | Xklusiv |
| Cabs 4 U | T4 Taxis | Cabs 4 Kids |
| Wair2 Travel | U Need A Taxi | |

**Puns**

| | | |
|---|---|---|
| B-Line Taxis | Air & Back | Fareway Taxis |
| All-Ways Taxis | | |

**Uses of "k" for "c"**

| | | |
|---|---|---|
| McKab Taxis | Kiddie Kruises | Kipling Kab |
| Kwikasair | Kidz Karz | Klutch Kargo |
| Kwik Cars Ltd | Kazy's Cabs | |
| City Kabs | Klass Kars | |

**Initials**

| | | |
|---|---|---|
| A.S.A.P. Taxis | Jay-Gees | P.D.Q. Taxis |

**Familiar novel spellings**

| | | |
|---|---|---|
| Rite Taxi | Starlite Taxi | Air-n-Port Cars |
| Comfi Cars | Airport Carz | Top Flyte Taxi |
| Speedicars | Taxifone | |
| Out 'n About Shuttle | Airports "R" Us | |

**Others**

| | | |
|---|---|---|
| Parceline | AL On Time | Bizzi Citiwide |
| Afaster Taxi | Kestral Taxis | Grabacab |
| Wideopen Air-n-Port Cars | Supacars | 1st Andycabs |
| | Gaz Cabs | Cozy Cars |

Excellancy
Happicabs
Air-Connex
Intime Private
    Hire
Jeteck
Croozer Cab

Aircomuter
Luxecabs Ltd
    Caffe De Taxi
HandiCabs
Ekco Taxi's
Ms Taxi
New-Moow Taxis

ACAB
Zed Cars
Taxifast
Bettacars
Exxtra's Limousine
    Service

# HAS AMERICAN SPELLING IMPROVED?
## The Lewis and Clark Diaries

\* \* \*

These spellings are taken from the diaries of Meriwether Lewis, William Clark and their companions during their expedition from Mississippi to the West in 1804–1806.

**Changes in Spelling Since 1806**
- —"c"+"k": publick, cholick/Chorlick/collick, Pacifick, Carthlick, musick
- —double "l": barrell, devill, untill
- —"-our": colour, labour, neighbouring

**Variations on names**
Sioux: Seouex, Shew, Soues, Sues, Soux, Scioues, Seaux, Souix
Pawnee: Pania, Paunees, pawne, ponies
Kansas: Caszes, Kances, Kanses, Kansis, Kanzus
Missouri: Mesury, Missor, Mussiry, Misoureis, Missourue, Missorea

**Mistakes with Words with the Same Sound but Different Spelling (Homophones; see p. 40)**
bare/bear, grate/great, pore/pour/poor, meat/meet, tale/tail, read/red, sore/saw, their/there, Greece/grease

**Doubling or Not Doubling Consonants (see p. 96)**
aproach, apeared, seting, midle, arival, imediately, submited, faithfull, maned (manned), verry, untill, aflicted, comming, oppinion, burried, flagg

**Other Mistakes**
dryed, ellegent, lieing, messinger, samon, swet, muddey, warr, beavour, rispect, previlege, nessy (necessary), behaveing, heavyly, purpendickler, destance, hickery, Pickture, buffalow/ buffaloe, trobelsom, Musquiters/Musquitoes/musquetoes/Musquitors, Roeing, adjasent, Warriers, butifull, Mockisons, Smallpoks, Instancetaniously

*Source American Speech, 75, 2, 2000 & on-line diaries*

# FROM ADDILOU TO VSETIN
*Spellings in Texan Place Names*

\* \* \*

The spelling of place names has always been much freer than the spelling of ordinary words. In North America they also reflect the languages of not only the incomers but also the indigenous inhabitants. Here are some of the more unusual Texas place names, taken from the Geographic Names Information System (GNIS). If you want to know how to pronounce them, ask a Texan.

| | | |
|---|---|---|
| Acebuche | Iraan | Speegleville |
| Addielou | Johhny Grave | Squier Cemetery |
| Bexar | Mountain | Tehuacana |
| Bieri | Katemcy Creek | Cemetery |
| Calabazar | Keechi Creek | Thiebaud Dam |
| Chiltipin Creek | Lawhon Springs | Tivydale |
| Chupadera Creek | Lazbuddie | Uhland |
| Dreyfoos | Lotspelch School | Vahlasing Lake |
| Dyess | Minjou Lake | Vrbas Lake |
| Echols Creek | Mulifest Creek | Vsetin |
| Eylau Siding | Okrob Heliport | Whangdoodle Pass |
| Fertitta Lake | Opdyke West | Wied |
| Fohn Hill | Opelika | XQZ Lake |
| Gholson Creek | Percilla | Yokum |
| Gruhlkey | Psencik Cemetery | Yoledigo Creek |
| Gyp Canyon | Quihi | Yznaga |
| Hlavacek Lake | Quitaque | Zimmerhanzel |
| Hopfs Creek | Raab Spring | Lake |
| Ijams Lake | Romayor | Zummo |

# THE INTERNATIONAL PHONETIC ALPHABET

\* \* \*

The International Phonetic Alphabet (IPA) uses special letter symbols to show the pronunciation of any language, usually enclosing the transcript in slash marks / /. The number varies slightly from one accent of English to another, usually around 40. The following shows a version of IPA for General American English, with some alternatives sometimes found in American books (see Roca and Johnson, 1999, p. 190).

1. /ɪ/ bit
2. /ɛ/ red
3. /æ/ fat
4. /ɒ/ lot
5. /ʌ/ fun
6. /e/ or /eɪ/ date
7. /ʊ/ good
8. /ɔ/ cloth
9. /i/ sea
10. /ə/ about
11. /ɜ/ bird
12. /o/ or /oʊ/ cone
13. /u/ food
14. /aɪ/ bite

15. /ɔɪ/ boy
16. /aʊ/ bout
17. /p/ pip
18. /b/ bob
19. /t/ tot
20. /d/ date
21. /k/ kick
22. /g/ got
23. /f/ fine
24. /v/ vote
25. /s/ cease
26. /z/ zoos
27. /ð/ the
28. /θ/ think
29. /ʃ/ or /š/ shush

30. /ʒ/ or /ž/ genre
31. /m/ mime
32. /n/ noon
33. /ŋ/ ring
34. /tʃ/ or /č/ church
35. /dʒ/ or /ǰ/ judge
36. /w/ wind
37. /h/ hot
38. /j/ or /y/ yes
39. /l/ lull
40. /ɹ/ roaster

Hamlet: /tə bi ɔɪ nɒ tə bi ðæt ɪz ðə kwɛstʃən
weðəɹ tɪz nobləɹ ɪn ðə maɪn tə sʌfəɹ
ðə slɪŋz ən æɹoʊz əv aʊtɹeɪdʒəz fɔɹtʃun
ən baɪ əpoʊzɪn ɛn ðəm/

52

# ROCKIN' 'N' ROLLIN'
## "-ing" and "-in"
* * *

The "-ing" in "taking," etc., can be said either as "ing" like "sing" or as "in" like "sin." The "in" pronunciation of "ing" is said to be more masculine and less formal. There is also a traditional association between "in" and "huntin'" in the southern United States.

**Advertising Slogans**
Tennessee Sippin' Whiskey, LEXUS CATERS FOR THE HUNTIN', FISHIN', SHOOTIN' CLASS, finger lickin' good, I'm lovin' it

**Song Titles by Sidney Bechet (New Orleans)**
Sobbin' and Cryin', Walkin' and Talkin' to Myself, Laughin' in Rhythm, Slippin' and Slidin', Preachin' the Blues, Foolin' Me, Groovin' the Minor

**Walkin' People**
Walkin' Jim Stoltz (a wilderness walker), Beats Walkin' Western Swing Band, Always Walkin' Horse Locators, "Walkin' Down the Line" (Dylan song), *Walkin' the Dog* (Mosley book), Walkin' South (country music Web site)

**Huntin' and Fishin'**
Coon Huntin', Billy Bob's Huntin' n Fishin' (Gameboy game), the huntin, shootin, fishin brigade

Big truck tires, huntin', fishin', tractor pulls, country music, Charlie Daniels, and rebel flags are just a few words that might describe a redneck.

**Don Marquis, *Noah an' Jonah an' Cap'n John Smith***
Noah an' Jonah an' Cap'n John Smith, . . .
Settin' up in Heaven, chewin' and a-chawin'
Eatin' their terbaccy, talkin' and a-jawin'; . . .

# FROM ȝERE TO YEAR
*Changing Letters of English*

\*   \*   \*

**OLD ENGLISH (OE)** *5th to 10th century* A.D.

    ð **(eth)/þ (thorn)** = both voiced and unvoiced "th" (this/
    theme): þe (the), þinȝ (thing), ðinȝ (thing), oðꝛe (other)

    ȝ **"open" "g"** = spoken "g," "j" and a fricative no longer used:
    ȝæſꞇ (ghost), ꝺæȝ (day), laȝu (law)

    ƿ **(wynn, from runic alphabet)** = spoken "w":
    ƿiſ (wife),ƿæꞇeꞃ (water)

    æ **(ash)** = spoken short or long "a":
    ſæꝺeꞃ (father), ſǣ ("sea"), æſc (ash)

    *letters used rarely in OE or as variants:* x, k, q, z, g, j, v

    *little punctuation:* low dot **.** = short pause; high · = long

**MIDDLE ENGLISH (ME)** *11th to 15th centuries*

    þ = spoken "th" in both forms (no ð): þat (that), þenk
    (think), deaþ (death); open top ȝ: ȝᵉ (the)

    ȝ/g **"open"** ȝ = "j" ȝere (year); "closed": "g" = "g"; gere (gear),
    g after vowels = now lost fricative ryȝt (right)

    *letters used only as variants:* **u** (for "v"), **j** (for "i")

    *punctuation:* low **.** = short pause; ⁊ = medium; / = long

**EARLY MODERN ENGLISH (EME)** *16th to 17th centuries*

    **v/u** one letter till about 1630 = spoken "v" or "u":
    vnkle, haue, vgly, receiue, giue, vnder, diuell, vs

    **i/j** one letter till about 1640 = spoken "i" or "j":
    ioy, iudge, iigge, iackedaw, ieloosie, iniurie

    ſ used in print for "s" until late 18th century long "s":
    ſoule, ſo, monſtrous, Paſſion, ſlaue, diſtraction

    **y/ie** = interchanged medially in some words:
    myraculous, dye (die), nimph: "ie" finally in some words:
    Maie, heavie, eie

    *punctuation:* ' = contraction, ? = question, ! = exclamation

# FIFTEEN-YEAR-OLDS
# AND SPELLING

\*   \*   \*

**TYPES OF ERRORS MADE BY 15-YEAR-OLDS**

| | | |
|---|---|---|
| **Insertion** (adding letters) | untill/until | 17% |
| **Omission** (leaving letters out) | occuring/occurring | 36% |
| **Substitution** (replacing letters) | definate/definite | 19% |
| **"Grapheme substitution"** (alternative sound-based spelling) | thort/thought | 9% |
| **Transposition** (switching letters) | freind/friend | 5% |
| **Other** | | 3% |

**MISTAKES BY 15-YEAR-OLDS IN TEN LINES OF WRITING**

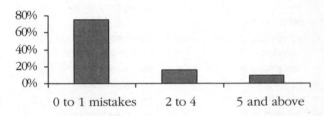

**MISTAKES BY 15-YEAR-OLD BOYS AND GIRLS IN TEN LINES OF WRITING**

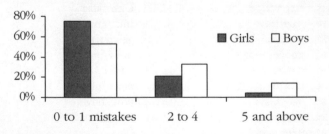

*Source: Brooks et al. 1993*

55

# ORTHOGRAPHIC
# REGULARITIES TEST

\*    \*    \*

As well as the rules about how sounds connect to letters, English spelling also has many rules about which combinations of letters are allowed in a particular part of the word, called "orthographic regularities." None of the following is a real English word, but one word out of each pair is a *possible* word in that it conforms to these orthographic regularities. Check the possible words. Page 155 gives the answers and explanations.

1. blar/blarh
2. ckole/kole
3. leck/ckel
4. snove/snov
5. tcheb/cheb
6. chig/tchig
7. blic/blick
8. fanq/fanque
9. ster/sterh
10. gneit/teign
11. nowh/whon
12. flij/flidge
13. huz/huze
14. pluze/pluz
15. staj/stadge
16. truv/truve
17. whar/rawh
18. gnope/nope
19. dgain/jain
20. jarn/narj
21. blav/blave
22. gnil/lign/
23. lutch/tchul

24. nait/gnait
25. wras/sawr
26. qish/quish
27. quong/qong
28. lerh/rhell
29. forh/rhoff
30. smaze/smaz
31. sniv/snive
32. frak/frack
33. spiwh /spiw
34. plawh/plaw
35. terque/terq
36. squol/squl
37. dgoll/joll
38. klaze/klaz
39. nuft/gnuft
40. gewr/wreg
41. prew/prewh
42. nartch/ tcharn
43. plock/ploc
44. blive/bliv
45. wrof/fowr

*Sources: Cook, 2004; Olson et al., 1985.*

# THE LETTERS OF THE ALPHABET
*Richard Mulcaster,* The Elementarie *(1592)*

\* \* \*

**E,** besides the common difference of time and tune, is a letter of
marvellous use in the writing of our tongue. . . . Which "e,"
though it be sometimes idly written, either of ignorance, if
the writer be unlearned, and know not how to write, or of
negligence, if he be learned, and mark not his hand, yet most
times it is written to great purpose, even where it seems idle.

**C** is strong like to "k." before "a," "o," "u," either simple vowels, or combined in diphthongs, as *cankard, cautele, concord,
coward, cunning,* or when it ends a foresyllable before any
other consonant as "c" "q" "k" "t" as in *succede, acquaint,
acknowledge, expecting.* "C," is weak like "s," before "e" and
"i," either alone or in diphthong, as *cease, deceit, surcingle,* or
before the qualifying silent "e," in the end, as *acceptance,
whence, once.*

**H** is an aspiration, whose force before all vowels and diphthongs is easy to be perceived, as *Henrie, hunter.* . . .

**O** is a letter of as great uncertainty in our tongue, as "e," is of
direction both alone in vowel, and combined in diphthong.

**Q** serves only in the nature of "k," or the strong "c," to go before
the single or double "w," both consonantlike in force, and
indifferent in place, as *quill, quail,* . . . *squint, squall, squat,
squese,* or with the double "w," *qwail, acqwaint, qwik,* . . .

**W** The double "w" is a letter that hath accompanied our tongue
from the original Germane, and is used sometimes as a
vowel, sometimes as a consonant. It is never a vowel but in
the diphthongs as, *draw, knew, throw,* . . .

**X** begins no English words, but ends many, as *wax, vex, yex,* and
goes into the middle of their derivatives, as *waxing, vexeth, yex-
ing,* and with the qualifying "e," *iaxe,* without *ax, pax, wax.*

**Y** likewise is sometimes consonantish, sometimes vowellish.
Consonantish, when it leads a vowel, as, *yonder, young,* . . .

**Z** is a consonant much heard amongst us, and seldom seen . . .

# NORRIF AND XIRYC
*Dungeons and Dragons Names*

*  *  *

To play D&D you have to have an appropriate persona. Here are some of the names of current players.

| | | |
|---|---|---|
| Agallela | Jeydrienne | Rehcran |
| Ahhzz | Johannixx | Rhomdruil |
| Astros | Kai-Raega | Shandakul |
| Bahagi | Kerahk | Shijin |
| Berdoingg | KouAidou | Slasiter |
| Boobooruboo | Leafgoodbread | Thyrwyn |
| Ceresco | Leariel | Tkolhoff |
| Chidebol | Legynd | uNtz!! |
| DaGreatJL | Loztastic | Vetrpger |
| Darvank | Lyferocks | Vrecknidj |
| Dhruin | Lynxara | Waqas |
| Ergazh | Mesclion | Welderd |
| Fallnwlf | Mysttic | Wyrmyone |
| Fraon | Nalancray | Xenobenzes |
| Gikar | Norrif | Xiryc |
| Gnarlo | Nyneve | Ynnep |
| Gnatetgnome | Oinkus | Zaxh |
| Griznuq | Oortoort | ZideX |
| H3llz Fire | Pneema | Zushoen |
| Hillelr | Raark | Zyguh |
| IkusaGwai | Ravenspoe | |

# BROCCOLI AND LETTUCE
*History in Garden Plants*

\* \* \*

The spellings for plants grown have varied considerably over the years. (Dates from the *Oxford English Dictionary*.)

| | |
|---|---|
| **chili** | chille (1662), chile (1676), chilli (1685), chili (1818) |
| **daisy** | dayeseye (1000), daysye, daysy, deysy, dasye, daizy |
| **thyme** | thyme (1398), tyme (1420), time (1563) |
| **sunflower** | sonne flower (1562), sunflow'r (1652), sunflower (1794) |
| **squash** | from Narragansett asquutasquash (1643) |
| **okra** | ocra (1707), ochre (1713), ockro (1750), okra (1777) |
| **alyssum** | alysson (1551), alasum (1840), alyssum (1876) |
| **cabbage** | cabache (1440), cabbyshe, cabidge, cabige, cabbach |
| **lettuce** | letuse (1290), lettuse, latewes, letews, letuce, lattice |
| **garlic** | garleac (1000), garleek, garlick [source: "gar" (spear) "leek"] |
| **parsley** | petersilie (1000), percil (originally Latin "petro" rock) |
| **cucumber** | cucumer (1382), cowcumber (1584), cucumber (1688) |
| **cauliflower** | cole florie (1597), cawly-flower, collyflower |
| **peony** | pioine (1265), pyone, piane, pyonie, piony, peiony |
| **spinach** | spynnage (1530), spenege, sippanage, spynach, spinech |
| **pea** | (originally "pease" was both singular and plural); pyse (1000), peose, pees, pes; (new singular) pea (1611) |
| **onion** | unyonn (1356), uniowns, oynyons, hunyn, oignion, ingyon |
| **broccoli** | broccoli (1699), brocoli (1732) |
| **carrot** | carette (1533), caret (1565), carrootes (1634) |

## REASONS FOR ODD SPELLINGS IN PLANT NAMES

1. *dialect variation in Middle English:* e.g., 15th century spellings of pease, pees, pease, pyson, pesone, peise, pese, peas

2. *borrowings from Latin and Greek:* chrysanthemum, gladiolus
3. *wrong ideas about word forms:* pease (singular, but changed to "one pea/two peas")
4. *plant names based on proper names:* dahlia (Dahl), fuchsia (Fuchs), poinsettia (Poinsett), wistaria (Wistar), cinchona (Chinchon)

# TEST
*British Versus American Newspapers*

\*   \*   \*

Which are British newspapers, which American?

1. . . . at the county's day labor hiring area, some workers said they might not be able to qualify for the program . . .
2. The sheer size of the voids would also allow visitors to experience something of the physical dimension of the trade center towers.
3. It makes no difference if they are real fur or fake, but it's worth checking that it won't moult too dramatically.
4. I've been eager to open up a dialog with Okrent.
5. Five-year-old Alyasa Klotz wanted a new wagon for Christmas.
6. THE QUICK actions of a Newquay mother helped save the life of her neighbour.
7. The FBI are hunting a bank robber who's struck eight times this year with only a pencil-drawn moustache as a disguise.
8. This Red Cross blood drive is also in honor of all public servants, past and present, who serve and protect every day.
9. The price of petrol at government stations in Iraq is about one cent per liter.
10. The LME launched its own internal investigation into aluminium trading in August.
11. But if we look at the report through our skeptic's goggles, combined catalog and internet sales increased 11.4%.
12. New Doping Rules Favour GAA Cold Sufferers.
13. Most plums are preserved without the addition of sulfur dioxide, a chemical which causes an allergic reaction in some people.
14. Travelling people are being given cameras and training to document their lives, it was announced today.

*Answers on page 156.*

# NO3ODY's $$$$s

*Substitutes for Letters*

\* \* \*

Characters other than letters of the alphabet can stand in for letters, such as "@," "$," "£" and "+."

# YE OLDE TUCK SHOPPE
*Olde Tyme Spelling*

\* \* \*

The examples come from the United States, Australia, Ireland, Canada and the United Kingdom—Olde Tyme spelling affects all parts of the English-speaking world. Some names go with genuinely old institutions, such as eighteenth-century pubs like "Ye Olde Admiral Rodney" in Cheshire. Others are modern "jokes": "Ye Ole Karaoke Web."

Around 1400 A.D. Middle English used the letter "Y" for "th" sounds in words like "this" and "think"; it resembled the modern letter "y." The word "the" was thus written as Yᵉ though pronounced more or less as now. This letter "Y" became confused with the letter "y," so that "the" is written as "ye" in spelling that is supposed to look quaint. Other ways of suggesting antiquity are:

- **add an "e" at the end of words**, "olde," "shoppe," another holdover from Middle English where the "e" at the end of words like "love" was pronounced rather than silent.
- **use old-looking fonts, Ye Old Court Yard.**
- **revive spellings once possible in English**, such as "fayre," used up to 1602, "tyme" up to 1552—though never with an "h" (the herb "thyme" has had an "h" since about 1500)—or "musick," used up to 1800. Usually the "antique" form is only one of the many possible alternative historic spellings. For example, "musique," "musyque," "musycque," "musik," "musyce," "musyk," "musicke," "musiq" all occurred in English.

Ye Olde Tuck Shoppe

The Publick Musick (group)

Ye Olde Admiral Rodney

Psychic Fayre

Ye Olde Cheshire Cheese Inn

Never Enough Thyme
Shoppe

Ye Olde Chimney Sweeps

Thee Newe Worlde Inne

*Ye Olden Days* (Mickey Mouse
film, 1933)

The Publick Theatre (Boston)

Ye Essex Baebes (medieval
music singers)

MAGICK MUSICK
MUSEUM

Ye Olde London Cab Hire
Service

Olde Thyme Photographs of
the Ladies of the House of
Negotiable Affections

Ye Ole Karaoke Web

Olde Worlde Santas

OLDE WORLDE LACE

Ye Olde Tyme Radio Trading
Post

Ye Olde Den of Iniquity

Olde Thyme Fayre

Ye Olde Directory Shoppe

Ye Olde Green Dragon

Wild River Pub and Publick
House

Ye Olde Tea Shoppe

Olde Thyme Aviation

Ye Olde Trip to Jerusalem

### *Ye Olde Marquis*
**REAL FOOD**

Ye Olde Slide and Popcorn
Night

Ye Olde Fish & Chippe
Shoppe

The University Towne House

Goose Fayre

Ye Olde George Inn

Olde Musick and Cokery
Books

Ye Olde Crosse

Southampton Publick House

Ye Olde Soap Shoppe

# HINTS ON PRONUNCIATION
# FOR FOREIGNERS

\* \* \*

This anonymous poem illustrating the problem words for English spelling has circulated constantly among teachers of English.

I take it you already know
Of *tough* and *bough* and *cough* and *dough*?
Others may stumble, but not you,
On *hiccough*, *thorough*, *lough* and *through*?
Well done! And now you wish, perhaps,
To learn of less familiar traps?
Beware of *heard*, a dreadful word
That looks like *beard* and sounds like *bird*,
And *dead*: it's said like *bed*, not *bead*—
For goodness sake don't call it *deed*!
Watch out for *meat* and *great* and *threat*
(They rhyme with *suite* and *straight* and *debt*).
A *moth* is not a moth in *mother*,
Nor *both* in *bother*, *broth* in *brother*,
And *here* is not a match for *there*
Nor *dear* and *fear* for *bear* and *pear*;
And then there's *dose* and *rose* and *lose*—
Just look them up—and *goose* and *choose*,
And *cork* and *work* and *card* and *ward*,
And *font* and *front* and *word* and *sword*,
And *do* and *go* and *thwart* and *cart*—
Come, come, I've hardly made a start!
A dreadful language? Man alive!
I'd mastered it when I was five!

# DIRECTION OF WRITING

\* \* \*

Arabic and Hebrew writing go from right to left; traditional Chinese and Japanese characters go from top to bottom. Does English go just from left to right? Signs from several English-speaking countries:

# THY THIGH
*The "th" Rule*

\* \* \*

The "th" combination of letters is pronounced in two different ways in "this" and "thistle." The "th" sound in "this" is "voiced," the sound in "thistle" is "unvoiced." The difference is the vibration from the vocal cords with the "th" in "this" but not with the "th" in "thistle." The pairs of words below differ chiefly by having one or other of these two sounds.

| the | therapy | that | thatch | thou | thousand |
| there | theory | this | thistle | those | thong |
| their | theft | thus | thud | thence | theorem |
| them | thematic | than | thank | though | thought |
| these | thesis | then | Theo | thy | thigh |

## THE "TH" RULE

The words with voiced "th" like "the" and "than" are called "structure" words because they link words together in phrases—"*that* man with *the* beard." The words with unvoiced "th" are ordinary nouns and verbs, etc., that need to be linked with structure words to make a phrase, called "content" words: "thesis," "thistle" and "thatch"—"the *thesis* about *thistles.*"

## EXCEPTIONS TO THE "TH" RULE

- words with silent "th": asthma, isthmus
- the structure word "through," said with unvoiced "th"
- words where "th" is pronounced "t": Thames, thyme, Thai
- pairs of nouns/verbs, etc., differing only over which "th" sound is used: bath/bathe, breath/breathe, wreath/wreathe, ether/either (for some people), loath/loathe, etc.

# SNACK-TASTIC STEAK-O-RAMA
## *Word Endings*

\*   \*   \*

New words with unusual spellings are created by adding particular word endings.

**tastic** (presumably from "fantastic")

| | | |
|---|---|---|
| scan-tastic | Carb'Tastic | Snack-Tastic |
| friendstastic | *Tan-tastic!* | Rant-tastic! |
| cam-tastic | ghetto-tastic | Pop-tastic |
| Kid-Tastic | fat-tastic | Can-tastic |

**tacular** ("spectacular")

| | | |
|---|---|---|
| Pet-tacular | crap-tacular | Snake-Tacular |
| Spa-Tacular | Mac-tacular | Pet'acular |
| Prank-tacular | Sports-tacular | |

**licious** ("delicious")

| | | |
|---|---|---|
| paw-licious | madonnalicious | dinner-licious |
| soapylicious | Ice-A-Licious | Carb-O-Licious |
| picklelicious | spa-licious | Moolicious Dairy Bar |
| tea-licious | Soy-licious | |

**teria** ("cafeteria")

| | | |
|---|---|---|
| Joke-a-teria | eat-a-teria | Gas-A-Teria |
| Snack-a-teria | wash-e-teria | Frame-a-teria |
| *Disk-O-teria* | Laugh-e-teria | wine-a-teria |
| book-a-teria | Dance-A-Teria | |

**delic**

| | | |
|---|---|---|
| Shag-A-Delic | Dance-A-Delic | punk a delic |
| Funk-A-Delic | Mr.Sick-O'Delic | Pop-a-delic |

Sci-fi-delic
psyk-E-delic
Rock-A-Delic

Psy-Cow-Delic
Cycle-Delic
retro-delic

Shop o Delic
glam-edelic

**a/o-rama** (originally from "panorama," invented in 1789)

Bounce-A-Rama
Blog-arama
Elvis-A-Rama
Liq-O-Rama
Kleen-o-rama

Putt-o-rama
Schlockorama
Floor-O-Rama
Beef-a-rama
Wig-o-rama

Wood-o-rama
Swap-o-Rama
Spell-o-rama
Steak-O-Rama
Stretch-O-Rama

# SUPADUPA KILLAH MOBB
## Hip-Hop Spelling

\* \* \*

"Rebellious" novel spelling abounds in Hip-Hop, partly to show a way of speaking.

### Hip-Hop Lyrics
Supadupa fly · Tell me whatcha gon do? · I'm in love wit chu · Rainbow Flava · it ain't nothin nobody can say cuz you're the one for me baby · they just wanna hold me Cuz im so supa · The rhythm on ya get yo groovin baby! · You know the old krumbsnatcha's in this land of decay · Got doe ma didn't know, good gracious alive! · Work 'til we break our back and you hear the crack of the bone to get by · my goals Just to stop smokin, and stop drinkin · Might of heard me spittin wit Cain and Fab playa · people killin people dyin children hurt and women cryin · Neva gave her tha cold shoulda' · if she's in the benz, I let her take ova' the Rova (vrrm-Vrrm!) · I ain't tryna wanna fight with ya man · IT PAYZ TO BE THA BOSS

### Hip-Hop Chat
Ja wuss hip hop now he juss pop in mah opinion · I seriosly ain't heard one good verse from this kat · TUPAC IS DA GANGSTA OF DA SKY, HE WOULD ALWAYZ STAY IN MA HEART AS DA BEST RAPPER ONCE ALIFE · neva heard Busta diss a kat but his spit was hott · U hit it rite on the money dawg! · Killah Mobb 4 Life! · Who do u guyz think is the most Influencial Artist out of everybody? · even though he aint a artist u still gotta give respect to tha ONE AND ONLY

# TEA-TIME OR TEATIME
# OR TEA TIME?
*Hyphens Joining Words*

*   *   *

*All the Words with Hyphens in the Brown Corpus of the
5,000 Most Frequent Words in American English*

1. year-old
2. long-range
3. over-all
4. so-called
5. long-term
6. part-time
7. anti-trust
8. twenty-five
9. Bang-Jensen
10. full-time
11. anti-Semitism
12. Anglo-Saxon
13. middle-class

*Longest Hyphenated Word in the British National Corpus*
oral-aggressive-anal-retentive-come-and-see-me-five-times-a-
week-for-years-at-vast-expense-or-how-do-I-know-you're-really-
committed (source: Leech et al., 2001)

**CHANGES OVER TIME** (*source:* Oxford English Dictionary)
Often a word changes over time from two words, "tea bag," to
one word with a hyphen, "tea-bag," to no hyphen, "teabag." The
form in boldface is the one given in *Webster's Unabridged*.

*   week end 1638, **weekend** 1793, week-end 1970
*   **won ton** 1948, won-ton 1952, wonton 1956
*   **hot dog** 1908, hot-dog 1920
*   **tea bag** 1898, tea-bag 1936, teabag 1977
*   time-table 1820, time table 1838, **timetable** 1970
*   **cooperate** 1616, co-operate 1762
*   head maister 1576, **headmaster** 1776, head-master 1791
*   screw driver 1779, **screwdriver** 1840, screw-driver 1842
*   lamp shade 1850, lamp-shade 1877, **lampshade** 1960
*   **air port** 1919, airport 1924
*   **sight-see** 1824, sightsee 1913
*   back stroke 1876, back-stroke 1908, **backstroke** 1958

# TEST
## Words That Are Commonly Misspelled
* * *

Circle the correct one.

1. choize — choice — choise
2. sincerely — sincerly — sincerelly
3. thier house is . . . — there house is . . . — their house is . . .
4. really — realy — reelly
5. develope — divelop — develop
6. kindergarten — kindegarten — kindergarden
7. becuse — becase — because
8. diffrint — different — diferent
9. govemment — goverment — government
10. busines affairs — busyness affairs — business affairs
11. knowledge — noledge — nollidge
12. profesional — professional — proffesional
13. wold — wou'd — would
14. I don't know where to go. — I don't know were to go. — I don't know wear to go.
15. superseed — supercede — supersede
16. address — adress — adresse
17. cariere — carier — career
18. accommodation — accomodation — acomodation
19. particuler — particular — partikular
20. intergrate — integrate — intigrate
21. grammar — grammer — gramar
22. descripe — describe — discribe
23. begining — beginning — biginning
24. interesting — intristing — intresting
25. the book wich — the book which — the book witch

*Answers are on page 157.*

72

# ALPHA BRAVO CHARLIE
*Spoken Alphabets for English*

\* \* \*

For various military or police purposes, it is necessary to spell out crucial words, call signs or locations letter by letter in an unambiguous way over the radio or phone, etc. Two widely used variants are the "NATO" alphabet and the "Names" alphabet.

|   | NATO | Names |
|---|---|---|
| A | Alpha | Andrew |
| B | Bravo | Benjamin |
| C | Charlie | Charles |
| D | Delta | David |
| E | Echo | Edward |
| F | Foxtrot | Frederick |
| G | Golf | George |
| H | Hotel | Harry |
| I | India | Isaac |
| J | Juliet | Jack |
| K | Kilo | King |
| L | Lima | Lucy |
| M | Mike | Mary |
| N | November | Nellie |
| O | Oscar | Oliver |
| P | Papa | Peter |
| Q | Quebec | Queenie |
| R | Romeo | Robert |
| S | Sierra | Sugar |
| T | Tango | Tommy |
| U | Uniform | Uncle |
| V | Victor | Victor |
| W | Whiskey | William |
| X | X-ray | Xmas |
| Y | Yankee | Yellow |
| Z | Zulu | Zebra |

**Bookshops**

Bold Face Books

Hue-Man

Murder Ink

Apocalipsis

Rhythm & Muse

**Plumbers**

The Drain Surgeon

Lone Drainer and Pronto

Go with the Flow

Clog Busters

Royal Flush

**Massage Therapists**

A Kneaded Massage

Bodiwerks

Have Chair Will Travel

Tangible Results

A Touch of Class

Hands On Therapeutics

**Delis**

Crepe Vine

Love N Haught

Hugs & Quiches

Mega Bites

New Deli

Pasta T' Go-Go

**Cafés and Coffeehouses**

Uncommon Ground

Beanocchio

Bean There

Belly Good Cafe

Chock Full of Nuts

Grind N'brew

**Boarding Kennels**

Cat Calls

See Spot Run

Bark Avenue

Leash We Can Do

Citizen Canine

Barking Lot

Punning Shops and Restaurants from Different Countries

# WHY ARE AMERICAN AND BRITISH STYLES OF SPELLING DIFFERENT?

\*   \*   \*

The differences come from a small number of sources.

## Noah Webster

Webster's 1828 *American Dictionary of the English Language* argued for:

**"-or" rather than "-our"**: odour/odor. Webster blames Dr. Johnson for standardizing on "-our" in words like *favour* and *labour* rather than the traditional "-or."

**"-er" rather than "-re"**: centre/center. Webster suggests returning to the earlier "-er" spelling in words like *centre*.

**"-se" rather than "-ce"**: defence/defense. Webster's reasons for restoring the older "-se" to words like *defence* are partly the Latin sources, partly to make spelling uniform.

## National Education Association, 1898

In 1898, the National Education Association in the United States of America listed twelve words that should be changed, namely:

tho, altho, thru, thruout, thoro, thoroly, thorofare, program, prolog, catalog, pedagog, decalog.

While some have become American style ("program" and the "-og" words), others have not become standard written style even if they appear in informal contexts ("thru," "thorofare") (see p. 37).

### HOW MANY WORDS ARE AFFECTED?

The only words affected by Webster's three main changes in the top 5,000 words of the Brown Corpus of American English are the following, plus their derivatives:

**"-er"**: center, theater, fiber

**"-or"**: labor, color, behavior, favor, honor, humor, liquor, neighbor, harbor

**"-ize"**:  realize, recognize, organize, authorize, characterize,
emphasize but also "-ise" (Webster's): exercise, surprise
(or surprize), enterprise, advise, arise, compromise
Other words in the top 5,000 that differ between American and
British styles: program, tire, defense, license, jail, mold, wagon

# CHEESE PATTER WITH ASIDES
*Mistakes on Menus*

\* \* \*

### OUR COUSINE
we serve food the taditional way . . . we would ike our patrons to order an entree per person · Traditional cousine · It's surpisingly filling · Experience Kyoto with tongue! · Open all days except on suday · we want your back

### SNACKS AND APPERTIZERS
Toated Bagel · hand held breadfast · egg sandwiches garnished with luttuce · Hot Hors D'peivres · Gratinated snails · gourmet pig feet · herborized cheese · Shirimp Cocktail

### APPETIZERS
Read Bean Soup with Lotus Seed · Bouilla Baisse · a teast of Olive oil · Egg Drip Soup · Oister soup · Ceasar salad · tuned salad

### MAIN COURSES
fried wantons · whit-bean stew · unfrozen beef-rips · chilly chicken · Fried Port Chop · Buffer Dirn Sum · Carmelized salmon fillet · Spicy and sour chestnet · Veal knee · prawns and brocolli in an oyster sauce · Seasonal veges · Western Ommelette · With sundried tomatoe salsa · scramble eggs · beef or fishdessert served with spicy ranch · sizzerling dishes

### VEGETABLES
Chinese vegetables in space blend of white sauce · Served by itself or with two asides · Egg crocket groton style · Blanded tometos · Couliflower and Potato curry

### ASSORTED DESERTS
Australian and imported cheese patter · Crape with fruit · decadent emulsion of sugar · Wide selection of daily cakes and

confectionary · The French chef of our shop made it hand-made dessert of it combines be prosperous and eat that and whatever.

**DRINKS**
Roze wine · Clab soda

# TEST
*Sounds or Letters?*

\* \* \*

Written English becomes so much part of our lives that it has an effect on how we *hear* spoken English. People sometimes "hear" sounds because they know the letters in the word. To see how you are affected by this, quickly count how many *sounds* there are in each of the following words.

| | | |
|---|---|---|
| 1. bought ___ | 18. music ___ | 35. rich ___ |
| 2. box ___ | 19. judge ___ | 36. wing ___ |
| 3. thin ___ | 20. who ___ | 37. page ___ |
| 4. him ___ | 21. spend ___ | 38. unit ___ |
| 5. catch ___ | 22. age ___ | 39. me ___ |
| 6. the ___ | 23. it ___ | 40. cost ___ |
| 7. chop ___ | 24. think ___ | 41. she ___ |
| 8. crash ___ | 25. match ___ | 42. crop ___ |
| 9. of ___ | 26. chat ___ | 43. shock ___ |
| 10. edge ___ | 27. next ___ | 44. bat ___ |
| 11. fix ___ | 28. thought ___ | 45. let ___ |
| 12. do ___ | 29. land ___ | 46. trust ___ |
| 13. then ___ | 30. nothing ___ | 47. back ___ |
| 14. broccoli ___ | 31. ought ___ | 48. stamp ___ |
| 15. jet ___ | 32. win ___ | 49. past ___ |
| 16. light ___ | 33. stupid ___ | 50. washing ___ |
| 17. job ___ | 34. plant ___ | |

*Answers on page 158.*

# HIGH KLASS SHOPS
*Unusual Spelling in Shop Names*

\*   \*   \*

# THE GHASTLY KHAKI WALTZ
*Unusual English Spellings*

\* \* \*

"pph" = "f": sapphire, Sappho

"cch" = "ch," zucchini; = "k": gnocchi, Pinocchio, saccharine

"ch" = (silent), yacht, Crichton; = "sh," fuchsia (though derived from Leonard Fuchs)

"dh" = "d": dhobi, Gandhi, dhoti, dhall, dhow, dhurrie, jodhpur

"kh" = "k": khaki, khan, Khmer, sheikh, Sikh, Khyber

"rrh" = "r": diarrhea, hemorrhage, cirrhosis; (silent): catarrh, myrrh

"ae" = "air": aerial; = "ee": Caesar

"ltz" = "s": waltz; = "ts": seltzer, schmaltz

"ea" = "eh": great, break, steak, Yeats

"rtz": quartz, Hertz

"rgh" = "rg": sorghum, burgher, Pittsburgh

"gn" (initial)= "n": gnu, gneiss, gnostic, gnat, gnaw, gnome

"sth" = "s": asthma, isthmus

"gu" = "gw": guano, Guinevere

"gm" = "m": phlegm, paradigm, diaphragm

"th" = "t": thyme, Thames, Thompson, Thomas, Esther

"oeu": hors d'oeuvres

"mn" = "m": autumn, column, condemn, damn, solemn, hymn

"ieu" = "you": adieu, lieu

"gh" = "g": ghost, ghastly, Ghana, gherkin, ghetto, ghoul

"cz" = "s": Czar; = "tch": Czech

"ez" = "eh": chez, rendezvous, laissez-faire

"rr" = finally: burr, err, shirr

## SOME ONE-OFF WORDS

djinn, chamois ("shammy"), junta ("hunta"), colonel, Xhosa ("hosea"), England/English ("ingland/inglish"), of ("ov"), milieu ("mealyer"), ache ("ehk")

# TRAFFIC SIGNS FROM SEVERAL COUNTRIES

* * *

**Notice**
CONTINUAL AGGRESSIVE TAGGING IN FIRE ROUTE IS IN EFFECT EVERYDAY

Motorists Beware Ducks On Road Beyond Bridge

PED XING

# WELCOME COMPLIMENTS
*Two Common Mistakes*

\*    \*    \*

**Compliment** = a remark intended to praise or please
**Complement** = something that fills up or completes (*Webster's*)

## Complimentary Food

Dinners are complimented with the appropriate condiments.

Rosettes of Smoked Norwegian Salmon complimented with a duo of Relishes

Mouthwatering flavors of red raspberry, currant, plum jam and raisins are complimented by spicy pepper and herb notes.

Enjoy a complimentary pastry when ordering any hot beverage.

No dessert menu is complete without Ice cream though, so we have chosen a variety of fabulous flavours to compliment the menu.

Complex with a good balance of ripe berry flavors, low acidity & soft tannins complimented by a long finish.

## Other Compliments

. . . full time teachers . . . are complimented by highly respected part time teachers from the business community.

Luxuriant tropical gardens and attractive landscaping are complimented by the tall palms and majestic flamboyant trees.

NATO and the EU army are complimentary, not competitive.

The bedroom is complimented by a king sized brass bed.

## Wellcome to My Web Page

    Wellcome to Bavaria (wellcome to yodelling area).
    Hopefully we can soon wellcome you here again.
    Wellcome to Life, Wellcome to Geneva
    Scarecrow grapevine wreath will give a warm wellcome!
    Wellcome I really want to know that is your opinion.

Various people, objects and shapes can be used as letters.

# SHAKESPEARE AND SPELLING

\*   \*   \*

## Shakespeare's Name
All these spellings for Shakespeare—the writer rather than other people with the same name—are found before 1616, the year of his death:

Shakespeare, Shake-speare, Shakspeare, Shaxberd,
Shakespere, Shak-speare, Shakspear, Shakspere, Shaksper,
Schaksp., Shakespear, Shakespheare.

## To Be or Not to Be
*The Tragedie of Hamlet* First Folio, 1623, original spelling (not necessarily Shakespeare's), using the long "s" ſ used by English printers in the seventeenth and eighteenth centuries.

To be, or not to be,that is the Queſtion :
Whether 'tis Nobler in the minde to ſuffer
The Slings and Arrowes of outragious Fortune,
Or to take Armes againſt a Sea of troubles,
And by oppoſing end them : to dye,to ſleepe
No more ; and by a ſleepe, to ſay we end
The Heart-ake, and the thouſand Naturall ſhockes
That Fleſh is heyre too? 'Tis a conſummation
Deuoutly to be wiſh'd. To dye to ſleepe,
To ſleepe, perchance to Dreame; I, there's the rub,
For in that ſleepe of death, what dreames may come
When we haue ſhuffel'd off this mortall coile,
Muſt giue vs pawſe

*Different versions of this speech are on page 131.*

## Other Familiar Quotations from the First Folio of Hamlet
• There are more things in Heauen and Earth, *Horatio*,
  Than are dream't of in our philoſophy
• Something is rotten in the State of Denmarke.
• Goodnight ſweet Prince,
  And Flights of Angels ſing thee to thy reſt

# SPELLING GAMES
*Set 2*

\*   \*   \*

## Matching Letters
Each of two players writes down a six-letter word, say,
C O M M O N

The aim is to discover the other person's word. Each player
produces another six-letter word, say O R I G I N

They score one point for each letter that is in *exactly* the same
place in the target word, in this case I for the last letter, N.
Repeat until the word is found. Proper names and plurals are
not allowed for the target word but can be used in the test
words. A four-letter version of the same game can be played by
two people in a car.

## Last and First
The aim is to supply a word of the appropriate category that
begins with the last letter of the preceding word. So if players
choose countries as a category, the sequence might be:

   Japan > Nigeria > Afghanistan > New Zealand > . . .

Players lose a point when they cannot supply a word.

## I Love My Love with an A
Each player describes his or her love with words starting with a
given letter of the alphabet, following the formula:

   I love my love with an A because she is Athletic. I hate her
   with an A because she is Artful. Her name is Amanda and
   she comes from Alaska.

Players go through the letters of the alphabet: X, Y and Z are
optional. This game goes back at least to Samuel Pepys (1669).

\* \* \*

Handwritten notices in streets and on blackboards, doors, etc., are prone to error.

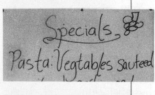

# THE EIHGTEEN-MILLION-DOLLAR SUPPRISE

* * *

Here are specimen spelling mistakes from 75 versions of the spam e-mail inviting you to accept millions of dollars. These may, of course, be deliberate attempts to appear naive or to evade spam detectors.

*The Preamble*
YOU MAY BE SURPRISE TO RECEIVE THIS LETTER • I ONLY GOT YOUR CONTACT ADDRESS FROM INDISCREET SEARCH

*The Money*
THE SUM OF EIHGTEEN MILLION UNITED STATE DOLLARS (US$18,000,000,00.)

*The Background*
THE CHAIRMAN ... IS NOW HIDDING IN A FORIEGN COUNTRY • he fore saw the looming danger in Zimbabwe • he was shoot by hired killers • many people in other state knows on what this perpatrate against christian • [my cancer] has defiled all forms of medical treatment • you will understand my plige

*Your Involvement*
you will advice on areas of investment • At this time I can not devulge further information • WE HAVE BEEN RELIABLY INFORMED OF YOUR DISCRETENESS

*Legal Arrangements*
my words is my bond • I will involve my confidant lawyer • once the layer have your consent and trust then he can proceed immediately • the funds will be donated to a discreted trust fund for the purchase of arms and amunnitions

## An Alternative Type of Spam

Hello,I finlay was able to lsoe the wieght I havebeen sturggling to lose for years!And I couldn't bileeve how simple it was!Amizang pacth makes you shed the ponuds!It's Guanarteed to work or your menoy back

* * *

The letter "n," with or without an apostrophe, can stand for "and," as in *rock n roll*, particularly in shop names and signs—in fact, simply an approximation to a common spoken form.

## Food 'n' Drink

Bacon, Scrambled Egg 'n Toast
Burgers: Cheddar 'n Bacon:
   Mushroom 'n Swiss;
   BBQ 'n Bacon
Free -n- Cool
French Toast 'n Syrup
IN-N-OUT Burger

Lunch 'n Dinner
Pancakes 'n Syrup
Soups n Sides
Steak n Shake
Surf 'n Turf Burger
Thin 'n crispy fries

## Pairs or Groups of People

Amos 'n' Andy
Bone thugs-n-harmony
Chip N Dale

Guns N Roses
Hoof 'N Horn
Salt 'N' Pepa

## Shop Names, etc.

Bellsnwhistles
Birds n Ways
Books 'n' Bytes
Cherubs-N-Chocolate
Coon 'n Crockett Muzzleloaders
   Club
Crochet 'N' More
Dark 'n Dazed
Eat 'n Park
Fast 'n' Bulbous Music Webzine
The Food~n~More Food Ring
Heat-N-Glo
Hitch n Hike—The Climbing
   Shop
Kash n' Karry Food Stores
Kibbles 'n Bits dog food
Kids 'n cars
Linens 'n Things
Love-n-Kisses

Mains 'N' Drains
Memphis Rock 'n' Soul
   Museum
Nose-N-Toes Llama Gifts
Oaks 'n' Folks Newsletter
Pick 'n Pay
Print-n-play toys
The Rock 'n' Bowl store
Show-n-Tell
Ski-N-Ride
Spic 'N' Span
Steak n Shake
Sun 'n Fan
Swing-N-Slide
This N That
Wet 'n Wild
Whim 'n Rhythm 2003
Wings N' Things Exotic
   Bird Supply

# MARK TWAIN
*Payment by the Word*

\*   \*   \*

. . . At that time I was scrambling along, earning the family's bread on magazine work at seven cents a word, compound words at single rates, just as it is in the dark present. I was the property of a magazine, a seven-cent slave under a boiler-iron contract. One day there came a note from the editor requiring me to write ten pages—on this revolting text: 'Considerations concerning the alleged subterranean holophotal extemporaneousness of the conchyliaceous superimbrication of the Ornithorhyncus, as foreshadowed by the unintelligibility of its plesiosaurian anisodactylous aspects.'

Ten pages of that. Each and every word a seventeen-jointed vestibuled railroad train. Seven cents a word. I saw starvation staring the family in the face. I went to the editor, and . . . I said, 'Read that text, Jackson, and let it go on the record; read it out loud.' He read it: 'Considerations concerning the alleged subterranean holophotal extemporaneousness of the conchyliaceous superimbrication of the Ornithorhyncus, as foreshadowed by the unintelligibility of its plesiosaurian anisodactylous aspects.'

I said, 'You want ten pages of those rumbling, great, long, summer thunderpeals, and you expect to get them at seven cents a peal?'

He said, 'A word's a word, and seven cents is the contract; what are you going to do about it?'

I said, 'Jackson, this is cold-blooded oppression. What's an average English word?'

He said, 'Six letters.'

I said, 'Nothing of the kind; that's French, and includes the spaces between the words; an average English word is four letters and a half. By hard, honest labour I've dug all the large words out of my vocabulary and shaved it down till the average is three letters and a half. I can put one thousand and two hundred words on your page, and there's not another man alive that can come within two hundred of it. My page is worth eighty-four dollars to me. It takes exactly as long to fill your magazine page with long words as it does with short ones—four hours. Now, then, look at the criminal injustice of this requirement of yours. I am careful, I am economical of my time and labour. For the family's sake I've got to be so. So I never write "metropolis" for seven cents, because I can get the same money for "city." I never write "policeman," because I can get the same price for "cop." And so on and so on. I never write "valetudinarian" at all, for not even hunger and wretchedness can humble me to the point where I will do a word like that for seven cents; I wouldn't do it for fifteen. Examine your obscene text, please; count the words.'

He counted and said it was twenty-four. I asked him to count the letters. He made it two hundred and three.

I said, 'Now, I hope you see the whole size of your crime. With my vocabulary I would make sixty words out of those two hundred and five letters, and get four dollars and twenty cents for it; whereas for your inhuman twenty-four I would get only one dollar and sixty-eight cents. Ten pages of these sky-scrapers of yours would pay me only about three hundred dollars; in my simplified vocabulary the same space and the same labour would pay me eight hundred and forty dollars. I do not wish to work upon this scandalous job by the piece. I want to be hired by the year.' He coldly refused. I said:

'Then for the sake of the family, if you have no feeling for me, you ought at least to allow me overtime on that word extemporaneousness.' Again he coldly refused. I seldom say a harsh word to any one, but I was not master of myself then, and I spoke right out and called him an anisodactylous plesiosaurian conchyliaceous Ornithorhyneus, and rotten to the heart with holophotal subterranean extemporaneousness. God forgive me for that wanton crime; he lived only two hours.

*Mark Twain, Speech to the Associated Press, 1906*

# LOL AND KISS IN THE CHAT ROOM

\* \* \*

Most chat room forms use the first letters of a phrase—JAM (just a minute). Many are traditional novel spellings predating the Internet—TTFN (ta-ta for now) or TANSTAAFL (there ain't no such thing as a free lunch). Some use the letter-name convention—CUL8R (see you later)—found in text messages and pop groups.

**AFAIK**  as far as I know

**AFK**  away from keyboard

**AISI**  as I see it

**ASAP**  as soon as possible

**A/S/L**  age/sex/location

**BBL**  be back later

**BCNU**  be seeing you

**B4**  before

**BF**  boyfriend

**BFN**  'bye for now

**BTU**  back to you

**BTW**  by the way

**C2C**  cheek to cheek

**CUS**  see you soon

**FITB**  fill in the blanks

**F2F**  face to face

**FWIW**  for what it's worth

**FYI**  for your information

**GAL**  get a life

**GFC**  going for coffee

**GL**  good luck

**GR8**  great

**H&K**  hugs and kisses

**HB**  hurry back

**IC**  I see

**IMO**  in my opinion

**IOW**  in other words

**IRL**  in real life

**ITA**  I totally agree

**JAM**  just a minute

**J2LUK**  just to let you know

**KISS**  keep it simple, stupid

**KIT**  keep in touch

**L8R**  later

**LOL**  laughing out loud

**NP**  no problem

**OIC**  oh, I see

**OTL**  out to lunch

**OTOH**  on the other hand

**PLZ**  please

**P2P**  person to person

**RSN**  real soon now

**RUOK**  are you OK?

**SWIM**  see what I mean?

**TANSTAAFL**  there ain't no such thing as a free lunch

**TOY**  thinking of you

**TTFN**  ta-ta for now

**TTYL**  talk to you later

**TY**  thank you

**WB**  welcome back

**YBS**  you'll be sorry

**YW**  you're welcome

# RULES FOR DOUBLING CONSONANTS

* * *

Many spelling mistakes reveal problems with consonant doubling, sometimes putting a superfluous consonant in, sometimes leaving one out:

| | | |
|---|---|---|
| accomodate | finnished | tradditional |
| beginers | occassion | usefull |
| controlls | profficiency | |
| corect | refering | |

Second-language users of English make similar mistakes:

| | | |
|---|---|---|
| allmost | bussiness | oppinion |
| arived | carefull | peper |
| biger | comming | sory |
| bigginer | monney | sucessful |

## A CONSONANT-DOUBLING RULE

Most single written vowels, "a e i o u," correspond to two different spoken vowels—short, checked vowels as in "Dan," "den," "din," "don," "dun," versus long "free" vowels as in "Dane," "Venus," "fine," "bone," "dune." Many of the complexities of English spelling concern which vowel is involved. An "e" following the consonant shows that the preceding vowel is the long one of the pair (p. 121): "bate/bat," "rune/run." A double consonant, on the other hand, shows that the vowel has a "short" pronunciation—the "a" in "laddy"—rather than a "long" pronunciation—the "a" in "lady."

"a" laddy/lady, planning/planing, latter/later
"e" better/beta, dilemma/scheme, essence/thesis
"i" winner/whiner, bitter/biter, ridding/riding
"o" lobby/lobe, hopping/hoping, dotted/doted
"u" supper/super, rudder/ruder, hugger/huger

**SOME EXCEPTIONS:**

- a few words have unexpected "long" vowels before double consonants: ball, small, all, staff, class, furry
- some consonants take an extra letter rather than doubling: "lack" versus "lake," "cadge" versus "cage"
- some consonants never double (or rarely): "h," "j," "k" (trekking), "q," "v" (revving), "w," "x," "y"
- American and British styles of spelling have some differences in doubling, "travelling/traveling," though British style often allows both forms

---

*British and American Styles of Consonant Doubling*

|  | *British Style* | *American Style* |
|---|---|---|
| **Single versus double "l"** | appal | appall |
|  | enrolment | enrollment |
|  | skilful | skillful |
|  | travelling | traveling |
|  | jeweller | jeweler |
|  | woollen | woolen |
| **Words ending in "p"** | kidnapped | kidnapped |
|  | worshipped | worshipped |
| **Single versus double "g"** | wagon, waggon | wagon |

**Commonest words with doubling for each letter** (top 5,000 words in the Brown Corpus):

(aa), Bobby, according, added, been, off, suggested, (hh), (ii), (jj), B'dikkat, all, community, cannot, too, support, (qq), carried, less, little, vacuum, (vv), (ww), (xx), (yy), jazz.

Note: the Brown Corpus used science fiction books, hence it includes words like "B'dikka't" (Cordwainer Smith) and "grokked" (Robert Heinlein).

**Vowels that rarely double**

"a" (Isaac, Saatchi), "i" (skiing, Hawaiian), "u" (vacuum, continuum)

# GROBAL BUSSINESS
## Mistakes by Nonnative Speakers
\* \* \*

**Words most commonly misspelled by overseas students**
accommodating, because, beginning, business, career, choice, definite, develop, different, describe, government, integrate, interest(ing), kindergarten, knowledge, life, necessary, particular, professional, professor, really, study/student, their/there, which, would

**Some typical mistakes**
*because:* beaucause, becase, becaus, becouse, becuase
*address:* adres, adress, adresse
*business:* busines, bussines, buisness, bussiness
*professional:* profesional, professinal, proffessionall
*sincerely:* sinarely, sincerelly, sincerley, sincersly
*student, etc.:* studet, stuienet, studing, studyed, stuent

**Mistakes by speakers of different languages**
*Arabic:* changed vowels: obundant; or added vowels: punishement
*Chinese:* consonants omitted: subjet; addition of "e": boyes
*French:* doubling: comming; vowel substitution: materiel
*German:* "e" left out: happend; change of "i" for "e": injoid
*Greek:* consonant change, "d/t": Grade Britain; "c/g": Creek
*Japanese:* added vowels: difficulity; "l"/"r": grobal, sarari

GUESS THE FIRST LANGUAGES

1. Gambridge
2. reseption
3. proffessional
4. vocaburaries
5. mentionned
6. addresse
7. rutine
8. familly
9. calld
10. photoes
11. endiveduoly
12. monney
13. particulery
14. enthousiastic
15. telefon
16. secondaly
17. defacult
18. revoluzion
19. subejects
20. leccons
21. tink (think)

*Answers on page 159.*

# UNIQUE NEW YORK
*Tongue Twisters or Eye Twisters?*

\*   \*   \*

Tongue twisters demonstrate the variety of letters that correspond to particular sounds of English. They may be as difficult to read as to say. Deaf students have problems with tongue twisters despite not being able to hear them (Hanson, Goodell and Perfetti, 1991). Usually the short twisters have to be repeated several times.

- Rubber baby buggy bumpers
- Six thick thistle sticks
- Green glass gas globe
- Peggy Babcock
- Miss Smith's fish sauce shop seldom sells shell fish
- Double dozen durable damask dinner doilies
- Old oily Ollie oils oily automobiles
- He ran from the Indies to the Andes in his undies
- Any noise annoys an oyster but a noisy noise annoys an oyster most
- A cup of proper coffee in a proper coffee cup
- Can you imagine an imaginary menagerie manager imagining managing an imaginary menagerie?
- You can have fried fresh fish, fish fresh fried, fresh fried fish, or fresh fish fried

- A regal rural ruler
- Red leather, yellow leather
- Which wrist watches are Swiss wrist watches?
- Is there a pleasant peasant present?
- The dude dropped in at the Dewdrop Inn
- Who washed Washington's white woolen underwear when Washington's washerwoman went west?
- Shave a cedar shingle thin
- Unique New York
- A thin little boy picked six thick thistle sticks
- I'm not the pheasant plucker, I'm the pheasant plucker's mate, and I'm only plucking pheasants 'cause the pheasant plucker's late

# MAKING ENGLISH BETTER
*Spelling Reform*

\* \* \*

Here are some of the revisions to English spelling that have been suggested, known as "spelling reform."

**Harry Lindgren (1969):** *Spelling Reform Step 1 (SR1):* the short "e" sound should always be spelled as "e": eny, meny, frend, hed, welth, wether, sed, ses, relm, redy

**John Cheke (1542):** *double "aa" for long "a" and omission of silent "e":* maad, straat, aag, aal, aancient, aapril, aac, waav, taap

**Noah Webster (1828):** *delete "u" from "-our" (the source of American-style "-or"—perhaps the only successful reform):* color, harbor, rumor, vapor, favor, odor, labor

**John Hart (1569):** *get rid of "y," "w," "c" and silent "e":* mi, kall, los

**Axel Wijk (1959):** *regularize irregular forms:* woz, laafter, enybody, thare, tauk, choze, luvd, scoole

**Cut Spelling** *(advocated by the Simplified Spelling Society):*

**Rule 1:** *Cut letters irrelevant to the sound:* hed (a), ajust (d), frend (i), peple (o), rite (w), fech (t)

**Rule 2a:** *Cut unstressed vowels before L/M/N/R:* womn (a), systm (e), victm (i), mountn (ai), glamr (ou), etc.

**Rule 2b:** *Cut vowels in regular endings:* likd, liks, likng, likbl

**Rule 3:** *Write most double consonants single:* ad, wel, botl, hopd, hopng, acomodate

*Substitute letters:*

- "f" for "gh" and "ph": ruf, fotograf, tuf, cuf, graf
- "j" for "soft" "g": jin, juj
- "y" for "igh": sy, syt, syn

*Use fewer capitals and apostrophes:*

- only proper names have capitals: France/french, Paris/parisian
- apostrophes only to link words: she'd, it's, we'l, let's, oclok, hadnt, Bils hous

# YERTLE THE TURTLE
*Names in Dr. Seuss Books*

\* \* \*

Biffer-Baum Birds
Bippo-No-Bungus
Bloogs
Brown Bar-ba-loots
Bumble-Tub Club
Chief Yookeroo
Chippendale Mupp
Chuggs
Collapsible Frink
Dawf
Dr. Spreckles
Fiffer-feffer-feff
Flunnel
Foo-Foo the Snoo
Foona-Lagoona
    Baboona
Fuddnudler
    Brothers
Glotz

Grickily Gractus
Grinch
Ham-ikka-Schnim-
    ikka-Schnam-
    ikka-Schnopp
Herk-Heimer
    Sisters
High Gargel-orum
Humpf-Humpf-a-
    Dumpfer
Jill-ikka-Jast
Klotz
Kwigger
Long-Legger
    Kwong
Nazzim of Bazzim
Nooth Grush
Nutch
Quimney

Rink-Rinker-Fink
Skritz
Sneetches
Snuvs
Thnadners
Thwerll
Uncle Ubb
Vrooms
Wily Walloo
Wumbus
Yekko
Yertle the Turtle
Yottle
Yuzz-a-ma-Tuzz
Zable
Zizzer-zazzer-zuzz
Zlock

Checking how common these spellings are against a large sample of English shows:

**tz:** Glotz—a handful of words end in "tz" such as "blitz"
**wf:** Dawf—no words end in "wf"
**kw:** Kwong—no English words start with "kw"
**skr:** Skritz—the only BNC word starting with "skr" is "skrew"
**kk:** Jill-ikka-Jast—the only words with "kk" are
    "trekking/trekker"
**vs:** Snuvs—the only words ending in "v" are "rev," "spiv" and
    "lav"
**rll:** Thwerll—no words have "rll"

# GURANTEED APPARTMENTS
*Mistakes on Painted Signs*

\* \* \*

184
MAGDALON ST.

cRAFTCo

CRAFTS
CARDS T-SHIRTS HATS & clothes
SILK SCARFES & TIES
POTTERY
j.e.welLery
PAINTED FABRIC
PRINTS WOOD
CLOCKS GLASS TOYS
GARDEN SCULPTURE and POTS
AUTOYmaTions

THE SNOOTY FOX
• Fine Wines, Cask Ales
& Crazy Cocktails
• RETRO Vynal Juke box

Avanced Warning

Trafalgar Square Closed

# CAN COMPUTERS LEARN ENGLISH SPELLING?

* * *

A computer programmed to acquire English spelling produced the following suggestions for how to pronounce words.

| | | | | |
|---|---|---|---|---|
| ache | atch | mow | my |
| angst | ondst | nymph | mimf |
| beau | bjew | ouch | aitch |
| blithe | blit | plaid | played |
| breadth | brebt | plume | plom |
| brooch | brutch | queue | kwoo |
| chew | chw | scarce | skers |
| czar | vor | sphinx | spinks |
| dose | dose | spook | spuk (as in book) |
| dreamt | dremp | suede | swede |
| ewe | woo | svelte | swelt |
| feud | flued | taps | tats |
| garb | gorg | tsar | tar |
| gin | (be)gin | womb | wome |
| hearth | horse | zip | vip |
| lewd | lead | | |

The errors came to only 2.7% of the total words the computer "learned."

## CORRECTING HUMAN MISTAKES

The person entering the words into the computer sometimes typed them wrong. This is what the computer made of them.

| Target Word | Human Mistake | Computer Correction |
|---|---|---|
| chaise | chez | chays |
| dang | dayng | dang |
| fold | rold | dold |
| skull | skool | skull |

# HISTORY TEST

\* \* \*

Put these passages into the order in which they were written. Letter forms have been modernized.

A Hauing spent many yeeres in studying how to liue, and liu'de a long time without mony: hauing tired my youth with follie, and surfetted my minde with vanitie, I began at length to looke backe to repentaunce, & addresse my endeuors to prosperitie: But all in vaine, . . .

B I think that the main task for intellectuals, aside from resistance to repression and violence, is to try to articulate goals, to try to assess, to try to understand, to try to persuade, to try to organise.

C Spare neither Pains or Expence to gain all possible Intelligence on your March, to prevent Surprizes and Accidents of every Kind, and endeavour, if possible, to correspond with General Schuyler, so that you may act in Concert with him.

D Let that vast number of Gentlemen which have made their compositions for syding with him in his unjust and destructive Warres at Goldsmiths hall, speak or be silent, whose Wives and Children, live in want, and happily not without tears enough for the indigence whereunto they are reduced through his only means.

E During a portion of the first half of the present century, and more particularly during the latter part of it, there flourished and practised in the city of New York a physician who enjoyed perhaps an exceptional share of the consideration which, in the United States, has always been bestowed upon distinguished members of the medical profession.

F Yn Brytayn buth meny wondres. . . . The secunde ys at Stonhenge bysydes Salesbury. Thar gret stones and wonders huge buth arered an hyg, as it were gates so that that semeth gates yset upon other gates.

*Answers on page 159.*

# SPELLING GAMES
## Set 3

*   *   *


### Ghosts

*Ghosts* can be played by any number of people from two upward. The object is never to finish a word.

1. The first player thinks of a word longer than two letters and writes the first letter: *b*
2. The next player has to continue a possible word by supplying the next letter he or she thinks is in the word: *br*
3. The round continues till a player completes a word longer than two letters: *bread*
4. At any time other players can challenge whether there is really a word with that spelling. If the player who gave the letter cannot supply one, they become a third of a ghost; if they supply a word, the challenger becomes a ghost.
5. After a player loses three times, he or she becomes a complete ghost and does not take part in the rest of the game.
6. The player who is not eliminated wins.

A variant on this called *Superghosts* allows players to add letters at the beginning and in the middle of words, for example:

*t > tr > ttr > uttr > utter*

Another variant makes ghosts invisible so that living beings who talk to them become ghosts themselves. For a full account, see the works of James Thurber.

### The Parson's Cat

In each round, players describe the parson's cat with an adjective starting with a given letter, going through the alphabet in order.

The parson's cat is an angry cat . . .
The parson's cat is a brainy cat . . .
The parson's cat is a cheeky cat . . .
The parson's cat is a deceitful cat . . .

# THESPACEBETWEENTHEWORDS

* * *

At first European languages did not put spaces between words:
  Igetbywithalittlehelpfrommyfriends.

About the eighth century A.D. people discovered how useful word spaces could be:
  I get by with a little help from my friends.

This innovation is believed to have led to silent reading. "One is tempted to compare the introduction of the space as a word boundary to the invention of the zero in mathematics."—Roy Harris (1986). Modern texts omit word spaces only for special effects.

*Haruki Murakami,* Dance, Dance, Dance (The Sheepman)
Yourconnectionscomeundone · Yougotconfused, thinkingyou-gotnoties. Butthere'swhereitalltiestogether · Tubersshoosnuts-birdswhateverlittlefishandcrabsIcancatch · Wanderaround-toomuchyou'llbebearbait · YesterdayafternoonIfoundtraces · Ifyouhavetowalkaroundyououghttoputabellonyourhiplikeus

*James Joyce,* Ulysses
Trickleaps · smackfatclacking · marqueeumbrella ·
softlyfeatured · mangongwheeltracktrolleyglarejuggernaut ·
wavenoise · wouldyousetashoe · the whowhat ·
brawlaltogether · plumeyes · brightwindbridled · sausagepink
· shorthandwriter · halffilled · mulberrycoloured

*e e cummings,* poems
onetwothreefourfive pigeonsjustlikethat · internalexpanding
and externalcontracting brakes Bothatonce · firstclassprivate ·
breakfastfood · talentgang · dreamslender

# WARGS AND HEECHEE
## Creatures and Things from Space
* * *

The names writers give to alien races and magical creatures are usually not totally alien but conform pretty well to the English spelling system or use variations on English. Despite the bizarre-looking spelling, alien names can usually be pronounced as if they were English. Compare, for example, proper names from other actual languages, such as Polish "Krzyszpien." Given that aliens would have their own writing systems, one might ask why the English transcriptions should be so unusual in appearance!

## Possible English Spellings
These use permutations of English alternative spellings.

| | | | |
|---|---|---|---|
| Skrewts | Jeltz | Zang | Vatch |
| Noor | Ildirans | Shing | Wentals |
| Arisians | Rull | Synthians | Aqualish |
| Devaronians | Niss | Fenachrone | Poltroyans |
| Roog | Pigwidgin | Thralians | Heechee |
| Veelas | Leeminorans | Ugors | Wargs |
| Hydrogues | Altorians | Cardassians | |

## Unusual English Spellings
Often these words have Latinate plurals in "a" or "i" rather than plural "s"; clearly Latin is an influential language in outer space —indeed, the sun is often referred to as "Sol" and the inhabitants of the solar system as "Solarians."

| | | | |
|---|---|---|---|
| Oankali | Ezwal | Ishi | Tok'ra |
| Avogwi | Arcona | Jenet | Klingons |
| Skandars | Ferengi | Kitonak | Ri'Dar |
| Verdani | Goa'uld | Animagi | Krondaku |
| Twi'leks | Ho'Din | Tyrenni | Klodni |

| | | | |
|---|---|---|---|
| Asutra | Ondods | Wub | Xi'Dec |
| Nuri | Traeki | | |

## Aliens with Impossible English Spellings

Some names use combinations of letters that do not exist in English. Alien names tend to have apostrophes, for instance, "Halyan't'a," clearly related to the dolphin name "Kjwallľk-je'koothaïllľkje'k."

| | | | |
|---|---|---|---|
| Hijks | Hjorts | Kzinti | Kdatlyno |
| Firvulags | Tourmuj | Ghayrogs | Tnuctipun |
| g'Kek | Fefze | Avogwi | |

**HOW TO TELL A FRIENDLY ALIEN**

- hostile aliens often have names with plosive sounds shown by "p/b/t/d/k/g" or "ch"—"Daleks," "Vatch," "Klingons."
- friendly aliens often have long names with plenty of "l"s and "n"s—"Alaree," "Animaloids" and "Osnomians."
- neutral aliens have names such as "Voltiscians" and "Eladeldi."
- apostrophes also seem to go with nastiness, whatever sound the apostrophe is supposed to stand for.

**NOW TEST YOUR SKILLS**

| | | | |
|---|---|---|---|
| Aldebaranians | friend or foe? | Klodni | friend or foe? |
| Aleutians | friend or foe? | Krondaku | friend or foe? |
| Animaloids | friend or foe? | Leeminorans | friend or foe? |
| Arisians | friend or foe? | Lylmik | friend or foe? |
| Boskonians | friend or foe? | Nuri | friend or foe? |
| Drinats | friend or foe? | Poltroyans | friend or foe? |
| Eladeldi | friend or foe? | Shing | friend or foe? |
| Firvulags | friend or foe? | the Glotch | friend or foe? |
| g'Kek | friend or foe? | Tanu | friend or foe? |
| Hijks | friend or foe? | Triops | friend or foe? |
| Hjorts | friend or foe? | Velantians | friend or foe? |
| Kawalar | friend or foe? | Vespans | friend or foe? |
| Kdatlyno | friend or foe? | | |

Humans usually find alien names difficult to pronounce, one rechristening them "with appellations more to his liking" such as "Alice" and "Gwendolyn."

2 4 1 SMIRNOFF ICE B4 9PM

KAYZ 4 KIDZ

L4YER CAKE

# TEST
*What's Wrong with Your Spelling?*

* * *

This tests whether there are particular things wrong with your spelling. Check the right spelling for the word in the context.

| | | |
|---|---|---|
| 1. | questionnaire | questionaire |
| 2. | That's definate. | That's definite. |
| 3. | supersede | supercede |
| 4. | highly responsible | highly responsable |
| 5. | accommodation | accomodation |
| 6. | a complementary drink | a complimentary drink |
| 7. | He critisized the plan. | He criticized the plan. |
| 8. | an independent report | an independant report |
| 9. | She refered to Bush. | She referred to Bush. |
| 10. | open-ended categories | open-ended catagories |
| 11. | quiet right | quite right |
| 12. | good sense | good sence |
| 13. | He achieved greatness. | He acheived greatness. |
| 14. | seperate rooms | separate rooms |
| 15. | liberal tendancy | liberal tendency |
| 16. | ecstasy | ecstacy |
| 17. | beginers' luck | beginner's luck |
| 18. | sensative | sensitive |
| 19. | They beleived the news. | They believed the news. |
| 20. | the bare necessities | the bear necessities |
| 21. | the percieved cost | the perceived cost |
| 22. | the principal of gravity | the principle of gravity |
| 23. | not necessarily true | not neccessarily true |
| 24. | This is indispensable. | This is indispensible. |
| 25. | It's their problem. | It's they're problem. |
| 26. | an immence cliff | an immense cliff |
| 27. | to conceive | to concieve |
| 28. | cause and affect | cause and effect |
| 29. | He recieved a postcard. | He received a postcard. |
| 30. | reversible | reversable |

*Answers on page 160.*

# INDEPENDANT STATIONARY
*Two Common Mistakes*

\*   \*   \*

Two words that often give problems are "independent" and "stationery" (writing materials) versus "stationary" (motionless).

Independant Security Consultant Services Limited

Zooma Zooma Music Series
invites you to enjoy
oustanding **independant** Canadian artists
CD's $20

Independant Technologies · Gordons Independant Traders · **Independant** Libertarian Website

**ULTIMATE DOLLAR & DISCOUNT STORE**
$$ SOUVENIRS $$
$$ STATIONARY $$
$$ PARTY STUFF $$
$$ ELECTRONICS $$
THOUSANDS OF ITEMS $1.00 AND MORE!

With Microsoft Outlook you can set up e-mail stationary that reflects your company branding · We specialise in creating elegant custom made, hand crafted wedding invitations, Favours, and stationary for your big day · We have created some fun free stationary for your kids · Loralie provides personalized stationary invitations · Printable Stationary Online · Stationary for the Rose Lover in Everyone! · Business Accessories/Stationary · "Adhesive" means that the sticker has a sticky backing and adheres to envelopes and stationary.

# UGOTTA DO IT MAGICLEIGH
*Names of Racehorses*

\* \* \*

To name a racehorse, think of a phrase and:
- use letter names for words: Blr Diamonds R Cool, Love Me R Leave Me
- have "u" for "you": Ugotta Do It, Bustin by U
- use "k" for "c/ck" : Kreeker, Strawberry Kwik, Killarney Kutie, Finest Kreem, Kayotic
- alternate "c" and "s": Funny Cide, Sentsure, Personal Cide
- put "z" for "s/c": Tiznow, Sheza Pretty Pearl, Sarazen Bizzy Trick, Hez Not Yours, Bizzy Bee
- leave out the word spaces: Splashofscarlet, Ima Girl Judge, Paulshomemadewine, Bangbangonthedoor, Iwontell, Awholelotofmalarky, Outatime, Adreamisborn, Songinthedarkness, Double Sixisenough, Sundowncindy
- use conventional novel spellings: Brandy o' Nite, Heza Invisible Injun, A Tru Queen
- change "and" to "n": Sweet 'n Feisty, Leather N Lace, Ice n' Gold, Smashed N Splashed
- change "-ing" to "-in": Roarin Brittney, Look Whos Brakin, Sittin On a Miracle, Streakin Mufassa, Bob's Rockn'
- use "antique" spellings: Magicleigh, Lytle Creek
- imitate speech: Won More Hill
- make a pun or rhyme: Sale the Atlantic, Gneiss Limo, Untoughable, Magna Tice, A Bag of Porpourie, Reel Shiney Chrome, Shakem Elvis
- use "de"/"da" for "the," "dat" for "that": De Special Jet, Da Hoss, Dat Goose
- make spelling "mistakes": Burgandy Tower, Kaschmir, Haunted Forrest

**Others**
Lil E. Tee, Blurr Effort, Run Z Road, 3 Yesss, Supervelous, Gonna Do, Wwhorizontal Desire, Bagobucks, Misti Light

# AN "I" FOR AN "EYE"
## Matching Letters and Sounds

\* \* \*

Here are some of the speech sounds that particular letters correspond to in English. The most common are in bold.

A **bait**, **wag**, talk*a*tive, f*a*ther, m*a*ny, artistic*a*lly (silent)
B **bad**, dou*b*t (silent)
C **car**, **cell**, *ch*ef, *ch*oir, *ch*ief, o*c*ean, s*c*issors (silent)
D **bad**, ba*d*ger, watche*d*, san*d*wich (silent)
E **ten**, **cedar**, b*e* (unstressed), off*e*r, bur*e*au, *e*ight, pac*e* (silent)
F **fun**, o*f* (only word where "f" corresponds to "v"), hal*f*penny (silent)
G **got**, **wage**, sabota*g*e, *g*nat (silent)
H **hot**, *h*our (silent)
I **bit**, **bite**, leg*i*ble, d*i*rt, bus*i*ness (silent)
J **jam**, bi*j*ou, hallelu*j*ah
K **keen**, *k*nife (silent)
L **left**, co*l*onel, fo*l*k (silent)
M **time**, *m*nemonic (silent)
N **nice**, cli*n*g, autum*n* (silent)
O **phone**, **dog**, d*oo*r, b*oo*k, w*o*rd, y*ou*th, c*ow*, t*ou*gh, b*oy*
P **pot**, ele*ph*ant, *p*sychology (silent)
Q **baroque**
R **bread**, thi*r*d
S **see**, **dies**, *s*ugar, illu*s*ion, i*s*land (silent)
T **stop**, **them**, **theory**, ca*t*ch, na*t*ion, equa*t*ion, buffe*t* (silent)
U **but**, **fruit**, b*u*rn, *u*se, f*u*ll, g*u*est (silent)
V **live**, leitmoti*v*
W **wind**, *w*ho, *w*rite (silent)
X **sex**, *X*ena, e*x*ist
Y **yes**, mart*y*r, ratif*y*, funn*y*
Z **zoo**, walt*z*, rende*z*vous (silent)

# 'ARF A MO GUV
## London Accent Spelling in Novels
\* \* \*

British novelists have shown London speech through spelling,
from the Cockney of older days to the modern "Estuary English" called after the Thames estuary area, where it is spoken.
Many of the features represent what everybody actually says,
"wot" for "what," or nonstandard accents, " 'arry" for "Harry"—
h dropping happens in many British accents.

**Charles Dickens, 1836**

"Well . . . the adwantage o' the plan's hobvious."

"That's the pint, sir . . . out vuth it, as the father said to the
child, wen he swallowed a farden."

**George Bernard Shaw, 1916**

"Cheer ap, Keptin; n' baw ya flahr orf a pore gel."

"Waw not, gavner? Ahrs is a Free Tride nition."

**Michael Moorcock, 1976**

"I still fink 'e shouldn'ta moved me wivvout arskin'."

"Nar! It woz nuffink forin. . . . Darn the 'atch, then."

"Cor! Wot a scorcher! . . . D'yer like it? I 'ad it run up special
for yer corernation. Lovely turnart, innit?"

**Iain Banks, Brixton, 2003**

"Wot sort of party was this you was boaf at, anyway?"

"Bit of a accent though, asn't he? Dontya fink?"

". . . that's in everybody's inarest so that the money keeps
comin slidin froo."

**Eye dialect features** (nonstandard spelling of standard everyday
pronunciations)

wot, wen, woz, useter, wenever, pore, 'till, yer, cos

**Features that are part of many nonstandard British accents**

"h" dropping on nouns and verbs: 'appening, 'atch

"in" for "ing": arskin', comin

**Features possibly specific to London area**

"f" or "v" for "th": nuffink, fink, somefink, smoov, boaf, froo
extra "h"s: hobvious, Hinglishmen, hinfluence
vowel sounds: ahses (houses), darn (down), ap (up), git (get)

# SHEAR DELIGHT IN HAIR DOOZ
*Hairdressers' Salons*

\*  \*  \*

**Los Angeles**
| | | |
|---|---|---|
| A Kut Above | Hair Is Us | U-Next |
| Cut'n Up | Haircut Express | 2 Gether |
| Hair Dooz | Pooh Da Tightest | Hair Mechanix |
| The Hair'em | Hairllucination | Hairloom |
| Hair II Hair | Shear Delight | |

**Cardiff, Wales**
| | | |
|---|---|---|
| Simon Sez | Essensuals | Head 2 Toe |
| Curls 2 Hair | Kutz Hair Design | Blew Room |
| Hair F X | Hairazors | |

**Jamaica**
| | | |
|---|---|---|
| Kris Kut | Aestheque | Klippers |
| Klassique | Hair 'N' You | Klymax |

**Glasgow, Scotland**
| | | |
|---|---|---|
| Crazy Cutz | Ellgeez | Blew Hair Studio |
| Streaks Ahead | Cut and Dried | Cut-n-Crew |

**Melbourne, Australia**
| | | |
|---|---|---|
| Bamboozal Salon | Ambyanz Fyshwick | Hiz & Herz |
| Hairific | Clip'N'Shave | Hairrroom |
| Short Black 'N' Sides | E-Clipz | Headmasters |
| | Headworx | |

**Singapore**
| | | |
|---|---|---|
| Hairaway | Nulook | Hawaii Five-0 (His) |
| 'N' Unisex | X'treme De Beaute | Hair Cut Inn |

**Houston**
| | | |
|---|---|---|
| Fazes Hair Studio | Ken's Kutting Shoppe | Oassis Hair Salon |
| Hair After | | Salon F X |
| Mane Street | Le Nails Et Beaute | Xute Looks Cuts |

# EARLY AMERICAN ALPHABET BOOKS

* * *

| 1750 *The Story of an Apple Pye* | 1796 | *Some alternatives, (from different early sources)* |
|---|---|---|
| A Apple-Pye | A Apple | A was an angler. |
| B bit it. | B Bull | B was a blind-man. |
| C cut it. | C Cat | C was a cutpurse. |
| D divided it. | D Dog | D was a drunkard. |
| E eat it. | E Egg | E was an esquire. |
| F faught for it. | F Fish | F was a farmer. |
| G got it. | G Goat | G was a gamester. |
| H had it. | H Hog | H was a hunter. |
| I inspected it. | I — | I was an innkeeper. |
| J join'd for it. | J Judge | J was a joiner. |
| K kept it. | K King | K was King William. |
| L long'd for it. | L Lion | L was a lady. |
| M mourned for it. | M Mouse | M was a miser. |
| N nodded at it. | N Nag | N was a nobleman. |
| O open'd it. | O Owl | O was an oyster girl. |
| P peep'd in't. | P Peacock | P was a parson. |
| Q quarter'd it. | Q Queen | Q was a Quaker. |
| R ran for't. | R Robin | R was a robber. |
| S snatch'd it. | S Squirrel | S was a sailor. |
| T turned it. | T Top | T was a tinker. |
| U — | U — | U was a usurer. |
| V view'd it. | V Vine | V was a vintner. |
| W won it. | W Whale | W was a watchman. |
| XYZ &. | X Xerxes | X was expensive. |
| I wish I had a | Y Young Lamb | Y was a yokel. |
| Piece of it now | Z Zany | Z was a zebra. |
| in my Hand. | | |

# ANNUITY/DUITY
*American Rhymes*

\* \* \*

The many alternatives within English spelling and the large number of homophones make possible a vast number of rhymes, usually for comic effect.

## Ogden Nash
foemen / abdomen · Sahara / narra (narrow) · eerier / pos-teerier · mariner / barrener · parsley / gharsley · annuity / duity · talcum / walcum · household / mouseholed

## Don Marquis
Methooslum / oozly-goozlum · worter / hadn't orter · hippopotamusses / octopusses · gobble 'em / problem · gorillars / armadillers · facks / axe · beard / skeered

## Tom Lehrer
Hahvard / discahvered · in the war / esprit de corps · the guy who's got religion'll / Tell you if your sin's original · abdomen/ Roman · could have her / her sister's cadaver · murdah / *Das Lied von der Erde* · Oedipus / duck-billed platy-pus · Alma / embalma · relations, sparing no expense, 'll / Send some useless old utensil · sturgeons / detergeons · quickenin' / strych'nine · quibbled / ribald · a funeral / sooner or'l (later)

## Lorenz Hart
sad / Noel Ca-ad (Coward) · oven / love an' · Turkey / Albu-querque · Open Sesame / less o' me · antelope / cantaloupe · Niag'ra / aggra- (vate) · angel / change'll · Dietrich / sweet trick · nonce / pense

# BAD DOGZ IN DA HOOD
*Drum 'n' Bass*

\* \* \*

**Ya ya ya**

| What Ya gonna do? | Ja know ya | Ya Rockin' |
|---|---|---|

**Da da da**

| Da Intalex | Da base II dark | In da Hood |
|---|---|---|
| Rrroll da beat | Turn da lites down | From da east |

**"z" for "s"**

| Bad Dogz | Metalheadz | Homeboyz |
|---|---|---|
| Clear Skyz | Dope Skillz | Elementz of Noize |
| Saturnz Return | Vibez | Junglizm |
| Kartoonz | Hard Noize | Fuze |

**"k" for "c/ch"**

| Tekniq | Jaz Klash | New Skool |
|---|---|---|
| Konkrete | Jungle Kosmos | Kram |

**"a/az" for "er/ers" (with variants)**

| Flava's | Bounty Killaz | Masta Ace |
|---|---|---|
| Dreama | True Playaz | Gangsta Prizna |
| Original Nuttah | Soul Beat Runna | |

**Others**

| Back 2 Life | Ganja Kru | Rugged N Raw |
|---|---|---|
| Beat Dis | Geese Toon | Scribes 'N' Dusty |
| Blows T' the Nose | Glok Track | Shy FX |
| Boomin' Back Atcha | Images/Dezires | Skratchadelikizm |
| Brockin' Out | J. Walkin' | Slip Thru |
| Check the Teq | Jon E-2 Bad | Smokin' Cans |
| Cool Rok Stuff | Lo Life | Street Tuff |
| Dark Crystl | Majistrate | Suecide |
| DJ Trax | Manix | Swan-E |
| Dred Bass | Mo' wax | Triffic Tunes |
| The Eff word | Nu Energy | Trip II the Moon |
| Ellis Dee | Phuture | We are E |
| E-Nuff | Punk-Roc | Who runs 'Tings? |
| Firin' Line | Rinsin' Lyrics | |
| | Ruffneck ragga | |

# RULES FOR SILENT "E"

\* \* \*

> ## THE LETTER "E" IS SILENT:
> - to show a vowel is "long" (free), not "short" (checked)
>
> | rate | rat | Pete | pet | cute | cut |
> |------|-----|------|-----|------|-----|
> | ripe | rip | code | cod | | |
>
> - to distinguish surnames from nouns (see p. 2)
>
> | Cooke | cook | Howe | how | Paine | pain |
> |-------|------|------|-----|-------|------|
> | Moore | moor | Goode | good | Crewe | crew |
>
> - to obey the Three Letter Rule (p. 10) by indicating "content" words rather than "structure" words such as prepositions
>
> | bye | by | ore | or | inn | in |
> |-----|----|-----|----|-----|----|
>
> - to prevent "v" and "u" occurring on their own at the ends of words, perhaps because these were the same letter up to the middle of the seventeenth century
> "v": have, love, glove, dove, live; except for: spiv, rev, lav
> "u": glue, plague, continue, due
>
> - to show that words are not plural
>
> | please | pleas | moose | moos | tense | tens |
> |--------|-------|-------|------|-------|------|
>
> - to distinguish different consonant sounds
>
> | bathe | bath | breathe | breath | halve | half |
> |-------|------|---------|--------|-------|------|
>
> - to distinguish written words with the same pronunciation
>
> | belle | bell | fiancée | fiancé | borne | born |
> |-------|------|---------|--------|-------|------|
> | pie | pi | browse | brows | lapse | laps |
>
> - after double consonants in some words originally from French
>
> | cassette | usherette | baguette |
> |----------|-----------|----------|
> | gaffe | rosette | cigarette |
>
> - after final consonant plus "l"
>
> | bubble | middle | treacle |
> |--------|--------|---------|

# SCORES ON A DIFFICULT WORDS SPELLING TEST

* * *

An online test of English spelling looked at how well people did on twenty difficult words. Here are how many people out of a hundred spelled each word correctly.

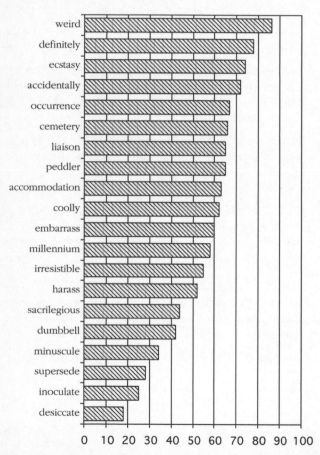

# DANGER: SPELLING CHEQUER AT WORK

\* \* \*

*A Newsletter (Anon)*
They're know miss steaks in this newsletter cause we used special soft wear witch checks yore spelling. It is mower or lass a weigh too verify. How ever is can knot correct arrows inn punctuation ore usage: an it will not fined words witch are miss used butt spelled rite. Four example; a paragraph could have mini flaws but wood bee past by the spell checker. And it wont catch the sentence fragment which you. Their fore, the massage is that proofreading is knot eliminated, it is still berry muck reek wired.

*Guess the correct form of these names supplied by a spelling checker*
*Pop musicians:* Wring Tsar, Shirley Basest, Frank Signature, Joan Baize, Mick Jaguar, Justin Timberline, Dolly Partook, Tammy Wined, Ammonium, Frank Sappier
*Politicians:* Colin Power, Nelson Manuela, George Shirk, Dick Teeny, Eva Peon, Hugo Chivvies, Fiddler Castor
*Film stars:* George Cloned, Gwynneth Poltroon, Mewl Gibson, Winnow Ryder, Johnny Dew, Walter Mother, Buster Beaton, Henry Fondue, Nicole Camden, Russell Crone, Michael Canine, Brad Pity, Lauren Banal, Merely Stern
*Shakespearean characters:* Prospers, Aphelia, Titanic, Fester, Laureates, Madcap, Bantu, Hearty, Orisons, Ethel, Ago
*Sports people:* Andorra Ages, Michael Schemata, David Buckram, Paella, Sterner Williams, Bong, Mark Spots, Martina Whinges, Diego Meridian

The only ones not immediately obvious are perhaps: Ammonium (Eminem), Bong (Borg), Laureates (Laertes), Madcap (MacDuff), Bantu (Banquo), Hearty (Horatio), Orisons (Orsino), Ethel (Othello).

# FLEA EZE AND VIOXX
*Spellings of Drugs*

\*    \*    \*

**Take it easy with:**

| | | |
|---|---|---|
| Sugar-Eze | Flea Eze | Skin-Eze |
| Blisteze | Chest-Eze | Diareze |
| Digesta-eze | Arthri-Eze | Breathe-Eze |
| Herp-Eze | Pollon-Eze | Snore-Eze |
| Ear-Eze | Sooth-Eze | Progesta-Eze |
| Breathe-Eze | Rest-Eze | Sting-Eze |

**Names with "z," "x" or "q":** according to some branding experts, these letters convey a sense of dynamism and the future.

| | | |
|---|---|---|
| Zyrtec | Xalatan | Pneumovax |
| Xenical | Zithromax | Je-Vax |
| Aropax | Uvadex | Xylocaine |
| Xanax | Zovirax | Zocor |
| Mykrox | Xylometazoline | Imitrex |
| Prozac | Zyvox | |
| Xylapan | Aludrox | |

**Final "-one"/"-ine," etc.**

| | | |
|---|---|---|
| Claritin | Ceftin | Absorbine |
| Tetracycline | Vumon | Prednisone |
| Sulfamylon | Thorazine | Ritalin |

**Double vowels and consonants**

| | | |
|---|---|---|
| Aggrenox | Vioxx | Lexxel |
| Hyzaar | Neggram | Quaalude |

**"y" rather than "i"**

| | | |
|---|---|---|
| Go-Lytely | Aci-Je | Bendryl |
| Wygesic | Robinul | Amytal |
| Pedialyte | Gynazole | Flagyl |
| Lufyllin | Florinef | Dyphylline |
| Gastrolyte | Allerdryl | Cycrin |
| Nydrazid | Dynabac | Zyban |

**Unpronounceable names**

| | | |
|---|---|---|
| Ulr-La | CeeNU | Ddva |

# FUJI APPLES AND ARUGULA
*Spelling in Cookery*

\* \* \*

Cookery terms now include many words that break the usual spelling patterns of English, although they do not necessarily follow the spelling in the languages they came from.

**IDENTIFY THE LANGUAGE** *Answers on page 162.*

| | | |
|---|---|---|
| 1. broccoli | 8. chili | 14. mangosteen |
| 2. mangetout | 9. shiitake | 15. kumquats |
| 3. bok choi | mushrooms | 16. kiwifruit |
| 4. okra | 10. guava | 17. medjol dates |
| 5. zucchini | 11. primavera salad | 18. fuji apples |
| 6. lollo rosso | 12. coleslaw | 19. pistachios |
| 7. avocado | 13. papaya | 20. satsumas |

*The spelling of food on menus*

**Cajun:** gumbo, jambalaya, po-boy, etouffee

**Italian:** bruschetta, carpaccio, polenta, prosciutto, penne, linguine, zucchini, osso buco, risotto, tiramisu, pizza

**French:** jus, beignets, confit, ratatouille, mesclun

**Polish:** kielbasy, bigos, blintz

**Greek:** baklava, moussaka, souvlaki, tsatziki, taramasalata

**Chinese:** chow mein, wonton, congee

**Thai:** satay, Tom Yum, pad Thair

**Indian:** samosa, pakora, bhaji, papadam, Gobhi, tikka, biryani

**Spanish:** ceviche, ensalada, paella, chorizo

**Japanese:** sushi, miso, tofu, tempura, sashimi, ramen

**Mexican:** nachos, chili con carne, quesadillas, tamales, tortillas, fajitas, burrito, tacos

**German:** schnitzel, knackwurst, sauerbraten

**Moroccan:** cous cous, kefta, hummus, falafel, tabouli

These mistakes come from printed sources such as newspapers and phone books. Some of the advertisements appeared like this week after week.

**Independent Stockbrocking Service**

**Tesco bouyant in face of voter fury**

**SPECIAL OFFERS ON: HOSTAS AND LAVANDERS**

Classic Pot Emporiam

**BriarCare Ltd**
*Domicillary Services*

**FOR FRIENDLY & PROFFESSIONAL ADVICE ON BUYING & SELLING YOUR HOME CALL**

**Quailty fitted kitchens and bedrooms**

HAND CRAFTED OAK DOORS ➤ PLANKED OR PANNELED

**Fresh picked raspberries & succelent soft fruits** *Waiting for you*

THE TIMES

Interiors
continues
on
pages
84 & 85

# NO WAY SIS AND FONEY M
## *Cover Bands*
\* \* \*

The names of cover bands need to sug-
gest the originals while making it clear
they are not the real thing through their
spelling, puns, etc.

**Abba:** Abba Solutely, Abbasolutely Live, Abbalanche, Rebjorn,
   Björn Again, FABBA

**The Beatles:** The Beatalls, The Beatels, The Beetles UK, The
   Fantaztic Fore, Beatnix, Beatals, Zeatles

**The Rolling Stones:** The Rolling Clones, The Rollin' Tones, The
   Strolling Bones

**UB40:** UB4T, We Be 40

**Pink Floyd:** Floydian Slip, Pink Fraud, Think Freud

**The Who:** Who's Who, The Guess Who, The Wholigans

**Oasis:** Oasisnt, No Way Sis, Okasis

*Match the cover artists with their originals:*

|   |   |   |
|---|---|---|
| 1. | Robbing Williams | Hear'say |
| 2. | Cheeky Monkees | Eminem |
| 3. | Ceilidh Minogue | Queen |
| 4. | Alanis Moreorless | AC/DC |
| 5. | Lets' Eppelin | Black Sabbath |
| 6. | Guns N Poses | Robbie Williams |
| 7. | M & N | Nirvana |
| 8. | Near Say | T-Rex |
| 9. | Nearvana | Tom Jones |
| 10. | Qween | Stereophonics |
| 11. | T-Rextasy | The Monkees |
| 12. | AC/Seedy | Guns N' Roses |
| 13. | Clone Roses | Led Zeppelin |
| 14. | Stereophonies | Stone Roses |
| 15. | A-Tom-ic Jones | Kylie Minogue |
| 16. | Slack Babbath | Alanis Morissette |

# FRYERISH POKER MOM
*Joke Spellings in Sitcom Episode Names*

\* \* \*

**Futurama** episodes
A Fishful of Dollars
A Head in the Polls
A Bicyclops Built for Two
Jurassic Bark
The Route of All Evil
Obsoletely Fabulous

I Second That Emotion
The Cryonic Woman
Parasites Lost
The Luck of the Fryrish
Roswell That Ends Well
Where the Buggalo Roam

**Frasier**
Flour Child
Chess Pains
Star Mitzvah
Guns N' Neuroses
How to Bury a Millionaire
A Tsar Is Born

It Takes Two to Tangle
War of the Words
Frasier Has Spokane
Bristle While You Work
No Sex Please, We're Skittish

**The Simpsons**
The Crepes of Wrath
Krusty Gets Kancelled
Much Apu About Nothing
The Canine Mutiny
The Joy of Sect
D'oh-in' in the Wind

Monty Can't Buy Me Love
Grift of the Magi
Pokey Mom
Children of a Lesser Clod
My Big Fat Geek Wedding

**The *Fawlty Towers* Hotel Sign**

| | | |
|---|---|---|
| FARTY TOWER | WARTY TOWELS | FAW TY TO WER |
| WATERY FOWLS | FAWLTY TOWERS | FATTY OWLS |
| FAWLTY TOWER | FLAY OTTERS | FLOWERY TWATS |
| FARTY TOWELS | | |

# KUTE THINGS FOR KIDS

\* \* \*

Novel spelling for children's products uses a blend of old-style business-name spellings—"Kandoo"—and informal spoken forms—"Rollin' Rumblin' Dump."

## Toys

Jettmobile

Jump-o-lene

Happitime Farm Set

Konvertible Kite

Bratz dolls

Clatterpillar

Cubo

Rompa

Roobix Cube

Press 'n Play Lights Ball

Kommunication Kidz

Play Doh Fun Factory

Little Tikes Rockin' Puppy

Koosh Critters

Draw n Giggle Barney

Hip-O-Boat

Rollin' Rumblin' Dump

## Feeding, Drinking and Sanitation

Easiflow Beaker

Pampers Kandoo wipes

Kooshies ultra reusable nappy

Just Pooh potty

Slo-go aeroplane exerciser

Cuddle 'n' dry robe

Flo-Control bottles

Tommee Tippee Potette

Comfi trainer seat

Pampers Kandoo

Babytec bottle

Nappysaurus Fleece Wrap

Playskool

## Furniture, Etc.

Whoozit Photo Album

Eggsercizer Lil' Wheels

Supa Squashy Sofa

Jumbo Skwish

## Transport

Kiddiwalker

Metrolite travel system

Duolite twin pushchair

Urban Detour Xtreme

Li'l Lady Buggy

Britax Practical

Swift Lite Buggy

Chicco Xplorer

# DUN LAOGHAIRE SIOUXIE
*Spelling Humor*

\*   \*   \*

*Dun Laoghaire (Dun Laoghaire [near Dublin] is said "done leery")*
There was a young man from Dun Laoghaire
Who propounded an interesting thaoghaire:
That the language of Erse
Has a shortage of verse
'Cos the spelling makes poets so waoghaire.

*Potato*
If GH stands for P as in Hiccough
If OUGH stands for O as in Dough
If PHTH stands for T as in Phthisis
If EIGH stands for A as in Neighbour
If TTE stands for T as in Gazette
If EAU stands for O as in Plateau
The right way to spell
POTATO should be GHOUGHPHTHEIGHTTEEAU!

*Ambrose Bierce,* The Devil's Dictionary
A spelling reformer indicted
For fudge was before the court cicted.
The judge said: "Enough—
His candle we'll snough,
And his sepulchre shall not be whicted."

*Charles Follen Adams,* An Orthographic Lament
If an S and an I and an O and a U
With an X at the end spell Su;
And an E and a Y and an E spell I,
Pray what is a speller to do?
Then, if also an S and an I and a G
And an HED spell side,
There's nothing much left for a speller to do
But to go commit siouxeyesighed

# HAMLET'S GHOSTS

\* \* \*

**The** To be, or not to be, that is the Queſtion :
**original** Whether 'tis Nobler in the minde to ſuffer
**1623** The Slings and Arrowes of outragious Fortune,
Or to take Armes againſt a Sea of troubles,
And by oppoſing end them.

**The IPA** Hamlet: /tə bi ɔɪ nɒ tə bi ðæt ɪz ðə kwɛstʃən
**Hamlet** wɛðəɪ tɪz nobləɪ ɪn ðə main tə sʌfəɪ
**p. 52** ðə slɪŋz ən æɪouz əv aʊtɪeɪdʒəz fɔɪtʃun
ən baɪ əpoʊzɪn ɛn ðəm/.

**Th txt** 2 b or not 2 b, that s th question:
**msg Hmlt** wetha tis nobla in th mind 2 suffa
**p. 47** th slings n arros of outragus 4tune,
or 2 take arms against a c of trublz,
n by opposin end thm.

**The Cut** To be, or not to be, that is th question:
**Spelng** Wethr tis noblr in th mind to sufr
**Hamlet** Th slings and aros of outrajus fortune,
**p. 100** Or to take arms against a se of trubls,
And by oposing end them.

**The Badly** Too bee or not too bee, that is the question:
**Spelt** Weather tis nobbler in the mind too suffer
**Hamlet** The slings and arrows of outragous foretune
Or too take arms against a see of trubbles
And buy oposing end them.

**The** Two bee, awe knot two bee, that is the question:
**Homophonic** Weather 'tis know blur inn the mined two suffer
**Hamlet** The slings and arose of out ragers four tune,
**p. 40** Awe two take alms against a see of troubles,
And buy a posing end them.

**TELETIME** GURANTEED LOWEST PRICES

**Competetive Rates of Commision**

ROGER DOGDER

# ELROND AND BOMBUR
## Tolkien's Names

\*   \*   \*

In the Middle Earth created by J. R. R. Tolkien in *The Lord of the Rings*, the *Silmarillion*, *Unfinished Tales*, etc., the characters come from several races that speak different languages, chiefly indicated by the spelling. Sort these out into the relevant languages. Warning: these come from the books, not necessarily the films.

| | Elves | Humans | Dwarves | Hobbits | Maiar | Others |
|---|---|---|---|---|---|---|
| 1. Balin | | | | | | |
| 2. Galadriel | | | | | | |
| 3. Eowen | | | | | | |
| 4. Gimli | | | | | | |
| 5. Aragorn | | | | | | |
| 6. Gandalf | | | | | | |
| 7. Arwen | | | | | | |
| 8. Bombur | | | | | | |
| 9. Saruman | | | | | | |
| 10. Bilbo | | | | | | |
| 11. Celeborn | | | | | | |
| 12. Meriadioc | | | | | | |
| 13. Fangorn | | | | | | |
| 14. Legolas | | | | | | |
| 15. Telchar | | | | | | |
| 16. Beren | | | | | | |
| 17. Frodo | | | | | | |
| 18. Sauron | | | | | | |
| 19. Theoden | | | | | | |
| 20. Glorfindel | | | | | | |
| 21. Beleg | | | | | | |

*Answers on page 162.*

*Maiar:* the first beings, the Ainur, consisting of Valar and Maiar
*Elves:* First Born race, immortal

*Humans:* Second Born race, mortal
*Dwarves:* race created in secret to be strong and unyielding
*Hobbits:* the Halflings (three and a half feet tall)
*Ents:* the tree-folk

# TEST
*Odd Word Out*

\*   \*   \*

One of the words in each of these lists has a different sound correspondence for the letters than the others, at least in a General American accent.

| | | | | |
|---|---|---|---|---|
| 1. | **ch** | chicken | cheese | chef |
| 2. | **ei** | weigh | ceiling | receive |
| 3. | **x** | Xena | X-ray | xylophone |
| 4. | **gh** | though | ought | gherkin |
| 5. | **ow** | cow | show | now |
| 6. | **c** | cent | call | Cuthbert |
| 7. | **s** | ask | bids | scan |
| 8. | **l** | bill | almond | almoner |
| 9. | **e** | ego | egg | bed |
| 10. | **m** | mnemonic | autumn | lemming |
| 11. | **th** | this | then | thin |
| 12. | **oa** | abroad | goat | load |
| 13. | **a** | father | chalk | Brahms |
| 14. | **oo** | food | book | brood |
| 15. | **ph** | physics | Ralph | shepherd |
| 16. | **y** | city | youth | you |
| 17. | **au** | sausage | bauble | saucer |
| 18. | **wh** | whole | whale | while |
| 19. | **o** | above | aroma | cover |
| 20. | **p** | corps | corpse | copse |
| 21. | **u** | bun | but | brute |
| 22. | **ae** | eon | aerial | anemia |
| 23. | **h** | house | honest | hour |
| 24. | **cc** | accept | succeed | broccoli |
| 25. | **gu** | tongue | disguise | guard |

*Answers on page 163.*

# MODERN TYPEFACES
# FOR ENGLISH

\* \* \*

The use of typefaces is a vital part of the modern English writing system, now that they are under the control of most writers. Fonts like Times New Roman, with cross-strokes (serifs) and varying line widths, are thought better for continuous text such as books. Fonts like Gill Sans and Verdana, without cross-strokes (sans serif) and with even width, are better for display and short pieces of text. Mistral tends to be used in posters.

**Times New Roman** *(serif, Stanley Morison, 1932)*
abcdefghijklmnopqrstuvwxyz?!&
ABCDEFGHIJKLMNOPQRSTUVWXYZ
The great enemy of clear language is insincerity.
Designed for *The Times* newspaper, derived from Plantin
and classical Roman letters.

**Verdana** *(sans serif, Matthew Carter, 1996)*
abcdefghijklmnopqrstuvwxyz?!&
ABCDEFGHIJKLMNOPQRSTUVWXYZ
The great enemy of clear language is insincerity.
Designed to be legible on monitor screens and massively used
in Web pages.

**Gill Sans** *(sans serif, Eric Gill, 1928)*
abcdefghijklmnopqrstuvwxyz?!&
ABCDEFGHIJKLMNOPQRSTUVWXYZ
The great enemy of clear language is insincerity.
Linked to Edward Johnston's font for the London Underground
(1916), an adapted form of which (New Johnston) is still in use.

*Mistral (joined-up brush strokes, Roger Excoffon, 1953)*
*abcdefghijklmnopqrstuvwxyz?!&*
*ABCDEFGHIJKLMNOPQRSTUVWXYZ*
*The great enemy of clear language is insincerity.*
*Perhaps the first to achieve an apparently joined-up effect.*

# TEST
*American Versus British Style Around the World*

\* \* \*

The spelling of English varies in different countries according to how much they favor British or American styles of spelling for particular words. Which of these newspaper examples seem more American style, which more British style?

1. ***Ghana:*** December 2004 would be the first time that a civilian government . . . is going to fulfil a full term.
2. ***Israel:*** Channel 2 does viewers a favor by offering a 23:05 rescreening of *Monsoon*.
3. ***Lebanon:*** Dubai has more than 600 jewelry shops, the densest concentration in the world.
4. ***Russia:*** The dialogue with Moscow, which is lately gaining momentum, is highly appreciated in Georgia.
5. ***Canada:*** The alliance will continue to plow ahead on its own.
6. ***China:*** Richard Pearson, an independent Canadian archeologist . . .
7. ***Australia:*** A Briton has been jailed for 15 years in Vietnam for murdering his travelling companion . . .
8. ***Borneo:*** Two unemployed local men pleaded guilty yesterday to stealing 29 kg of used aluminium.

*Labor (American)/Labour (British) Around the World*
***Korea:*** escalating labor unrest
***Canada:*** the restructuring would have to work around labour laws.
***Israel***: High-tech labor demand down 40% in 2003
***Thailand:*** The senior government official who fell to his death out of the Labour Ministry . . .
***New Zealand:*** Handcuffed labour criticised
***India:*** . . . labour commissioner MB Gajre . . .
***Singapore:*** Left-wing Labor MPs
***Bangladesh:*** child-labour education programme
***Czech Republic:*** the labor rights situation
***Nigeria:*** the Nigeria Labour Congress (NLC)
*Answers on page 163.*

## SAMUEL JOHNSON
*Preface to* A Dictionary of the English Language *1755*
\*   \*   \*

I found it necessary to distinguish those irregularities that are
inherent in our tongue, and perhaps coeval with it, from others
which the ignorance or negligence of later writers has produced. Every language has its anomalies, which, though incon-
venient, and in themselves once unnecessary, must be tolerated
among the imperfections of human things, and which require
only to be registered, that they may not be increased, and ascer-
tained, that they may not be confounded: but every language
has likewise its improprieties and absurdities, which it is the
duty of the lexicographer to correct or proscribe.

As language was at its beginning merely oral, all words of
necessary or common use were spoken before they were written; and while they were unfixed by any visible signs, must
have been spoken with great diversity, as we now observe those
who cannot read catch sounds imperfectly, and utter them neg-
ligently. When this wild and barbarous jargon was first reduced
to an alphabet, every penman endeavoured to express, as he
could, the sounds which he was accustomed to pronounce or to
receive, and vitiated in writing such words as were already
vitiated in speech. The powers of the letters, when they were
applied to a new language, must have been vague and
unsettled, and therefore different hands would exhibit the
same sound by different combinations.

From this uncertain pronunciation arise in a great part the
various dialects of the same country, which will always be
observed to grow fewer, and less different, as books are
multiplied; and from this arbitrary representation of sounds
by letters, proceeds that diversity of spelling observable in
the Saxon remains, and I suppose in the first books of every
nation, . . .

# THE FREQUENCY OF LETTERS IN AMERICAN ENGLISH

* * *

The letters of a language do not occur with the same frequency. The figures here are calculated from Mark Twain's *Huckleberry Finn* (109,000 words; 433,000 characters). The most frequent letter is "e" with 46,661 (10.8%), the least frequent is "q" with 173 (0.01%).

**LETTER FREQUENCIES FOR ENGLISH**

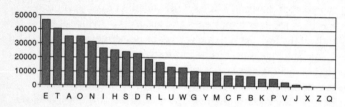

**DIGRAPH FREQUENCIES**

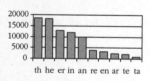

**TRIGRAPH FREQUENCIES**

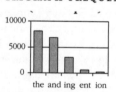

Such information helps code breakers to find out which language is concealed in a message and to work out which letters have been substituted for which, as described in Edgar Allan Poe's "The Gold Bug." Helen Gaines's *Cryptanalysis* gives the high frequency group as "e t a o n i r s h," the top ten digraphs as "th in er re an he ar en ti te," and the top five trigraphs as "the ing and ion ent," slightly different from those here.

# OUTLAWZ AND CUTE CAIT
*British and American Novel Spellings*

\* \* \*

The British and American editions of this book revealed differences over how novel spelling are handled in American and British English. Can you tell which are which?

## Pop Groups (see p. 22)

| | | | | | |
|---|---|---|---|---|---|
| Gorillaz | Am ☐ | Brit ☐ | Puddle of | | |
| 6 Teens | Am ☐ | Brit ☐ | Mudd | Am ☐ | Brit ☐ |
| Eminem | Am ☐ | Brit ☐ | 4-Hero | Am ☐ | Brit ☐ |
| Nuckledz | Am ☐ | Brit ☐ | Outlawz | Am ☐ | Brit ☐ |
| | | | Black II Basics | Am ☐ | Brit ☐ |

## Show Dogs (see p. 32)

| | | | | | |
|---|---|---|---|---|---|
| Knot-A-Yacht | Am ☐ | Brit ☐ | Mistymoor | Am ☐ | Brit ☐ |
| Miss B'Havin | Am ☐ | Brit ☐ | Up N'Adam | Am ☐ | Brit ☐ |
| For-U-To-N-V | Am ☐ | Brit ☐ | Justine Thyme | Am ☐ | Brit ☐ |
| Brite As A | | | Nice Tri | Am ☐ | Brit ☐ |
| Button | Am ☐ | Brit ☐ | | | |

## License Plates (see p. 38)

| | | | | | |
|---|---|---|---|---|---|
| 2FAST4U | Am ☐ | Brit ☐ | G1 RLY | Am ☐ | Brit ☐ |
| UNC 1E | Am ☐ | Brit ☐ | CYCOPTH | Am ☐ | Brit ☐ |
| CHZHED | Am ☐ | Brit ☐ | 81TCH | Am ☐ | Brit ☐ |
| S4 NDY | Am ☐ | Brit ☐ | P9 YCO | Am ☐ | Brit ☐ |

## Racehorses (see p. 114)

| | | | | | |
|---|---|---|---|---|---|
| Funny Cide | Am ☐ | Brit ☐ | Hez Not Yours | Am ☐ | Brit ☐ |
| Luvah Girl | Am ☐ | Brit ☐ | Nothin' Leica | | |
| Cute Cait | Am ☐ | Brit ☐ | Dane | Am ☐ | Brit ☐ |
| Iwontell | Am ☐ | Brit ☐ | Outatime | Am ☐ | Brit ☐ |
| | | | Scooby Who | Am ☐ | Brit ☐ |

## Hairdressers (see p. 117)

| | | | | | |
|---|---|---|---|---|---|
| Mane Street | Am ☐ | Brit ☐ | Hair Dooz | Am ☐ | Brit ☐ |
| Oassis Salon | Am ☐ | Brit ☐ | Curl Up 'N' Dye | Am ☐ | Brit ☐ |
| Split Enz | Am ☐ | Brit ☐ | Stylelistiks | Am ☐ | Brit ☐ |

## Song Titles (see p. 147)

| | | | | | |
|---|---|---|---|---|---|
| Bangin' Man | Am ☐ | Brit ☐ | You boyz | Am ☐ | Brit ☐ |
| Emale | Am ☐ | Brit ☐ | make big | | |
| Myzterious | Am ☐ | Brit ☐ | noize | | |
| Mizster Jones | Am ☐ | Brit ☐ | Bagg Up | ☐Am | ☐Brit |

*Answers on page 164.*

# MILLENIUM EXSTACY
*Spelling Mistakes on the Web*

\* \* \*

The percentage of incorrect spellings on Web pages compared to the correct spelling. Sometimes the incorrect spelling may be correct in another language and may distort the figures.

| | | |
|---|---|---|
| **minuscule** | (miniscule: labeled as "erroneous" in *OED*; as variant in *Webster's*) | 42% |
| **millennium** | (millenium, milenium, milennium) | 32.7 |
| **supersede** | (supercede, superceed) | 26.1 |
| **accommodation** | (accomodation, acommodation) | 19.7 |
| **irresistible** | (irresistable) | 13.7 |
| **ecstasy** | (exstacy, ecstacy) | 13.5 |
| **embarrass** | (embaras, embarass) | 12.2 |
| **desiccate** | (desicate, dessicate, dessiccate) | 10.6 |
| **definitely** | (definately, difinately) | 10.4 |
| **pronunciation** | (pronounciation) | 10.2 |
| **separate** | (seperate) | 9.7 |
| **necessary** | (neccesary, necesary, neccesary) | 9.1 |
| **broccoli** | (brocolli, brocoli—alternative in *Webster's*) | 7.1 |
| **address** | (adress, adres) | 6.5 |
| **cemetery** | (cemetary, semetary, but Stephen King book *Pet Semetary*) | 6.3 |
| **occurrence** | (occurence, ocurence) | 6.1 |
| **independent** | (independant) | 5.7 |
| **questionnaire** | (questionaire) | 4.8 |
| **liaison** | (liaision) | 4.7 |
| **useful** | (usefull) | 4.3 |
| **referring** | (refering) | 3.1 |
| **recommend** | (recomend, reccomend, reccommend) | 3.1 |
| **liaison** | (liason) | 2.7 |
| **parallel** | (paralel, parallell, paralell, parralel) | 2.3 |
| **receive** | (recieve) | 1.8 |
| **beginning** | (begining) | 1.6 |
| **paid** | (payed) | 0.7 |

Nouns with plural "s" in English do not have an apostrophe; that is to say, the plural form is "books" not "book's"; "teams," not "team's." However, street notices, shop labels and advertisements frequently advertise "melon's," "cauliflower's" and "carrot's"—hence this is often called the greengrocer's apostrophe.

I come now to another part of your letter, which is the orthography, if I may call bad spelling ORTHOGRAPHY. You spell induce, ENDUCE; and grandeur, you spell grandURE; two faults of which few of my housemaids would have been guilty. I must tell you that orthography, in the true sense of the word, is so absolutely necessary for a man of letters; or a gentleman, that one false spelling may fix ridicule upon him for the rest of his life; and I know a man of quality, who never recovered the ridicule of having spelled WHOLESOME without the w.

Reading with care will secure everybody from false spelling; for books are always well spelled, according to the orthography of the times. Some words are indeed doubtful, being spelled differently by different authors of equal authority; but those are few; and in those cases every man has his option, because he may plead his authority either way; but where there is but one right way, as in the two words above mentioned, it is unpardonable and ridiculous for a gentleman to miss it; even a woman of a tolerable education would despise and laugh, at a lover, who should send her an ill-spelled billet-doux. I fear and suspect, that you have taken it into your head, in most cases, that the matter is all, and the manner little or nothing. If you have, undeceive yourself, and be convinced that, in everything, the manner is full as important as the matter. If you speak the sense of an angel, in bad words and with a disagreeable utterance, nobody will hear you twice, who can help it. If you write epistles as well as Cicero, but in a very bad hand, and very ill-spelled, whoever receives will laugh at them; and if you had the figure of Adonis, with an awkward air and motions, it will disgust instead of pleasing. Study manner, therefore, in everything, if you would be anything.

\*   \*   \*

Elephants R Us
Babies R Us
the NIH Molecules R Us
   Utility
Bricks 'R Us
Bannerz R US
Disabilities-R-Us
Bald R Us
Danes-R-Us
asian-brides-r-us.com
Goats R Us
Amish-r-us.com

Fantasy Sports R Us
Ratz R Us
Owls "R" US
Cowhides R Us
Cells R Us
Squirrels R Us
Aliens R' Us!
Chats-R-Us
Grants R' Us,
Cats R Us
Vans-R-Us
Casinos R Us

**Extensions from the pattern**
The-Web-is-us.com
bikesrnottoys.com
Perfumeisus.com
Chartsisus.com
Hair Is Us
golfisus.net

# STREETZ 4 U AND EYE: SONG TITLES

* * *

The spelling of song titles often deliberately shows the singer's accent.

## Songs Performed by Prince

| | |
|---|---|
| If Eye Was the Man in Ur Life | Strollin' |
| What Do U Want Me 2 Do | Sensual everafter |
| Lovesexy | Damn U |
| I Would Die 4 U | Live 4 love |
| U Got the Look | Emale |
| Gett Off | Old friends 4 sale |
| Money Don't Matter 2 Night | Love 2 the 9s |
| Take Me with U | Anna Stesia |
| Anotherloverholenyohead | |

## Linton Kwesi Johnson (Jamaica and London)

| | |
|---|---|
| All Wi Don Is Defendin | If I Waz a Tap Natch Poet |
| Di Great Insohreckshan | Independent intavenshan |
| Dirty langwidge dub | It noh funny |
| Doun Di Road | Liesense Fi Kill |
| Dubbin Di Revalueshan | Sense Outta Nansense |
| Fite dem back | Tings an' Times |
| Forces of vicktry | Wat about di workin' claas? |

## Chingy

| | |
|---|---|
| Right Thurr | Holidae In |
| He's Herre | Sample Dat Ass |
| Wurrs My Cash | Mobb Wit Me |
| Bagg Up | |

**2PAC**

The Streetz R Deathrow
Heartz of Men
Ballad of a Dead Soulja
Letter 2 My Unborn
Ambitionz Az a Ridah
I Ain't Mad at Cha
Never B Peace

Heaven Ain't Hard 2 Find
Last Wordz
What'z Ya Phone No.
2Pacalypse
Now Keep Ya Head Up
2 of Amerikaz Most Wanted
How Do U Want It

# ANSWERS

* * *

# DIFFICULT WORDS SPELLING TEST

*(p. 4)*

| | | |
|---|---|---|
| 1. dessicate | (desiccate) | desicate |
| 2. (ecstasy) | exstacy | ecstacy |
| 3. milenium | millenium | (millennium) |
| 4. dumbel | (dumbbell) | dumbell |
| 5. seperate | (separate) | seperete |
| 6. necesary | neccesary | (necessary) |
| 7. (peddler) | pedler | (pedlar) |
| 8. (minuscule) | miniscule | minniscule |
| 9. adress | adres | (address) |
| 10. accomodate | (accommodate) | acommodate |
| 11. iresistible | irresistable | (irresistible) |
| 12. (liaison) | liaision | liason |
| 13. harras | harrass | (harass) |
| 14. (definitely) | definately | difinately |
| 15. ocurence | (occurrence) | occurence |
| 16. embarass | embaras | (embarrass) |
| 17. pronounciation | pronounceation | (pronunciation) |
| 18. independant | (independent) | indipendent |
| 19. (questionnaire) | questionairre | questionaire |
| 20. wiered | (weird) | wierd |
| 21. brocolli | broccolli | (broccoli) |
| 22. refering | (referring) | refferring |
| 23. (recommend) | recomend | reccommend |
| 24. (cemetery) | semetary | cemetary |

# AMERICAN OR BRITISH STYLE OF SPELLING?

*(p. 16)*

|  |  | American | British | Both |
|---|---|:---:|:---:|:---:|
| 1. | honour | ☐ | ☑ | ☐ |
| 2. | meter | ☐ | ☐ | ☑ |
| 3. | mediaeval | ☐ | ☐ | ☑ |
| 4. | catalyze | ☑ | ☐ | ☐ |
| 5. | labor | ☑ | ☐ | ☐ |
| 6. | waggon | ☐ | ☑ | ☐ |
| 7. | favour | ☐ | ☑ | ☐ |
| 8. | neighbor | ☑ | ☐ | ☐ |
| 9. | travelling | ☐ | ☑ | ☐ |
| 10. | encyclopedia | ☐ | ☐ | ☑ |
| 11. | moustache | ☐ | ☑ | ☐ |
| 12. | color | ☑ | ☐ | ☐ |
| 13. | paralyse | ☐ | ☑ | ☐ |
| 14. | extol | ☐ | ☐ | ☑ |
| 15. | center | ☑ | ☐ | ☐ |
| 16. | dialogue | ☐ | ☑ | ☐ |
| 17. | molt | ☑ | ☐ | ☐ |
| 18. | analyse | ☐ | ☑ | ☐ |
| 19. | plow | ☑ | ☐ | ☐ |
| 20. | sulphur | ☐ | ☑ | ☐ |
| 21. | vigour | ☐ | ☑ | ☐ |
| 22. | skeptic | ☑ | ☐ | ☐ |
| 23. | catalog | ☑ | ☐ | ☐ |
| 24. | enrol | ☐ | ☑ | ☐ |
| 25. | archaeologist | ☐ | ☐ | ☑ |
| 26. | fulfil | ☐ | ☑ | ☐ |
| 27. | glamour | ☐ | ☐ | ☑ |
| 28. | theatre | ☐ | ☑ | ☐ |
| 29. | saviour | ☐ | ☑ | ☐ |
| 30. | distill | ☑ | ☐ | ☐ |
| 31. | litre | ☐ | ☑ | ☐ |

# OLD ENGLISH SPELLING

(p. 24)

Note: The fact that the word still exists with an altered spelling does *not* mean it necessarily has the same meaning today.

1. æsc: ash
2. bedd: bed
3. cīese: cheese
4. cild: child
5. circe: church
6. clǣne: clean
7. cwēn: queen
8. dēofol: devil
9. ecg: edge
10. fisc: fish
11. flǣsc: flesh
12. folc: folk
13. gēar: year
14. hecge: hedge
15. heofone: heaven
16. hlāford: lord
17. hors: horse
18. hring: ring
19. hwæl: whale
20. hwȳ: why
21. lēoht: light
22. miht: might
23. mōnaþ: month
24. nacod: naked
25. niht: night
26. ofen: oven
27. riht: right
28. sǣ: sea
29. sceaft: shaft
30. scēap: sheep
31. scield: shield
32. scilling: shilling
33. scip: ship
34. seofon: seven
35. siextig: sixty
36. stenc: stench
37. tōþ: tooth
38. þe: the
39. þicce: thick
40. þing: thing
41. þrī: three
42. þurh: through
43. tunge: tongue
44. wæter: water
45. weg: way
46. weorþ: worth
47. woruld: world
48. wrītan: write

# THE E-CANCELLATION TEST

*(p. 41)*

**A** At th& b&ginning of th& tw&nti&th c&ntury, th&r& was a
larg& farm n&ar Los Ang&l&s call&d th& Hollywood Ranch.
A f&w d&cad&s lat&r, it was on& of th& most famous plac&s
in th& world. Th& first movi&s w&r& mad& in N&w York on
th& &ast Coast. But, as th&y us&d th& light of th& sun, th&
advantag&s of Los Ang&l&s soon b&cam& appar&nt, wh&r&
th&r& w&r& at l&ast thr&& hundr&d and fifty days of sun
&v&ry y&ar as w&ll as pictur&squ& natural sc&n&ry such as
mountains, b&ach&s and d&s&rt. Aft&r its h&yday in the
nin&t&&n thirti&s and nin&t&&n-forti&s, Hollywood had to
turn to t&l&vision films b&for& g&tting back to th& block-
bust&rs that dominat& movi& hous&s today. How&v&r its
position as th& plac& that produc&s most films has b&&n
ov&rtak&n by Bollywood in India. (93 "e"s.)

**B** Grac& Pain& liv&d in an isolat&d cottag& for most of h&r
lif&. In middl&-ag& sh& cam& to London, and was
astonish&d at city lif&. B&st of all sh& lov&d h&r cook&r
with its row of controls. On& day sh& told m& about h&r
amazing cook&r. Sh& had l&ft h&r whol& &v&ning m&al in
th& ov&n; at fiv& o'clock th& &l&ctric clock would switch it
on and by s&v&n a thr&& cours& m&al would b& r&ady to
w&lcom& h&r hom&. I almost &nvi&d h&r. But wh&n w&
n&xt m&t sh& r&lat&d what had actually occurr&d:
how&v&r automatic your cook&r, you hav& still got to
r&m&mb&r to turn it on. (66 "e"s.)

**REASONS**

Usually people fail to spot about five "e"s out of a hundred, i.e.
about seven in the two passages, mostly in the word "the." This
demonstrates that they pay attention to whole words rather than
just single letters. Some types of dyslexia are signaled by problems with "important" "e"s, such as the "e" in "den," which dis-
tinguishes it from "din" and "don" but not with "unimportant"
"e"s, such as the "e" in "waited," since there are no words spelled
"waitid" or "waitod."

# ORTHOGRAPHIC
# REGULARITIES TEST

*(p. 56)*

1. **blar**/blarh
2. ckole/**kole**
3. **leck**/ckel
4. **snove**/snov
5. tcheb/**cheb**
6. **chig**/tchig
7. blic/**blick**
8. fanq/**fanque**
9. **ster**/sterh
10. gneit/**teign**
11. nowh/**whon**
12. flij/**flidge**
13. huz/**huze**
14. **pluze**/pluz
15. staj/**stadge**
16. truv/**truve**
17. **whar**/rawh
18. gnope/**nope**
19. dgain/**jain**
20. **jarn**/narj
21. blav/**blave**
22. gnil/**lign**
23. **lutch**/tchul
24. **nait**/gnait/
25. **wras**/sawr
26. qish/**quish**
27. **quong**/qong
28. lerh/**rhell**
29. forh/**rhoff**
30. **smaze**/smaz
31. sniv/**snive**
32. frak/**frack**
33. spiwh/**spiw**
34. plawh/**plaw**
35. **terque**/terq
36. **squol**/squl
37. dgoll/**joll**
38. **klaze**/klaz
39. **nuft**/gnuft
40. gewr/**wreg**
41. **prew**/prewh
42. nartch/**tcharn**
43. **plock**/ploc
44. **blive**/bliv
45. **wrof**/fowr

## Explanations
- "wh" occurs only at the beginning of words: when
- "ck" occurs only at the end: black
- "j" occurs at the beginning, "dge" at the end: judge
- "wr" occurs only at the beginning: write
- "ch" occurs at the beginning, "tch" at the end: chat, catch
- "v" occurs only at the end with a following "e": love
- single "z" occurs only at the end with an "e": laze
- "q" has to be followed by "u": quick

- "gn" has to occur at the end: sign
- "rh" has to occur at the beginning: rhubarb

Of course there are exceptions, such as "gneiss," "shiv," "catarrh," "Iraq" and "celeriac."


# BRITISH VERSUS AMERICAN NEWSPAPERS

*(p. 61)*

1. American labor
2. American center
3. British moult
4. American dialog
5. American wagon
6. British neighbour
7. British moustache
8. American honor
9. American liter
10. British aluminium
11. American skeptic and catalog
12. British favour
13. American sulfur
14. British travelling

# WORDS THAT ARE COMMONLY MISSPELLED

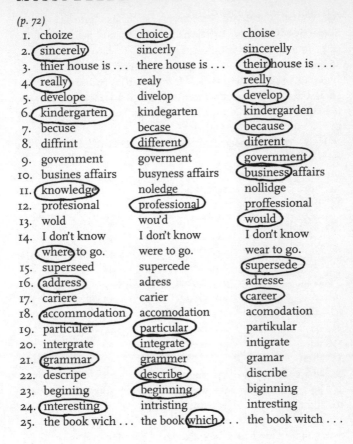

*(p. 72)*

1. choize — (choice) — choise
2. (sincerely) — sincerly — sincerelly
3. thier house is ... — there house is ... — (their) house is ...
4. (really) — realy — reelly
5. develope — divelop — (develop)
6. (kindergarten) — kindegarten — kindergarden
7. becuse — becase — (because)
8. diffrint — (different) — diferent
9. govemment — goverment — (government)
10. busines affairs — busyness affairs — (business) affairs
11. (knowledge) — noledge — nollidge
12. profesional — (professional) — proffessional
13. wold — wou'd — (would)
14. I don't know (where) to go. — I don't know were to go. — I don't know wear to go.
15. superseed — supercede — (supersede)
16. (address) — adress — adresse
17. cariere — carier — (career)
18. (accommodation) — accomodation — acomodation
19. particuler — (particular) — partikular
20. intergrate — (integrate) — intigrate
21. (grammar) — grammer — gramar
22. descripe — (describe) — discribe
23. begining — (beginning) — biginning
24. (interesting) — intristing — intresting
25. the book wich ... — the book (which) ... — the book witch ...

# SOUNDS OR LETTERS?

*(p. 80)*

## Answers and Explanation

Some words feel as if they had more sounds because of the extra letters. Many people judge "edge" to have more than 2 sounds (phonemes) because of its 4 letters. The same is true for "who" (2 sounds, 3 letters) and for "church" (3 sounds, 6 letters). In reverse, some words seem to have fewer sounds because they have fewer letters than sounds; "fix" seems to have fewer than 4, and "music" less than 6.

Here are the answers, giving the numbers of phonemes for each word.

| | | | | | | | |
|---|---|---|---|---|---|---|---|
| 1. bought | 3 | 18. music | 5 | 35. rich | 3 |
| 2. box | 4 | 19. judge | 3 | 36. wing | 3 |
| 3. thin | 3 | 20. who | 2 | 37. page | 3 |
| 4. him | 3 | 21. spend | 5 | 38. unit | 5 |
| 5. catch | 3 | 22. age | 2 | 39. me | 2 |
| 6. the | 2 | 23. it | 2 | 40. cost | 4 |
| 7. chop | 3 | 24. think | 4 | 41. she | 2 |
| 8. crash | 4 | 25. match | 3 | 42. crop | 4 |
| 9. of | 2 | 26. chat | 3 | 43. shock | 3 |
| 10. edge | 2 | 27. next | 5 | 44. bat | 3 |
| 11. fix | 4 | 28. thought | 3 | 45. let | 3 |
| 12. do | 2 | 29. land | 4 | 46. trust | 5 |
| 13. then | 3 | 30. nothing | 5 | 47. back | 3 |
| 14. broccoli | 7 | 31. ought | 2 | 48. stamp | 5 |
| 15. jet | 3 | 32. win | 3 | 49. past | 4 |
| 16. light | 3 | 33. stupid | 6 | 50. washing | 5 |
| 17. job | 3 | 34. plant | 5 | | |

*more sounds than letters:* box, fix, next, unit (depending on accent "u" may be one or two sounds)

*less sounds than letters:* bought, thin, catch, the, chop, crash, edge, then, broccoli, light, judge, who, age, think, match, chat, thought, nothing, ought, rich, wing, page, she, shock, back, washing

*same number of sounds and letters:* him, of, jet, job, spend, it, land, win, plant, me, cost, crop, bat, let, trust, stamp, music, stupid

# GUESS THE FIRST LANGUAGES

*(p. 98)*

Greek: Gambridge (1), revoluzion (18), leccons (20)
German: reseption (2), telefon (15), tink (21)
Spanish: proffessional (3), mentionned (5), photoes (10)
Japanese: vocaburaries (4), secondaly (16), subejects (19)
Italian: addresse (6), particulery (13)
Arabic: rutine (7), defacult (17)
French: familly (8), monney (12), enthousiastic (14)
Chinese: calld (9), endiveduoly (11)


# HISTORY TEST

*(p. 105)*

**F** 1400 John of Trevisa, *Marvels of Britain*

**A** 1592 Nash, Thomas, *Pierce Penilesse his supplication to the diuell.*

**D** 1651 Milton, John, *The life and reigne of King Charls*

**C** 1775 Washington, George, INSTRUCTIONS TO COLONEL BENEDICT ARNOLD

**E** 1880 James, Henry, *Washington Square*

**B** 1981 Chomsky, Noam (ed. C. Otero), *Radical Priorities*

# WHAT'S WRONG WITH
# YOUR SPELLING?

(p. 111)

| | | | spelling group |
|---|---|---|---|
| 1. | (questionnaire) | questionaire | 1 |
| 2. | That's definate. | That's (definite.) | 6 |
| 3. | (supersede) | super(cede) | 3 |
| 4. | highly (responsible) | highly responsable | 6 |
| 5. | (accommodation) | accomodation | 1 |
| 6. | a complementary drink | a (complimentary) drink | 2 |
| 7. | He critisised the plan. | He (criticised) the plan. | 3 |
| 8. | an (independent) report | an independant report | 5 |
| 9. | She refered to Bush. | She (referred) to Bush. | 1 |
| 10. | open-ended (categories) | open-ended catagories | 5 |
| 11. | quiet right | (quite) right | 2 |
| 12. | good (sense) | good sence | 3 |
| 13. | He (achieved) greatness. | He acheived greatness. | 4 |
| 14. | seperate rooms | (separate) rooms | 5 |
| 15. | liberal tendancy | liberal (tendency) | 5 |
| 16. | (ecstasy) | ecstacy | 3 |
| 17. | beginers' luck | (beginner's) luck | 1 |
| 18. | sensative | (sensitive) | 6 |
| 19. | They beleived the news. | They (believed) the news. | 1 |
| 20. | the (bare) necessities | the bear necessities | 2 |
| 21. | the percieved cost | the (perceived) cost | 4 |
| 22. | the principal of gravity | the (principle) of gravity | 2 |
| 23 | not necessarily true | not necessarily true | 1 |
| 24. | This is (indispensable) | This is indispensible. | 6 |
| 25. | It's (their) problem. | It's they're problem. | 2 |
| 26. | an immence cliff | an (immense) cliff | 3 |
| 27. | to (conceive) | to concieve | 4 |
| 28 | cause and affect | cause and (effect) | 5 |
| 29. | He recieved a postcard. | He (received) a postcard. | 4 |
| 30. | (reversible) | reversable | 3 |

*Explanations for What's Wrong with Your Spelling Test*
This test indicates whether people have problems with particular areas of English spelling. To find the type of mistake involved, circle the spelling group number in the right-hand column for each word spelled incorrectly and then see which group has the most mistakes.

1. *Letter doubling (words 1, 5, 9, 17, 23):* one reason for doubling consonants is to show that the preceding vowel is "short"— "din" versus "dinner." See page 96.

2. *Homophones (words 6, 11, 20, 22, 25):* words that have the same pronunciation, or nearly so, but different spelling, such as "whole" versus "hole." See page 40.

3. *"c" or "s" (words 3, 7, 12, 16, 26):* rules about whether to write "s" or "c" for an "s" sound. Usually "c" is said as "s" before "e/i/y." "Supersede" is difficult because English spelling kept the distinction between two Latin words "cedere" (to go) "intercede" and "sedere" (to sit) "supersede." There are variations between English and American styles for words like "defense/defence." See page 76.

4. *"ie" or "ei" mistakes (words 13, 19, 21, 27, 29):* "i" before "e" except after "c" when the vowel sound is "ee." See page 46.

5. *"e" or "a" (words 8, 10, 14, 15, 28):* the correspondences for these letters vary in unstressed syllables. The "-ant/-ent" spellings are said in the same way. Some words follow the French "-ant" ending, "descendant," some the Latin "-ent," "independent." Often both are possible, "dependant/dependent."

6. *"i/a" (words 2, 4, 18, 24, 30):* the correspondences for these letters are hard to predict in unstressed syllables. The difference between "-ible" and "-able" is tenuous. Some words, often ending in "s" sounds, follow the Latin "-ible"— "responsible." Others, tending to end in "d" or "t" sounds, follow the French "-able"—"dependable."

# IDENTIFY THE LANGUAGE

*(p. 125)*

Note: these are the languages, not the plants' places of origin.

1. broccoli **Italian**
2. mangetout **French**
3. bok choi **Chinese**
4. okra **West African (Fante)**
5. zucchini **Italian**
6. lollo rosso **Italian**
7. avocado **Spanish**
8. chili **Spanish**
9. shiitake mushrooms **Japanese**
10. guava **Spanish**
11. primavera salad **Spanish**
12. coleslaw **Dutch**
13. papaya **Spanish**
14. mangosteen **Bahasa Malaysia**
15. kumquats **Chinese**
16. kiwifruit **Maori**
17. medjol dates **Arabic**
18. fuji apples **Japanese**
19. pistachios **Italian**
20. satsumas **Japanese**

# TOLKIEN'S NAMES

*(p. 133)*

1. Balin **Dwarf**
2. Galadriel **Elf**
3. Eowen **Human**
4. Gimli **Dwarf**
5. Aragorn **Human**
6. Gandalf **Maiar**
7. Arwen **Elf**
8. Bombur **Dwarf**
9. Saruman **Maiar**
10. Bilbo **Hobbit**
11. Celeborn **Elf**
12. Meriadioc **Hobbit**
13. Fangorn **Other (Ent)**
14. Legolas **Elf**
15. Telchar **Dwarf**
16. Beren **Human**
17. Frodo **Hobbit**
18. Sauron **Maiar**
19. Theoden **Human**
20. Glorfindel **Elf**
21. Beleg **Elf**

# ODD WORD OUT

*(p. 135)*

1. **ch**   chicken   cheese   (chef)
2. **ei**   (weigh)   ceiling   receive
3. **x**   Xena   (X-ray)   xylophone
4. **gh**   though   ought   (gherkin)
5. **ow**   cow   (show)   now
6. **c**   (cent)   call   Cuthbert
7. **s**   ask   (bids)   scan
8. **l**   (bill)   almond   almoner
9. **e**   (ego)   egg   bed
10. **m**   (mnemonic)   autumn   lemming
11. **th**   this   then   (thin)
12. **oa**   (abroad)   goat   load
13. **a**   father   (chalk)   Brahms
14. **oo**   food   (book)   brood
15. **ph**   physics   Ralph   (shepherd)
16. **y**   (city)   youth   you
17. **au**   (sausage)   bauble   saucer
18. **wh**   (whole)   whale   while
19. **o**   above   (aroma)   cover
20. **p**   (corps)   corpse   copse
21. **u**   bun   but   (brute)
22. **ae**   aeon   (aerial)   anaemia
23. **h**   (house)   honest   hour
24. **cc**   accept   succeed   (broccoli)
25. **gu**   (tongue)   disguise   guard

# AMERICAN VERSUS ENGLISH SPELLING AROUND THE WORLD

*(p. 138)*

**British-style spelling:** 1. fulfil, 4. dialogue, 7. travelling, 8. aluminium

**American-style spelling:** 2. favor, 3. jewelry, 5. plow, 6. archeologist

# BRITISH AND AMERICAN NOVEL SPELLINGS

*(p. 141)*

**American pop groups:** 6 Teens, Eminem, Puddle of Mudd, Outlawz

**American show dogs:** Knot-A-Yacht, For-U-To-N-V, Mistymoor, Up N'Adam

**American license plates:** 2FAST4U, CHZHED, CYCOPTH, 8rTCH

**American racehorses:** Funny Cide, Iwontell, Hez Not Yours, Outatime

**American hairdressers:** Mane Street, Oassis Salon, Hair Dooz

**American song titles:** Emale, Bagg Up

# ACKNOWLEDGMENTS

\*   \*   \*

Major sources in putting together this book were the frequency list from the Brown University Corpus plus specific sources mentioned on individual pages, and indeed the streets of the places I have visited in the past five years in the United States, Canada, Ireland and elsewhere. The Web was an important resource, allowing one to discover hairdressers in Houston one minute, the number of wrong spellings for *receive* out of 37 million examples the next, the spellings of the original Shakespeare First Folio the next. Robert Cook searched out much of the information and coordinated its presentation. Some of the information and photos for this edition were kindly provided by Maria del Carmen De Avila; Nicky Cook; Iggy Roca; Cathy Walter and Dave, Robyn and Julie Newton.

Some of the same topics are treated in a more academic way in V. J. Cook (2004), *The English Writing System,* Arnold, and on the Web site *Writing Systems,* http://homepage.ntlworld.com/vivian.c/.

I am grateful to the Society of Authors, on behalf of the Bernard Shaw estate, for giving permission to quote from Bernard Shaw's preface to R. A. Wilson's *The Miraculous Birth of Language* (1941).

# SOURCES OF INFORMATION

\* \* \*

Brooks, G., Gorman, T., and Kendall, L. (1993) *Spelling It Out: The Spelling Abilities of 11- and 15-year-olds.* Slough, UK: National Foundation for Educational Research.

Carney, E. (1994) *A Survey of English Spelling.* London: Routledge.

Cook, V. J. (2004) *The English Writing System.* London: Edward Arnold.

Crain, P. (2000) *The Story of A.* Stanford University Press.

Diringer, D. (1962) *Writing.* London: Thames and Hudson.

Kucera, H., and Francis, W. N. (1967) *Computational Analysis of Present-day American English.* Providence: Brown University Press.

McIntosh, R. (1990) *Hyphenation.* Halifax: Hyphen House.

*Oxford English Dictionary* (OED) (1994) CD-ROM version 1.13, Oxford University Press.

Pound. L. (1926) "The Kraze for K." *American Speech* 1, 1, 43–44.

Roca, I., and Johnson, W. (1999) *A Course in Phonology.* Oxford: Blackwell.

Schwartz, A. (1974) *A Twister of Twists a Tangler of Tongues: Tongue Twisters.* London: Deutsch.

Seidenberg, M. S., and McClelland, J. L. (1989) "A Distributed, Developmental Model of Word Recognition and Naming." *Psychological Review* 96, 523–68.

Treiman, R. (1993) *Beginning to Spell: A Study of First-Grade Children.* Oxford: Oxford University Press.

Venezky, R. (1999) *The American Way of Spelling.* The Hague: Mouton.

# THEME INDEX

\* \* \*

To help readers to follow particular threads, the following list organizes the pages into themes.

**Alphabets:** alternative spoken alphabets 73, sources of the alphabet 1, changing letters of English 54, things as letters 85, International Phonetic Alphabet (IPA) 52, use of non-letters 62, early reading books 118

**American versus British styles of spelling:** word test 16, styles of spelling 42, newspaper test 61, world-wide newspaper test 138, reasons for differences 76, Noah Webster 5, quotations 21, novel spelling differences 141

**Apostrophe** (greengrocer's); in newspapers 126, in streets 144

**Computer Mediated Communication (CMC):** chat rooms 95, spam spelling 89, spelling checker 123

**History:** plants 59, Old English spelling 24, Shakespeare 86, dating test 105, "till/until" 27, changing letters of English 54, sources of the alphabet 1, words with two faces 6, individual words 12, *Hamlet* 131

**Learning:** stages in children's spelling 11, computer learning of spelling 104, 15-year-olds' mistakes 55

**Mistakes:** "compliments" 84, hotels 30, menus 78, natives 17, newspapers 126, non-natives 98, writers 8, "till/'til/until" 27, "stationary" 113, street signs (painted) 132, street signs (hand-drawn) 88, natives on computer test 122, Lewis-Clark diaries 50

**Novel made-up spellings:** space aliens 108, dungeons and dragons 58, cover bands 127, show-dogs 32, Dr. Seuss names 101, drugs 124, drum 'n' bass 120, sit com episodes 128, hairdressers 117, Tolkien's characters 133, classified ads 3, Hip-Hop 70, racehorses 114, "k"s 14, license plates 38, pop musicians 22, rock 'n' roll 91, shop puns 74, unusual shop names 81, taxis 48, "Toy's R Us" 146, "u" 137, antique "Ye Olde" 63, children's products 129, businesses 44

**Rules of spelling:** three-letter rule 10, doubling rule 96, silent "e" 121, "th" rule 67, "i before e" rule 46

**Spelling Games:** Set 1 34, Set 2 87, Set 3 106

**Street signs:** mysterious 83, mistakes 88, 112

**System of writing:** letters and sounds 115, "deep" spelling 7, direction 66, foreign words in cookery 125, homophones 40, homographs 20, hyphen breaks 28, hyphen links 71, letters used as words 38, word spaces 107, proper names 2, odd spellings 82, spelling reform 45, spelling reform success rate 37, silent letters 33, rhymes 119, letter frequencies 140, computer fonts 136, versions of "to be or not to be" 131, sources of the alphabet 1, tongue-twisters 99, Texan place names 51, word ending ("-teria," etc.) 68

**Tests:** American/British style words 16, counting sounds 80, finding out what's wrong 111, difficult words 4, e-deletion 41, American/British style newspapers 61, frequent errors 72, dates of passages 105, odd one out 135, orthographic regularities 56

**Texts:** pronunciation rhyme 65, Shaw preface 35, Twain speech 93, Mulcaster 57, Dr. Johnson 139, rhymes etc. 130, quotations on spelling 26, Webster 5

**Variety of spelling:** "ing" 53, London accent 116, song titles 147, American/British styles 42, reasons for American/British styles 76, quotations on American/British styles 26, New York 25, southern accents (Twain) 39, American/British novel spellings 141

No One Can Change
Your Life Except
for You

# No One Can Change Your Life Except for You

## How to be the hero of your own life

## Laura Whitmore

S

First published in Great Britain in 2021 by Orion Spring
an imprint of The Orion Publishing Group Ltd
Carmelite House, 50 Victoria Embankment
London EC4Y 0DZ

An Hachette UK Company

1 3 5 7 9 10 8 6 4 2

ISBN (Hardback) 978 1 3987 0167 0
ISBN (eBook) 978 1 3987 0170 0

Typeset by Born Group
Printed and bound in Great Britain by Clays Ltd, Elcograf S.p.A.

www.orionbooks.co.uk

For Stevie

## *She*

*She is strong, She is fierce,*
*She is smart, She is tough.*

*She is happy, She is sad,*
*She is polished, She is rough.*

*She is vulnerable, She is insecure,*
*She doesn't always know what to do.*

*But She learns, She grows,*
*She's a force to be reckoned with,*
*She is YOU.*

Laura Whitmore

# contents

Introduction   1

1. She is strong: just a girl   7

2. She is happy: the eternal optimist and finding
   perspective   31

3. She is sad: life after heartbreak
   (it does get better)   61

4. She is polished: expectations   91

5. She is vulnerable: open your heart   121

6. She is insecure: stop comparing   145

7. She doesn't always know what to do:
   faking it   175

8. She learns: we're in a constant state of
   evolution   203

9. She is you: the future   231

   Acknowledgements   255

   Credits   257

# introduction

> 'The most common way people give up their
> power is by thinking they don't have any.'
> **ALICE WALKER**

In 1990, when I was five, I asked my mother for Wilson Phillips' new album. Remember them? Three American women from the musical dynasty of the Mamas & the Papas and the Beach Boys. *Wilson Phillips* (it was self-titled) was to be the first album I would ever own. The first of many different albums I would accumulate over my life. And I've stacked a fair few so far.

I can't remember the first time I heard the song 'Hold On' from that album but I've never forgotten it since. On my BBC Radio show I do a segment called 'The Lyric I Live For', where I ask a well-known guest what

1

lyric means the most to them. It can be ANYTHING! A guilty pleasure or something with a deep meaning, but – whatever the song – it evokes for them a sense of inspiration or emotional connection.

I've had guests on my show say all sorts: Bob Geldof chose Little Richard's 'Tutti Frutti' ('Wop-bop-a-loom-a-blop-bam-boom!'); former president of Ireland Mary Robinson – I'll be talking about her lots later – picked 'The Times They Are a-Changin'' by Bob Dylan; and Sam Fender went with Bruce Springsteen's 'Reason to Believe'.

When my producer asked me which lyric I lived for, I was instantly transported back to listening to my first cassette by Wilson Phillips and that line from 'Hold On' which always stands out for me: 'No one can change your life except for you.'

As I was writing this book about learning to be your own hero, I knew the lyric would make the perfect title. But to use it I would have to get permission from the songwriters. Luckily, my radio team had surprised me with a birthday message from the Wilson Phillips girls (I'm aware they are women now but they still have that youthful charm that never ages) live on-air and I had their manager's details. Turns out this was the reason my producer asked for the lyric I live for. Sneaky and thoughtful – that's why I work with her!

We ended up getting lead singer Chynna Phillips and her husband Billy Baldwin (of Baldwin family fame!

OMG) to come on the show again and talk about the pressures of lockdown on their relationship. It was all very surreal. I mentioned to Chynna how much I loved that song's lyric – that despite everything that happens there is a comfort in knowing it is YOU who changes your life if YOU want to.

Chynna is now a devout Christian and said, 'Well, I used to think that way but now I think that no one can change your life except for . . . GOD.'

Ah. Didn't see that one coming.

But I guess if you are the religious type, God has a fair bit of sway. The lyric still has the same meaning for me, though. That's the beauty of song lyrics. Once written, the ownership goes to the listener to interpret as they wish. These words have got me through some pretty tough times. And I hope that whatever journey you are on, whatever your story may be, this book will help you.

Life can be shit. Believe me I know, I've been there. But no day is the same as the next and, if we all just give ourselves the time we need to grow or to heal, things will get better. This I promise.

We can blame the selfish or thoughtless actions of others for our circumstances, but we can't change those actions. We can change how we comprehend them and how we react. You have the power to grab life by the proverbial balls and recognise the ability inside you, even if it doesn't always feel that way.

I'm aware some of us have a head start in life – more privilege, more choice – be it because of where we are born, the family we are born into or the colour of our skin. But despite this, we ALL have some power and we get to choose how we use it.

Writing these nine chapters has been a journey – through loss, love, lockdown and new life. You really don't know what will get thrown at you as you progress from childhood to adulthood. We all have different journeys and different stories to tell. But one constant is, we can rely on ourselves to always be there. You show up for you.

I feel empowered as I reflect on the 'She' in the poem I wrote. She is all of us (men, I'm looking at you too). You are allowed to feel sad, and weak and vulnerable. That doesn't mean you can't be strong and tough and brave too. We are EVERYTHING.

My hope is that, in sharing what I have learned, I can perhaps inspire you to take back your power. Let me remind you to recognise that you'll never feel ready but that you can still do it.

At the end of every chapter is a reflection and an affirmation. The reflection is something I'd like you to consider and try to fulfil after every chapter. No pressure; it's there to help bring some of what we look at into your own life. Use it as much as you want or need.

The affirmation is a powerful message you can say out loud or repeat internally to help you stay focused.

I sometimes scribble an affirmation on a piece of paper beside my bed or in my notes on my phone as a reminder.

As I finish this book, I've learned that it doesn't end at chapter 9. There's a new chapter coming in my life in the form of a baby girl currently growing inside me. And that scares the shit out of me. I once swallowed a fly and was freaked out that there was a live bug inside me. A little live human is a whole new level of freaking out. But I'm excited. Because there is a lot of good in the world, there is a lot of potential, and I want to bring up a child knowing that she has her own story to write. She will be supported and loved, but she is the heroine of her own life, no one else.

We aren't built to have it all figured out. Imagine how boring a tale that would be! But we have the tools and capabilities to get through anything.

We are constantly learning and growing. And once you find your power, you will never let it go.

# chapter one

## She is strong: just a girl

'To be yourself in a world that is constantly
trying to make you something else is the
greatest accomplishment.'
**RALPH WALDO EMERSON**

My earliest memory is from when I was two years old.
My mother and I had just moved into a little red-brick
two-bed terraced house in Bray, a seaside town just
outside Dublin. I can still see my mother, fiercely independent, silhouetted in an eighties power suit, holding
my hand tightly as I stepped into the uncarpeted hall
and onto the pale cement flooring – so hard under my
tiny toddler toes. This was my new home.

I remember looking into the mirrored wardrobes in
my bedroom. I was getting my very own bedroom and

moving from the room my mother rented for me and her in a lady called Denise's house. The mirrored wardrobes were a massive bonus and the fanciest thing I'd ever seen. They made the room look double the size. I loved playing that game where you put half your body in to reflect the other half sticking out and make yourself really thin or fat.

If only it was that easy to change your shape. On a few occasions, the philosophical child that I was stared into that mirror and thought, 'Who am I?' Who is this girl looking at me? Who is this girl that I'm inside the head of? What am I all about?

Questions I still look into the mirror and ask . . . before spotting a random hair sprouting from my chin and thinking where the hell did that come from!!?

This face staring back at me is the one constant in my life. The face may get older, sprout more hairs – but it's the one face I can rely on to be there. Instead of waiting for other faces in my life to show up, I realise the most important face to show up is my own.

⚡ ⚡ ⚡

I didn't necessarily have a conventional upbringing, but I remember for the most part being happy and feeling loved, which I'm always thankful for.

And another thing I'm thankful for is that I was surrounded by strong women. As I've got older, I've realised women are strong because they don't really have a choice. Disparaging comments about appearing 'feminine' or 'fighting like a girl' suggest women are weak, but being a girl is tough. We have to be strong, and we are.

My nanny May raised my dad and his sister in a small flat in Temple Bar in Dublin. A far cry from the Temple Bar we know now of stag parties and bellowing buskers amid swarms of drunken crowds. Before the cobbled streets became a nightmare for hen-do-goers in stilettos, they were home to old Dublin in its rawest and oldest form. The flat had a small window that overlooked the Ha'penny Bridge, joining north and south Dublin where the River Liffey had rudely split it. Nanny lived there until she passed away when I was ten. She was the oldest in her family and raised most of her siblings after her mother – my great-grandmother Margaret – died tragically when Nanny was just fourteen.

I remember that she had a passion for Snickers bars. When she was older, she wasn't supposed to have them, because she couldn't chew the nuts with her false teeth; but she used to pick the bits of nuts out, suck them, and leave them in an ashtray on a little side table next to her armchair. Why she didn't just get a Mars bar I'll never know, but she loved a Snickers bar and, by God, she was going to keep having her treat for as long as she could. This woman swapped playtime to look after her younger brothers and sisters. The least she deserved was a Snickers in her old age.

It was only after she passed away that I realised having just two children in Catholic Ireland was quite rare. When she married my grandfather, she was at the ripe old age of thirty-five (can you imagine being single at thirty-five back then?!), and suffered many miscarriages which she endured and lived with privately.

I know how difficult it is to suffer a miscarriage in the twenty-first century, having been unfortunate to have experienced it myself; but there was no support for my nanny in those days. People were ashamed and dealt with things alone. They still do, I think, in some ways. It was a year before I spoke about my own loss. As I get older, I realise being strong doesn't mean dealing with things alone. It's about sharing your story to help others, and asking for help when you know you need it.

Back to twentieth-century Ireland. My mother gave birth to me in the eighties, out of wedlock. Again, single parents are common now but, back then, the youngest of thirteen children, she was the odd one out. She worked full-time as a civil servant from the age of seventeen until her recent retirement. When other mothers collected their children from the school gates, my mother was stuck in the office. I went to a childminder and then gradually started doing more and more extra-curricular activity – drama, Irish dancing, swimming. So I always think that her going out to work didn't affect me in a negative way, but it did give me a strong work ethic and the knowledge that having a child AND working is possible. For my mother, work was also a necessity – financially, and also, and just as important, so she still had her own life outside of being a mother.

I'm thankful to have a feminist father too. He had a strong mother, so what do you expect? But for me growing up as a girl never felt like something that held me back. I liked being a girl, and I looked forward to being a strong woman like my mum and my nanny. It was only as I got older and saw more of the world that I realised how being 'just a girl', or from a less privileged background, can have devastating, unjust repercussions.

Looking back, there was accepted behaviour that had wormed its way into becoming the social norm of my life – this seems to happen no matter what background you come from. No privilege is too great to escape it. I had my ass slapped when I was sixteen in a local club in Ireland and my older cousin Clair, who was with me, pushed the guy against a wall and made him apologise to me. He was shocked. He had never had that response before. That single moment comes back to me every time I feel violated in a similar way. No one has the right to do that to anyone. My body. My property. This I know. But sadly, I've experienced such behaviour repeatedly.

When I first moved to London, someone smacked my ass before I got on to a bus. I've had lewd remarks shouted at me. Every time I pass a group of guys alone, my stomach knots and I keep my head down because I worry they'll shout something and embarrass me. I am by no means a weak woman. I consider myself a strong person. Ask anyone who knows me. I'll fight for what I believe in, and I will always stand up for myself. But sometimes I feel I have to choose my battles, and other times I feel – like in that club – what's the point?

Sometimes it's about timing. Waiting until you feel strong enough and protected to speak up. Sometimes . . . you've just had enough.

⚡ ⚡ ⚡

As well as the strong female role models and supporters in my personal life, there are many other women who I've looked up to, who I've learned from and, ultimately, who I have decided to embrace and be inspired by.

I was asked recently to do a podcast about women in history hosted by my friend, the comedian Samantha Baines. I knew instantly who I wanted to talk about. I remembered back to being seven years old and doing a school project about my hero, Mary Robinson. I still feel now the same inspiration from her as I did back then.

In 1990 Mary Robinson became the first female president of Ireland. A former barrister advocating for human rights and women's equality in the Irish and European courts, she went on to become UN High Commissioner for Human Rights and founding member of The Elders (an international non-governmental organisation of kick-ass folk brought together by Nelson Mandela in 2007 to work for peace and human rights. As you can imagine, quite the group. I envisage their meetings as Knights of the Round Table meets *Star Wars*-esque Jedi conference calls, without the lightsabers, obvs).

In her inaugural address as president of Ireland, Mary Robinson said: 'I was elected by the women of Ireland, who instead of rocking the cradle, rocked the system.' What an absolute legend. She went on to say, 'As president directly elected by the people of Ireland, I will have the most democratic job in the country. I'll be able to look [the PM] in the eye and tell him to back off.'

How blessed I was to have her as a role model at such a young age. In the position of president she was respected, even by her enemies – which isn't the same for a lot of current heads of state. In 1992 she visited Somalia – a war-torn country where the most vulnerable suffered – and saw inhumanity and suffering in its rawest form. On the news she uncharacteristically broke down in tears. 'In a society where the rights and potential of women are constrained, no man can be truly free. He may have power, but he will not have freedom.'

At a time when crying, especially by a woman in power, was seen as a weakness, her tears on television, as witnessed by me as a seven-year-old girl as well as the rest of the world, showed there is strength in empathy.

In 2018, I met Mary Robinson. OM(F)G!

I had just been offered a summer series on BBC Radio and each week over six weeks I would interview someone of note. I have interviewed a lot of people over the years, usually very famous musicians and movie stars, but this time I had the opportunity to meet a true icon.

We were meeting to discuss her new podcast at an embassy in central London and I was overwhelmed by a mixture of excitement and absolute fear of shitting myself. What if I messed up the interview? What if I did, non-metaphorically, actually shit myself? I called my mother.

'Do you want me to post over that project you did about her when you were younger?' she suggested. 'You know, so you can show her.'

'Eh? No thanks. I'll stick with the questions.'

Mary Robinson was born Mary Bourke, and when she married her husband Nick she became Mrs Robinson. For many, taking her husband's name may have seemed as conflicting with her feminist views. But, in fact, she emphasised to me further the importance of choice. She decided to take her husband's name not because it was traditional, but because she had to fight to marry him. Taking your husband's name, wearing a skirt or make-up doesn't make you weak, or allow you to be open to attack.

The same year I met Mary Robinson another victory for Irish women was achieved. The Eighth Amendment of the Irish Constitution, which effectively banned abortion, was repealed. Something Mary herself had campaigned for.

I've never had to think about an abortion for myself. I've never been raped. I've never been in a position, for whatever circumstance, where I felt I had no other option. My mother, although out of wedlock when pregnant with me – which, thirty-odd years ago, was scandalous – was supported and in a position to raise a baby. But not everyone is so lucky. And we all have a duty of care to those who need it.

I've lived in London for over ten years, but growing up in the Republic of Ireland I witnessed a restrictive law that made it illegal for women to access abortion services even in extreme situations. This impacted many girls around me (some talked about it, most didn't). For many it didn't stop them having a termination. They simply travelled, usually alone, over to the UK, and didn't have aftercare or anyone to protect them.

When I was younger, I remember reading in the local newspaper about the body of a newly born baby being found in a field, left there by a distressed young mother. This news story always stayed with me. Then, in 2012, Savita Halappanavar, an Indian woman living in Ireland, died at thirty-one from septicaemia – an infection she developed after she was denied an abortion during a miscarriage. This sparked outrage across the country and gave momentum to a growing call for change.

On 25 May 2018 Ireland voted 'yes' to women's rights and 'yes' to reproductive freedom. Women were given a choice. We made history. The hard campaigning by so many incredible men and women paid off. I don't think I've ever been prouder of my country (and we've won seven Eurovisions!). In America, by contrast, there are states that are still effectively banning abortions and therefore taking away women's rights.

Abortion isn't an easy subject to talk about. After tweeting support for changing Ireland's abortion law, I received horrible abuse online. People tweeted that I had blood on my hands and was 'killing babies' because I wanted women to be able to make a choice safely. To be clear, access to safe and legal abortions is about giving people the right to choose. It's about allowing access to vital healthcare services. This is about basic women's rights. It is not about whether I believe an abortion in a particular situation is right or wrong.

We each have responsibility over our own life; we need to have control. I can't tell you what to do but I can help give you a choice. For too many years the decision had been taken out of women's hands by a patriarchal society. We now have it back. But the fight continues.

As women, we need to start celebrating ourselves and asserting our true worth. We are beautiful, complex creatures. We should not have to feel constantly on guard against oppression and abuse. I am lucky to have such strong and inspiring women in my life, as well as men who appreciate and respect women. I've always found it easier to speak up for others – but I now also acknowledge the importance of speaking up for myself.

As well as Wilson Phillips, I was always drawn to musicians like Dolores O'Riordan and Alanis Morissette. Like most teenage girls I had posters of boy bands and teen heart-throbs on my bedroom wall, but there was something about seeing these women making unapologetically angry music that appealed to me as I was growing up. Now, let's be clear, angry music doesn't mean they were consistently angry women. What I loved was their *agency*: they weren't the muse as many women are (and nothing wrong with that), they were creating this powerful sound and I was obsessed with it. Then I discovered Stevie Nicks, Patti Smith and Debbie Harry, who had come before. How lucky I am to have all these women as role models, even if Alanis Morissette had no idea that this little girl in Bray in Ireland, jumping on her bed to 'You Oughta Know', was slowly finding her voice.

## The Big Smoke

When I graduated in journalism from Dublin City University, I knew I wanted to see more of the world. You don't learn what you don't see, and I felt the need for a bigger horizon than my hometown offered. I had studied a semester abroad at Boston University the year before and loved it. I knew I needed to meet new people, understand different lifestyles and hear other people's stories.

I interned in a newsroom in Dublin for a few months. That was an incredible learning experience but also tough. I was one of a few young women and it was fast-paced with no time for explanations – you learned by doing. It's also where I met Samantha, one of my great friends and someone I admire hugely and look up to, who was also starting out on her career. Not all those you meet are 'your people', but when you find the gems hang on to them and learn from each other. The support and love of your peers is truly invaluable.

Life changed very quickly for me after this internship. I was given a permanent job and, after a month there, I entered an open competition to be the new 'face' of MTV – ah, sure, why not? I didn't tell anyone (except for Samantha and a few other close friends) and, to my surprise, I won the whole thing. I still haven't quite got my head around that to this day. I was definitely not cool enough and had no telly experience. But a somewhat naive enthusiasm and strong work ethic gets you far.

And when I look back at this time, I feel so proud that I just went for it and entered the competition. There were a thousand stories I could have told myself about how I wasn't likely to win, or that they would want someone different. Perhaps you are telling yourself a story right now about why your dreams are unlikely or impossible. Take it from me, the unexpected can happen. But it won't happen if you're not putting yourself out there.

When I started as a presenter in the MTV studios in London, I met some very interesting people. You can imagine. Some childhood heroes, some new acquaintances. I'll share a few of those stories later (there are others I'll probably never tell), but I'll always remember the day I worked on a project with a charity called Plan. A girl from the organisation came into the studio and handed me a leaflet with the header 'Because I Am a Girl'. They wanted support from media types to talk about their charitable work.

The flimsy pamphlet stated that '132 million girls around the world are out of school'. And something struck me. There are places in the world where you can't access education simply because you are a girl. It just never resonated with me until I saw the startling figures in black and white in front of me.

My biggest issue with being female at that stage of my life was that I needed at least an extra half an hour in the morning, to put some slap on my face and contain the crazy mop of hair on my head, to be socially acceptable. A bad day was my period making me grumpy, that I forgot to shave my legs or that the rude builder opposite work had wolf-whistled at me. But can you imagine getting your period and having no running water or sanitary products? Being forced into an arranged marriage as a child? Not having access to any of the opportunities made possible to us through education and literature? Being a girl is damn hard anyway, but this floored me. Compared to these women and girls, who stay positive in spite of so many obstacles, I feel guilty about the little things in life I get bogged down by.

I was so awkward growing up. I always wanted boobs. I actually once lit a candle at Mass and prayed for them (though I told my mam at the time it was for world peace – believe me, having boobs felt just as important at the time). They grew eventually, when I was seventeen . . . but not at the same time, of course. That would have made my life way too simple. Really should have asked for world peace, in hindsight. What I learned as I got older was that everyone seems to have had similar anxieties and freak-outs, even when our circumstances were very different.

In 2016 I travelled to Nepal with UNICEF to write about the aftermath of the devastating earthquake that struck the country in April the previous year. Over 8,000 schools were wiped out in forty-five seconds. That's all the schools in my home country of Ireland: gone, twice over.

The teenagers I met in Nepal were all ambitious like I was at their age. They all wanted careers. They saw world-class professionals in action as their country tried to deal with the trauma of this natural disaster. They dreamed of becoming doctors, civil engineers, social workers and aid workers. But I will never forget the silence that fell over a room in a Kathmandu slum when a sixteen-year-old girl called Kopila broke down in front of me.

It's very easy for me to say we can achieve anything, and to talk about being your own heroine, when I have the chance to do these things. What if you don't have the opportunity? Kopila told me she will likely never achieve her dream of becoming a doctor. As I sat there and tried to motivate her and her classmates, telling them that any dream is possible, I felt sick in my stomach. Kopila was right. She doesn't have the same opportunities that I had, because of something she had no control over – the country in which she was born. She has to leave school early to help her mother at home. It doesn't seem just. But I didn't see her as a victim. I saw someone who was speaking out. Who was asking for help. Who knew the world wasn't fair but wanted to do something about it. She taught me more than I could ever have imagined. I wanted to ask her so many questions. I asked her what was the toughest thing about day-to-day life. I assumed it would be lack of running water, financial support for basic necessities, trying to stay in school, but she immediately responded with 'catcalling'. The boys would jeer and shout lewd things at her when she took the bus to school. All the other girls in the room stoically nodded.

I naively thought I was coming to talk to young people who lived a different life to mine and here I was connecting with them on an obstacle that most girls face and hate no matter what country you're in. The routine abuse of women, the quiet remarks and injustices were constantly at the forefront of their minds.

I've had friends who have been the victims of horrific abuse. I've been frustrated when I see wrongdoings that I can't make right. Friends who are afraid to speak out and all I can say is, 'I believe you. I'm here and I support you.' Sometimes in life we have to let other people make their own choices, but we can control our reactions. We can be supportive, encouraging and, above all, we can listen.

All I can speak about is what I know – my personal experiences and things that may resonate with other women, and even men too. There have been so many things I've felt too embarrassed to talk about.

When I started to get more known as a presenter in London, there was a photographer who took pictures of me as I was getting out of a car outside my flat. It was a summer's afternoon and I was wearing a floral dress, carrying my dog and shopping bags. The article (I use the term loosely) that accompanied the images read 'near pants shot'.

For the next week, I again spotted a car with a photographer outside my flat. In fact, I even called the police one day as I have an elderly neighbour and didn't want to freak her out or have the front of my home printed in some newspaper – that's not what I signed up for, nor should I be coerced into it. It's embarrassing. The police officer told me that there was nothing I could do about it: a photographer was free to take pictures of me in public spaces and the footpath outside my home is public property – like I'm in some sort of urban zoo. I took a picture of the photographer in question, parked in one of the disabled bays, and posted it on Twitter (he wasn't happy about that), in the hope that it would have him moved. It didn't.

I remember wearing jeans for the next few days in case it might happen again. Imagine *that* being something you have to actually think about when you're getting dressed in the morning. In the past I've posed for fashion shoots in underwear on closed sets and in an environment I felt comfortable and empowered in. It was my choice. But that shouldn't make me a target for this behaviour, should it? I now worry: will a man put a camera under my skirt? How is this the world we live in? How is this legal?

This wasn't walking down a red carpet; this was walking outside my home. Besides, I like wearing dresses. Why shouldn't I be able to wear them without feeling constantly on guard?

Eventually he got what he wanted. If you follow someone around long enough, and shoot from a low angle on a day I'm wearing a dress, yes, you'll get the pants shot! Imagine this is actually someone's 'job'! What's worse, in a way, is that someone actually prints these pictures! Think about this: the moment there's a gust of wind is the moment that someone gets their money shot. It's awful.

To say that there are more important things going on in the world than the colour of my pants would be funny, if all of this weren't so invasive, so horrible, so cheap and nasty. On top of all that, the paper blurred my knickers, so it basically looked like I was wearing NO PANTS! The whole thing felt dirty and grossly, needlessly, sexualised.

I felt so humiliated at the time. I didn't want to say anything for fear of drawing attention to these awful, pathetically sordid pictures that were now posted online, with no way to remove them. So I was mortified in silence.

I am by no means the only woman to whom this has happened. In fact, most women I know in the entertainment industry have had similar ordeals. And some are affected by it more than others. Society has this female-shaming culture that seems to be acceptable. Why do we love to degrade women? 'Oh well, look what she was wearing, she was asking for it.' How is this a justification??! It isn't. Ever.

But this experience seems to be common among many women. Not just in showbiz culture. A few years ago I was contacted by a woman named Gina Martin who was trailblazing a campaign to make upskirting illegal.

**Definition: Upskirting** (n.)
A highly intrusive practice, which typically involves someone taking a picture under another person's clothing without their knowledge, with the intention of viewing their genitals or buttocks (with or without underwear).

It can take place in a range of places. For example, British Transport Police revealed they had seen a rise in reports of it happening on public transport. Anyone, and any gender, can be a victim and this behaviour is completely unacceptable.

The Voyeurism (Offences) Act, which was commonly known as the 'Upskirting Bill', was introduced on 21 June 2018. It came into force on 12 April 2019. The new law penalises cases where the purpose of the behaviour is to obtain sexual gratification, or to cause humiliation, distress or alarm. Perpetrators can face two years in prison. By criminalising this upsetting practice, the aim is that it will deter people from committing the offence. The new law sends a clear message that such behaviour will not be tolerated. But how the hell did it take so bloody long?

The short answer: because as a society we accepted it. It needed one person to be the change. Waiting for government bodies, the authorities, to make this needed change was pointless. You needed a spark to ignite the flame. Each of us has a responsibility to do what we can. The door to change doesn't open; we have to break it down, and usually it starts with one person having the courage to give the first push. That encourages more push from everyone else, and eventually this generates enough force for real change.

I spent most of my single days in the little limelight I've experienced, reading about my so-called dalliances with men. Pretty much every man I've ever crossed paths with, I may as well have been photographed straddling – from friends, to work colleagues, to actual boyfriends. This is supposed to be a measure of my worth? Not the fact that I have worked bloody hard in this industry and made a successful career, bought a house, supported my family, been a faithful girlfriend and lived my life as best I could, trying to be a kind person and standing up for others when I could?

A few years ago I read an extract from a newspaper where all the men were introduced in terms of their career, but the women were defined by their looks or who they've dated. This is a real clipping:

*Other stars to lend their support to the charity drive
include TV presenter Laura Whitmore who was once
linked to Leonardo DiCaprio, mature model Daphne
Selfe, sports presenter Ore Oduba, YouTube star Jim
Chapman and George Clooney's ex, Lisa Snowdon.*

All the guys are mentioned *sans* age or love-interest
details and not one woman is introduced without even
the most trivial of sex- or age-related reference. It's
effectively reducing women to an age or an act rather
than recognising them as stand-alone people.

People sometimes say to me, 'Ah, just ignore it.' Some
things may be ignored but they don't go away. They
affect you; they get buried deep down inside, gnawing
away at your soul.

The article was subsequently changed after I brought
this to the attention of the publication on a social media
platform. It was a small victory. But this isn't an isolated
incident, merely a small example of being 'just a girl'.

I know that compared to many people I have been
fortunate. I love this life and I've been blessed with
wonderful opportunities – but I've had enough of being
trivialised and gossiped about. Women are not play-
things – either of men or of the media – and should
not be treated as such.

I feel I owe it to that little girl in Bray with the
mirrored wardrobes and questionable posters on her

wall to speak up. That she needs to know it doesn't matter what shape she is or how much her body changes from a girl into a woman. People will judge you; people will tell you what to do, but the most important opinion is your own. Seek out role models who inspire you, who question you and who teach you.

I'm a bit jealous of my younger reflection. Because back then I was oblivious. I thought I could do anything. I actually impressed and inspired myself on a daily basis. I ran, jumped, swung, sang and danced openly without a care in the world, and without worrying about what everyone else thought of me. I didn't need anyone else's constant mirror; I had my whole life ahead of me and anything was possible. As I get older, I am losing a bit of that. My trigger used to be a fear of not being good enough or not fitting in. But now I don't want to fit in. In my late teens, when someone disapproved of me or laughed at me, I would do anything to avoid feeling not good enough. I felt helpless as a teenager, so feeling any degree of helplessness as an adult can still be a huge trigger for me. Comfort-eating or controlling what I ate made me feel fleetingly better, but it was empty. There are ways to reclaim control without hurting yourself or others.

I feel I'm still learning who I am, and I want to keep challenging myself as well as those around me. It's important to look ahead, but maybe we should learn from our carefree younger selves, before the realities of life sank in. Why our dreams became less exciting and we were told what we should feel, think and do. We don't have to have it all sussed out – sure, it's only chapter 1 after all.

REFLECTION: Who runs the world? Girls, reflect on the women in your life who have shaped you . . .

AFFIRMATION: I am beautiful. I am powerful. I am confident. I am the perfect age. I am the perfect size. I have the right to choose.

# chapter two

## She is happy: the eternal optimist and finding perspective

'Your success and happiness lies in you.
Resolve to keep happy, and your joy
and you shall form an invincible host
against difficulties.'

**HELEN KELLER**

Always look on the bright side of life.

I've always had this annoying habit of being optimistic. I'm one of 'those' positive people who I'm aware
can be rather annoying for the pessimists around them.
Sometimes I annoy myself. YES, I've spoken at length
about how fucking hard it is to be a girl in the previous
chapter; but I also think it's bloody *great*. I have always
seen the glass clasped by the female grip as being half-full

(preferably with Pinot Grigio) and forever ready and waiting for a top-up.

My mother once told me a great story about when my parents were still together and had gone on holiday to Tenerife before I was born. They were both in their early twenties and had spent a week away on what my mother remembers to have been a joyous and exciting adventure for them both. A few days after they returned to Dublin, they went to a friend's wedding together.

Sitting at one of those standard round tables, not knowing everyone and trying painfully to make conversation – let's be honest, wedding small talk can be a nightmare depending on who you get stuck beside – my parents' recent holiday and my mother's glowing fresh tan seemed to be a safe topic, and one that interested their fellow guests.

'How was your holiday?' someone asked.

My mother scanned through the memories, searching for which tale she'd tell. There were so many – the great dinners, delicious food or the beautiful weather, or perhaps the friendly hotel staff – but her thoughts were cut short by my father, who answered abruptly: 'CRAP! It was crap!'

My mother was confused. My father then carried on, describing a horrific holiday unfamiliar to my mother: 'Weather was shite! It rained the day we arrived.'

(Mother: 'Yes, but it was sunny every other day; and the first day isn't important, we didn't notice. In fact, we were lucky it turned for us.')

'The restaurant in the hotel forgot my order.' (Mother: 'Well, yes, but the waiter was polite and apologised. He sorted it all out AND included a complimentary panna cotta for dessert to make up for it.')

'The sand on the beach was so hot it scalded the soles of my feet.' (Mother: 'We had such beautiful weather, and a golden beach on our doorstep. It was paradise.')

My mother and father both experienced the same holiday. The only difference was . . . PERSPECTIVE.

Perspective doesn't always come easy. Especially if something terrible happens – a boyfriend cheats on you or a work colleague steals all your ideas. Some people are just arseholes and you can see them in all their shittiness. But coming out of the situation, YOU can control your reaction and how it affects you long-term.

How you choose to see a situation governs your mental outlook, which in turn determines how you choose to interpret it and how you decide your response. Remember those wise old words: 'change your perspective, change your world'.

There was a study I read in the papers a few years back. I remember it well because the headline jumped out at me: 'Pessimists are more likely to live longer.' FUCK. Well, I'm screwed (trying my best to be pessimistic to elongate my life)! At least all these years of negativity had served my father well.

The article was based on a wide-ranging study of the associations between people's expectations for their lives, and how accurate their predictions turn out to be; as well as various health outcomes. The study was carried out by researchers from the University of Erlangen-Nuremberg, the University of Zurich, Humboldt University of Berlin, the German Institute for Economic Research and the Max Planck Institute for Human Development (so it sounded legit!) and was published in a medical journal on psychology and ageing.

So was my father really going to double his life expectancy by seeing the world from his cynical stance? Eh? . . . Probably not.

On further investigation, the headlines declaring 'Being negative is good for you' do not really reflect the research results. The study did find that the more that people overestimated their future happiness (a group deemed 'optimists'), the higher their risk of disability and death. However, no significant differences were seen among individuals who underestimated their future satisfaction (dubbed 'pessimists'). So, headline writers would have been better off claiming 'pride comes before a fall'. But this isn't the first time (or last) that a head-line is miles away from the truth (curating the news you digest will come later). Imagine papers using a 'fake news' headline! It's more remarkable to see one encompassing the truth.

So thankfully this study does not prove that a dark and dreary outlook will lead to a long and healthy life. Praise be! I shall continue looking on the bright side of life.

One interesting thing from the study, however, is that younger people tend to be more optimistic about their future selves, and older people tend to be more realistic and veer towards the negative (probably because, realistically, they are closer to death).

Also, life experience affects us and taints our perspective. I always had an idealistic view of love, even though my parents weren't together. When an ex-boyfriend cheated on me, what upset me the most, besides the obvious betrayal of trust, was that it altered my view of love. I was genuinely scared it would make me a pessimist in future relationships. But what I eventually learned was that I could control how I look at the world moving forward. Easier said than done.

When I went to LA to 'take meetings', a fate most people in this industry usually suffer, I couldn't cope with the over-the-top 'positive vibes'. I was told to talk myself up more. Growing up in Ireland, that was somewhat frowned upon.

'Oh, you looked great in those pictures of Mary and John's wedding on Facebook, Laura!'

'Oh, Jaysus God, the state of me! My hair looked

like a bird's nest, and sure that dress was from Primark and clung to my stomach after the dinner, and everyone thought I was pregnant!'

It feels wrong to just say: 'Thank you. Yes, I did look fucking great!'

Where our American counterparts are notorious for their exhausting optimism, Irish folk and their neighbours in Great Britain tend merely to expect the worst.

I stumbled across another report in the papers more recently – though was wary of the boisterous headline. So I investigated further. According to the Boston University School of Medicine, optimists actually live longer than pessimists.[*] Maybe the Americans are on to a good thing.

Their long-term study of 70,000 older people found that, on average, the most optimistic participants lived 15 per cent longer. Though it's true that the upbeat individuals were more likely to take active steps to overcome life's challenges – going running if they became overweight, for example – the study showed that optimism alone accounted for a 9 per cent increase in lifespan, regardless of behaviour.

The theory is that optimists may find it easier to control emotions, and so be protected from the effects of stress. And researchers said pessimists could benefit

---

[*] Lewina O. Lee et al., 'Optimism is associated with exceptional longevity in 2 epidemiologic cohorts of men and women', *PNAS* (116: 37), September 2019.

from doing things like imagining a future where everything turns out well.

The study group's levels of optimism were assessed, as well as their overall health. They were also asked about exercise and diet, as well as whether and how much they smoked and drank alcohol. On average, the most optimistic men and women had an 11–15 per cent longer lifespan and were significantly more likely to live to eighty-five compared with the least optimistic group.

While a lot is known about the risk factors for disease and early death, far less is understood about what the researchers call 'positive psychosocial factors' that could enable healthy ageing. Professor Lewina Lee, associate professor of psychiatry at the Boston University School of Medicine, who worked on the study, said:

*Our findings speak to the possibility that raising levels of optimism may promote longevity and healthy ageing. Evidence from randomised control trials suggests that interventions, such as imagining a future in which everything has turned out well, or more intensive cognitive-behavioural therapy, can increase levels of optimism.*

However, exactly why optimistic people appear to live longer is still up for debate. But there is definitely a link between positivity and attracting good things to you if you truly believe in them.

Maybe optimistic people tend to have goals and the confidence to reach them. And even if they don't reach them, they have that hope and something to live for. Professor Bruce Hood from the University of Bristol runs a course called the 'Science of Happiness'. He said the study supported existing evidence of the benefits of positive thinking.

One causal mechanism could be that optimists cope better with stress by dealing with their emotions more effectively. Stress impacts on the immune system and so there is a possibility that this means that optimists cope better with infections. A number of studies have also linked stress with shorter 'telomeres' – a chromosome component that's been associated with cellular ageing and the risk of heart disease, diabetes and cancer.

Basically, in the tug-of-war between the world views of cheery optimists and dour pessimists, the happy people just got a big boost. Yay! Just what optimists need.

But what if you're not a natural optimist? Can I pretend or train myself to be one, you may ask? Well . . . kinda. Your mindset is about 25 per cent hereditary, according to Lewina Lee, the lead researcher of the University of Boston study. The rest is down to us.

Optimists generally expect good things to happen in the future and feel they can control important outcomes.

They tend to stay positive and to put the best spin on whatever comes their way. But remember we ALL have the ability to alter our thoughts, to be more optimistic.

So gloomy curmudgeons are not doomed to short, sad lives. There is hope – we can change our perspective. Hallelujah!

I know people may find eternal optimists insufferable. I was asked recently in an interview: 'How do you manage to always be so smiley?' I don't. Some mornings I wake up and, no matter what I do, I'll be in a bad mood. My perspective then shifts from how I'm feeling in the present to thinking I WILL feel better – so enjoy the dark depths of a little moan, but don't dwell there for too long. Sometimes it's important to acknowledge the bad mood without letting it completely devour you.

It is impossible to be positive ALL the time, but it is possible to shift one's perspective.

I was a guest on 'The Naked Professor' podcast which discusses mental health (give it a listen – it's really good). When it went out, one of the hosts, Matt Johnson, a brilliant activist and presenter, introduced me in the usual manner; but continued by saying that, unlike other guests who had been self-confessed alcoholics or heroin addicts, I hadn't gone through anything really bad. What he knew was someone who was happy and hadn't faced real adversity or struggle.

This isn't true. Negative things come in many forms. You can have a perfect upbringing and never go through a conventional trauma and still be damaged. The image you portray may not be the truth. Be careful judging an optimistic person, because it doesn't mean they are happy all the time – it just means their perspective is different and there are probably a lot more battles faced privately. The so-called obstacles and everyday problems faced can be the most difficult of all.

I can't tell you to be happy. It is impossible to be happy ALL the time. It's not in our nature as humans. Mick Jagger couldn't get it. Hamlet died for it. Angelica Schuyler in *Hamilton* toasts for it . . . But we will never truly achieve complete SATISFACTION.

And that's OK. What we CAN achieve is control over our outlook, our perspective.

## Seven Steps to Help Take Control of Your Perspective

As we are all unique individuals not all of these steps will necessarily work for you, but they may be beneficial to think about if you find yourself down in the dumps.

## 1. Watch your vocabulary

Look at the language my father used compared to my mother when speaking about their trip to Tenerife. There are a lot of people whose vernacular comprises negative words and phrases, or what I like to call 'bleak banter'. While many of us believe our happiness is based on external things, we're often the ones holding ourselves back. Many of us go through our days feeding ourselves negative messages we may not even be aware of, convincing ourselves we're 'not good enough', 'not clever enough' or 'not pretty enough'. Stop with the bleak banter and start thinking more positively.

Each chapter of this book ends with a reflection and affirmation. Affirmations are great things you can say to yourself to help tilt your perspective. If you keep saying you're going to fail, you WILL fail. If someone asks you a question, for example, 'How was your holiday?', and you immediately respond: 'Crap', you're setting yourself up for, well, crap.

Rather than saying you can't achieve something, why don't you say, 'I haven't achieved it YET.' Rather than telling people what you can't do, tell them what you CAN do.

Write down these positive affirmations and repeat them on a daily basis: 'Yes I can'; 'Yes I will'. It's not always what happens that determines your mood, but how you verbalise and express what happens that counts.

We are our own worst critics. We talk about being kind to each other but it must start with being kind to ourselves. So, say something nice to yourself. I remember once having a massive argument with a piece of IKEA furniture. I'm so shit at putting together IKEA. I usually buy myself milk and white chocolate to accompany the hours of torment constructing it, so I can pretend it's a giant Kinder Surprise egg and the *insert* [chest of drawers/side table/TV stand] is a very large toy.

Rather than beating myself up about it, I think: 'Either the instructions I'm following are unclear, or this project is going to require a bit more effort than I thought. Maybe I'm just having a rough day, maybe I'm better if someone helps me.' In other words, I use positive self-talk to keep the struggle outside myself.

The situation could have been very different if I'd used bleak banter, as in: 'I'm no good. I get everything wrong. I will never complete this.' The pessimist version of me would most likely have got me down, as I interpreted the same struggle as internal, widespread and everlasting.

Physical body language is also important. Your smile actually influences your mood in a positive way. When you feel down, your brain tells your face that you're sad, and your facial muscles respond by putting on a frown, which in turn conveys a message back to your brain that says you're sad. You can flip the switch on this internal reaction by adjusting your facial muscles into a smile so they don't correspond to what you're feeling. Obviously, this doesn't work on all occasions. If someone tells you your granny died and you start smiling like a Cheshire cat and laughing to yourself, you will just look like a crazy person.

But how we talk to ourselves is so, so important. If you say something enough and 'firehose' thoughts at your brain, you will believe them and they can become reality.

**Definition: Firehosing** (n.)
A propaganda technique in which a large number of messages are broadcast rapidly, repetitively and continuously over multiple channels (such as news and social media) without regard for truth or consistency. Since 2014, when it was successfully used by Russia during its annexation of Crimea, this model has been adopted by other governments and political movements around the world. (Wikipedia)

A lot of politicians use this technique of relaying false 'truths' to help gain voters. If they say something enough, even if it is untrue, we (and even they) start to believe it as fact. Look at Donald Trump's denial of the severity of the Covid-19 pandemic and the late response to tackling it. Firehosing is dangerous, but if we take the basic premise of it and use the above definition as a formula, it can have huge benefits for us.

This doesn't mean we are avoiding reality; this means we are encouraging our true potential. (Can't believe I've actually taken something positive from Trump!)

## 2. Focus on what you CAN do

Most of us will congratulate other people's successes and accomplishments ahead of our own. When it comes to our own talents we frequently play them down or just simply ignore them entirely. Yes, no one likes a 'show-off'. A certain decorum and level of modesty is classy. But in our own heads we need to stop listening to the inner critic all the time. Reflect on your past achievements and start to really appreciate your success and what you have to offer.

Some things I will get better at doing, such as writing – the more I do, the better I will get. Some things I will never be able to do. I can't bobsleigh. To be fair, I have little interest and never tried, but I have come to the conclusion I will not be a bobsleigher. Though in the early nineties, the Jon Turteltaub film *Cool Runnings* gave me a little bit of unrealistic hope.

But I'm not going to be a professional sports player in any form (is yoga a sport?). The lack of skills and the fact I'm now in my thirties has cemented that fact. And I am OK with that. And so is the world. No one's loss.

I know I'm a hard worker but I am not good at logistics. I will never read a whole call sheet, much to my agent's annoyance. If you send me an email, I'll only read the first two or three paragraphs before getting distracted. I'm better at being creative, so I work on honing my skills and working with people who complement my skill set (and send me short emails).

Often our negative thoughts are based on little more than our own fears, insecurities and low self-esteem. To help you overcome these, you need to constantly challenge your negative thoughts.

It is important to remember that it isn't events themselves that make us unhappy; it is our interpretation and reaction to them; and while you can't always change events, you can change your response. When negative situations occur, try to reframe them by focusing on the positives or what you can learn from the situation.

When I found out a boyfriend had cheated on me, I was in shock, but I couldn't control what had happened. However, I could control my reaction. I'd like to pretend I was level-headed about the whole thing, but I did throw his guitar in the bin. And to be honest I'd probably do it again. Sorry, not sorry.

I found comfort in knowing it doesn't define me, and what I chose to do was take back control. I could walk away from any toxic situation. Maybe we can gain inner strength and resilience or make stronger relationships through sharing heartbreak. We also learn something about ourselves. Try your best to focus on what you have learned and gained from your experience rather than what you have lost.

## 3. Surround yourself with people who lift you

Some people just bring out the worst in you, don't they? If you want to become an optimist, it can help to find yourself a positive circle to surround yourself with. Whether it is a colleague, close friend or even a well-known person, think of the most inspirational person you can. Good role models are important.

Also, spending time with negative people who continually see the bad in every situation is a sure-fire way to ensure you continue to feel negative too. You don't have to exclude these people from your life, especially if they are in your family. Maybe talk to them and say, 'Your negativity affects me.' Nobody wants to be miserable all the time. Or to be viewed in that way.

To stay feeling optimistic, you need to surround yourself with people who help you to appreciate the good in situations and in life in general. This also applies to other influences in your life, such as music, social media, newspapers, etc. You will find certain things can trigger you into 'bleak banter', so be wary.

'Did you see the news last night?'

'Yes, another murder. We are all doomed!'

You are only as good as the company you keep, and misery loves company. If you spend too much time around negative people, there's a strong chance you won't find much to be happy about. Do yourself a favour and dodge other people's negativity. Surround yourself with positive, emotionally supportive friends and spend time together doing things that make you smile.

Optimism is a learned habit, and it is completely contagious. So, surround yourself with people who could infect you with their positivity, and then pass your new good mood on to a friend or stranger with kind words and deeds.

'Sharon, you look great today!' Give compliments. Sharon may always look great, but don't assume someone has told her that. Do nice things – let somebody have that parking space, let that person with only a few items cut in front of you at the supermarket. The simple act of doing something for those around you will help create more positive people to interact with.

The bottom line is that life is way too short to waste time with people who don't treat you right. Surround yourself with people who lift you up when you're down, and then return the favour when you're able.

I have a WhatsApp group with two mates, Alex and Ryan. It's called 'Therapy'. At least once a month one of us feels down, and it is the responsibility of the other members of the group to cheer and lift up whoever is feeling lost. The following month it could be someone else. We all have a duty to lift AND be lifted. Thankfully we've never all been in a low state at the same time. When that happens, more people may be added to the group.

## 4. Where can I go from here?

Pessimists tend to focus on problems while optimists look for solutions. While it is tempting to dwell on your problems or disappointments, remember that this will not change your situation. The situation may not feel great and it may not seem fair; but what has happened has happened, whether you like it or not. Rather than reflecting on what could have been, let go of regrets and negative thoughts (and that binned guitar), get proactive and start planning where you can go from here.

I always like to think, to a certain degree, that everything happens for a reason. That there are certain paths we are destined to take, should we wish to. Look out for signs. Maybe your life wasn't running as smoothly as you thought and needed shaking up.

Whatever is going on, think: how can I make it better for me and those I care about? Have faith and trust in your purpose (purpose is one of my favourite words and I'll be mentioning it again later).

When I was eighteen, I was in a model competition that I didn't win. I was about three inches shorter than the other girls but what I lacked in height I made up for in enthusiasm. Enthusiasm doesn't win you modelling competitions, though, does it? I did, however, get signed by an agent and was sent to all sorts of auditions.

I remember everything from roller skating for a juice commercial I tried to blag – and didn't get booked; I was a bad roller skater – to being sent to an audition for an E4 show about a girl band. As the last Irish girl from the castings, I was brought over to London and got down to the final eight. Sadly, there wasn't to be an Irish girl in that band. I think they had one or two series and supported Girls Aloud before they disappeared into pop oblivion.

Looking back, if I'd landed the girl band gig, I wouldn't have got the MTV job two years later (or finished my degree in journalism), and would probably not be where I am now. Always keep looking forward to the path in front of you rather than where you've just been. There might just be something more suited to you.

## 5. Fake it till you make it

Optimism isn't something that comes naturally to most of us, and you may find that it takes time to change your mindset. Try putting the action before the feeling and faking a more positive outlook. Studies have found that it is possible to trick yourself into feeling optimistic by going through the physical motions. If I can trick myself into liking Diet Coke over full-fat Coke, anything is possible.

So, rather than going with your natural instinct of 'I have no idea what the hell I'm doing with my life', try to project a more confident outlook. I learned a long time ago that no one really knows what they are doing, and most people doing significant jobs have impostor syndrome (let's talk about this later).

No one is good at something straight away (unless you are Mariah Carey and born with that voice, but even Mariah has had to navigate her way through a cut-throat industry that is only partly about 'the singing'). When I won 'Pick Me MTV', MTV's search for the face of MTV Europe, I had never interviewed someone on the telly. My first day of the job involved flying to Los Angeles to cover the MTV Video Music Awards at the Gibson Amphitheatre. I had never been to LA. I had no experience, no hairstylist, no make-up artist and no clothes. I borrowed a Topshop skirt and top from my friend Medb, who I knew from university and was living in London. I attempted to do my make-up (albeit badly) and my GHD curls were my only saving grace when it came to red-carpet glam. Thank God I had done that tutorial on YouTube.

I felt like a fraud. But I knew I had an incredible opportunity; and if I acted like a fraud, I would be treated that way. So I had to battle with my internal dialogue telling me I didn't belong there, and convey the image of someone who very much should be where she was standing.

The first band I ever interviewed was Coldplay. Chris Martin didn't know it was my first day, so maybe I could just pretend I knew what I was doing and was an experienced MTV VJ.

When I got to the venue, all the acts were rehearsing, and I was ushered into their dressing-room compound. LA is hot. And I remember feeling the sweat accumulating under the layers of cheap foundation I had caked on. Thankfully that stuff was impenetrable, and not one droplet of perspiration emerged to freedom out into the Californian air to escape my flushed complexion. I had succeeded. No one knew I had no idea what I was doing.

As Coldplay's frontman and I relaxed and chatted while the cameraman set up, I felt I had completed my mission unnoticed. Then my producer James turned and blurted out to Chris, 'You know it's Laura's first day?'

NNNNNNNNNNOOOOOOOOOOOOOOOOOOO
OOOOOOOOOOOOO!!!

I had been outed as the fraud I was. Thankfully, Chris Martin is one of the nicest men in the music industry and ended up asking *me* loads of questions and being very forthcoming in his interview.

I continued to fake it until I could make it for many years. You never really know when it exactly happens but one day you realise . . . I'm actually not faking it as much as I think I am!


## 6. Respect yourself

As a child, I thought I could do anything. I didn't need anyone else's constant approval. Looking back at the little girl reflected in the mirrored wardrobes in Bray, I had my whole life ahead of me and anything was possible. As I get older, I've become jaded.

As we grow into adulthood, the pressure of popular media, our friends and society as a whole begins to wear on us. We start to compare ourselves to everyone around us. We constantly judge. We measure our lifestyle, our career and our bodies against other people's. And when we realise that many of these people have things that we do not, jealousy sets in and we gradually stop appreciating all the great things we do have in our life.

To stay optimistic as adults, we need to retain an element of childlike naivety and enthusiasm. We need to get back to trusting our own intuition when it comes to daily activities. To STOP ASKING FOR EVERYONE'S APPROVAL and simply do what we know in our hearts feels right. Optimists don't judge themselves against a set of unrealistic ideals pushed on to them by the outside world, they stay in their own lane and focus on their own dreams rather than everyone else's. We need to hold on to the belief that we are always good enough, just the way we are. We are constantly growing and evolving. We are constantly improving ourselves.

If we can't respect ourselves, how can we expect others to?

## 7. Happiness does not come from achievement

In order to be optimistic, you have to be relatively happy with your life. In order to find this contentment, you have to look within yourself.

Optimists can still be realists. Sure, you may never succeed – but that depends on your definition of what success is. Getting a promotion at work, or a text from the boy you fancy may give you an instant burst of happiness; but there is no longevity in it if success is left in the hands of other people and their decisions.

You get to choose if you are happy. Not someone else. Optimists disconnect achievement from happiness. They can give themselves permission to be happy in each moment, without the need for anything more. This isn't to say that they are lazy and make do with what life has handed them. They still set goals, work hard, help others and grow; but they learn to indulge joyously in the journey, not in the destination. I've had relationships that haven't worked out, lost friendships, but they have been so important in my becoming the person I am now. I didn't start a friendship thinking of where we'll be in ten or twenty years. The fun is the life experience, the good memories, the adventures shared. When you change your mindset to that mode, the world seems that bit brighter.

Just because you're an optimist doesn't mean you're not going to have bad days. You will, that's reality. Life isn't always rainbows and butterflies. A foundation of realism keeps things in perspective and helps prevent things from being blown out of proportion. Also, if you're happy all the time, you won't appreciate your happiness. Life's ups require life's downs. Prepare for the downs but capitalise on the ups. The former make you sensible, and the latter make you an optimist.

Most of us are pessimistic in order to protect ourselves from disappointment. But by trying to insulate yourself from life's difficulties, you're missing out on something else, too . . . all the possibilities.

## A Little Word About Hope

Always believe that something wonderful will happen.

Hope is my favourite word in the English dictionary. Well, actually it's my second. I really like the word 'discombobulate' because it sounds funny to say, especially after a few glasses of Pinot Grigio, when not only are you saying the word, you look like it too. But hope has my favourite meaning.

Hope does not depend on certainty. Hope is merely the belief that there is the potential for something good to happen. That something good is not anything specific. It is merely the idea of a positive outcome. As Desmond Tutu once said: 'Hope is being able to see that there is light despite all of the darkness.'

It's hard to be motivated in the morning. Staying in bed can feel safe and comforting. The outside world throws obstacle after obstacle at you. But you *hope*, once you're up, you'll feel better. That you'll achieve something or at least feel better as the day progresses. Hope not only helps you to believe that something better is coming, it gives you the belief that you are the person who can make that something better come true. It is difficult to have negative thoughts and be hopeful at the same time.

You don't need the desired outcome, just the possibility. Goals are important for our journey to happen but reaching the goal is actually only secondary. When I think of hope I reflect on the 2000 movie *Cast Away* with Tom Hanks – before Tom Hanks was using his plasma to find a vaccination for Covid-19. Hanks plays Chuck Noland, a FedEx systems engineer whose personal and professional life are both ruled by the clock. Something a lot of us could relate to before the coronavirus pandemic. Always too busy and never present. His fast-paced career takes him all over the world, to far-flung destinations and away from his girlfriend, Kelly, played by Helen Hunt (remember her in *Twister* and *Mad About You* – where is she now? LOVED HER!).

On one of Chuck's many trips, the small plane goes down in the middle of the Pacific Ocean and he becomes stranded on a remote, uninhabited island. He is the only survivor. I was sixteen when I first saw this movie and even my scattered teenage attention span was gripped by one man and pretty much no dialogue for most of the film.

With no one there to dump him off the island and most definitely no coupling up, Chuck makes the best of it. First, he must find a way to meet basic human needs. After failing many times, he finally makes 'FIIIIRRRRREEEEE'. There are lots of FedEx packages from the plane wreckage that he opens and uses. However, there is one package with an angel wing logo on it that he doesn't open and vows to return (still can't help but think a mobile phone could have been in there!). Along with a picture of Kelly, the package becomes a symbol of hope and a reason to endure.

In the midst of a desperate situation, with no end in sight, Chuck manages to maintain a sense of hope during his four years on the island. When he is finally rescued and returns to his beloved Kelly, she has moved on. She thought he was dead, she grieved for him, the man she lost she had laid to rest already. Chuck accepts this and thanks her for being his reason to hope. The picture and the idea of her was more important than actually ending up with her. Reflecting on fate's provision, Chuck concludes that we must always maintain hope, because we never know what we can achieve.

Firstly, the core message of this film is redeeming: we should never give up hope. We know from experience that many circumstances that seem hopeless today are the very things that empower us to succeed later on. Secondly, and as important, we learned that Tom Hanks is a legend.

I met Tom Hanks a few years ago when I was working for MTV and he was promoting a film that was nowhere near as good as the hit *Cast Away*. I had hoped he would be as lovely as I wished, even if his new film wasn't. I was ushered into a room of a decadent London hotel, with lots of people holding clipboards faffing about, and there he was tucked away in a corner under a huge beaming light.

At least I think the light was beaming, it may just have been his Hollywood 100-watt smile that lit up the room.

I wasn't disappointed. He ended up showing me his go-to robot dance move. He was engaged in our conversation. He remembered my name . . . and I suspected that he knew his film was shit and brushed it off with respectful humour. My hopes for Tom Hanks being sound were met. Praise be! Chuck might have 'gotten over' Kelly moving on, and the hope of her may have been enough in the movie *Cast Away*; but I'm not sure I'd have got over Tom Hanks not living up to my expectation in real life.

They say that in certain tragic situations only crazy people can keep their hope alive. But it's that little spark which eventually pulls us from the depths of despair. Hope has the power to make you do the impossible.

While it's hard to be optimistic during difficult times, think of it as your only weapon. Use it to fight, and you'll eventually find your way out. Don't just sit there waiting for the worst to happen, because there's always one more thing that you can do. Like what Mariah Carey sings about in that 'Hero' song about it not being anyone else you need to look for, the hero is inside you all along. Mariah not only has a blazing vocal range, her lyrics hit the spot too. And while, yes, they are as cheesy as a baked camembert, they speak truth.

Shift your gaze from what you can't do to what you can. Pay attention to those you're with when you feel at your best. And when all else fails ask yourself . . . What would Tom Hanks do?

**REFLECTION:** For every negative thought that comes into your head, flip it into a positive. You can't stop the obstacles but you can overcome them.

**AFFIRMATION:** I am in charge of how I feel and today I choose to be happy.

# chapter three

## She is sad: life after heartbreak (it does get better)

'Where there is no struggle,
there is no strength.'
**OPRAH WINFREY**

My 'Achy Breaky Heart'. Sadness is a feeling no one can avoid. It doesn't matter how optimistic you are, or how thick those rose-tinted glasses are, at some point or another you will be sad. Sad is a word that we use a lot, often very loosely, yet its meaning is quite complex. The state of sadness covers a wide range of emotions, from a moment of being slightly disgruntled to the more serious condition of clinical depression. It is important to acknowledge and identify what we are feeling and, more importantly, WHY we are feeling it.

Sometimes I feel really sad – so much so that it engulfs me and eats me up. However, usually the sadness is connected to something – there is a stimulus, such as a heartbreak. It is OK to feel sad if you can understand why you are unhappy, and you know it's temporary. It's harder to bear if your sadness feels all-consuming, and disconnected from a specific trigger. I am not an expert on clinical depression; although there have been people in my life who have been on antidepressants and dealt with various scales of mental health, it is also important to distinguish 'feeling down' in all its forms without judgement.

Life coach Iyanla Vanzant says, 'Trouble comes to pass, not to stay.' I love that.

You may be having a miserable time in life. Perhaps you can't get around some problem. Someone may have caused an incredible amount of damage to your heart, your total state of being. Like being overcome by a storm, you may be snowed in, bogged down, flooded out by fear, anger or emotional destruction. I sometimes feel ashamed for feeling sad.

'People have it worse,' I tell myself. The idea that you have to have something specific happen to you, or to have no happiness in your life to experience sadness is just not true. But that emotion of guilt is real and I have to deal with my sadness in spite of it.

Before I got together with my first boyfriend, I fancied him from afar. One night I was out and saw him coming out of Eamonn Doran's, a small music venue in Dublin. I literally dropped to the ground and hid behind a car. My mate Orla was with me and thought I'd gone mad. For so long all I wanted was to bump into him 'organically' . . . then I had my chance and all I could do was hide behind a car.

I'm an idiot. I was just too nervous and didn't know what to say. Instead I grazed both my knees on the pavement. We eventually went out for a few years before we broke up and I moved to London. I remember feeling guilty for feeling sad because I had just won the MTV search, and should have been happy about this brilliant opportunity; but the end of this relationship felt traumatic to my younger self. I was convinced I would never love again.

At that stage I had only slept with one guy, and I thought my little heart would never experience that type of adoration and intimacy again. Until it did. Life moves on, even though at the time it might not seem possible.

But back then those were real feelings that caused me lots of pain and many sleepless nights. It's easy to dismiss feelings of heartbreak as something you should just 'get over', but I say these feelings should be recognised and not brushed away as meaningless emotions. Anything you feel has meaning.

There's no real end to any story. It continues.

No happy ever after, just a constant selection of twists,

turns and possibilities. I've learned not to look for the happy ever after, but to look for the happy in what I'm doing NOW. I have a tendency to be constantly moving, like a wanted woman in some sixties crime thriller – I must keep moving or they'll catch me. But maybe I'm not running away from something. Maybe I'm not even running towards something. MAYBE I'm just running because it's fun to run.

Remember as a kid you'd run so fast you couldn't breathe; you're moving so fast you think you could just fall over? THAT feeling. That's my favourite feeling.

A year ago I drove across America, road-tripping west coast to east coast and staying in whatever town we happened to end up in for the night. In my perfect state of movement, my safe space.

Road trips mean playlists – and, my God, do I love a playlist! A song for every mood. Tina Turner, Mariah Carey, Wilson Phillips (of course), all part of the playlist. My windswept hair blowing, in the driver's seat of a convertible Ford Mustang GT, channelling Diana Ross in The Supremes, though not quite as glamorous but definitely with the same volume.

I loved leaving the highway, coasting along against a backdrop of boundless landscape. Manoeuvring on to the smaller roads, the side streets, taking in the surroundings and thinking: 'Who lives here? What's their purpose, their daily hang-ups and their virtues?'

A year before that drive I found out I was pregnant. Handbrake pulled. Car screeching to a halt.

I was in Italy on a job (in my usual state of travel flux, just like Tom Hanks in *Cast Away*) and my boobs were MASSIVE. I mean, they looked great. Extra-full, but they weren't fitting in my bras. So I did a test that I got from a local Italian pharmacy, and there it was in black and white. INCINTA. Translation: PREGNANT. Shit.

Or was it shit? Age thirty-three and a third; in a relationship; owns own property — it's hardly scandalous. My mother did it in far tougher circumstances. That much I knew.

But did this mean my constant state of movement would slow down or, worse still, stop? Would I lose my sense of identity? Would I be good enough as a mother?

So, I wrote a short film called *Sadhbh* (just to really confuse everyone outside Ireland, that's the actual spelling of a girl's name) about a young mother and the pressures of not being good enough. Of struggling. I surely wasn't alone with these thoughts. During those early few weeks, the hardest part was trying to hide the fact that I wasn't drinking. Isn't that obscene?! That was my biggest worry.

I went to the doctor to confirm the pregnancy, was handed a pile of faded pamphlets and told it's a good time to become pregnant, as the older you get, the harder it can be. That night were the *GQ* Awards – a fancy awards ceremony in London – and I wore a little black dress and super-stilettos (I mean, I may as well enjoy it while I can!). I didn't want my life to change. I can still be fun Laura *and* pregnant. Can't I?

But how the hell would I get through the night without anyone noticing I wasn't drinking? There were journalists everywhere and people were drinking A LOT. I grasped a half-full glass of champagne, my comfort blanket, with the rim orbiting but never actually touching my lips. Whatever your views are on drinking during pregnancy, it wasn't something I wanted to chance. My mother agreed . . . well, except for a glass of Guinness, which – back in 1985 – the doctor had told her she should consume weekly. But, as she insisted, 'THAT WAS FOR THE IRON, LAURA!'

So, there I was, sober at the awards do, my boyfriend running late – and I bumped into my ex-boyfriend. My now chipped manicured nails clawed at the champagne flute as we did the usual 'Oh how great to see you! Aren't you looking well' routine through fixed smiles. I really could have done with a drink. But there was no Guinness in sight.

The next few weeks I learned a lot about sobriety. I didn't have a hangover, which was great, but people are very untrusting of someone who doesn't drink, and HATE being drunk in front of them. Especially if you're Irish.

Non-Irish person: 'What are you drinking?'

Me: 'Just a lemonade would be great.'

Non-Irish person: 'But I thought you were Irish?'

Me: 'I am.'

Non-Irish person: 'Whiskey it is, then.'

Honestly, it just became easier to accept the drink, take it to the toilets and flush it down the loo. A lot of good-quality alcohol was wasted during this period and for that I'm truly sorry! Then I learned: if you are buying people drinks, they don't actually notice you're not drinking. So that's what I did. I was very popular.

At twelve weeks I did my first meet with the midwife and spent two hours going through all my options for the birth. The first scan was scheduled in another two weeks, as that was the earliest we could get. I was going away at the weekend, so I decided to get a private scan at Harley Street that evening. In the scanning room I could see on the screen the outline of what looked like a jelly baby – just like in the movies. Then silence.

'I'm sorry, there's no heartbeat.'

I wasn't sure how I was supposed to react. Should I cry? Was I allowed to be emotional for something unplanned? The things that go through your mind. Actually, I had just spent two hours planning with the midwife earlier that day. That handbrake again. Things spinning. Then the strangest thing happened. The doctor went out to the reception and brought in a puppy. She offered it to me for a cuddle. It was a new puppy that happened to be in the clinic that day – not a usual circumstance. But she hoped it would make me feel better. When in doubt, get the puppies out.

The doctor told me that miscarriages happen to one in three women. I didn't know this, because most people just don't talk about it. Now I'm part of that statistic. I hadn't planned the pregnancy in the first place, so should I be sad? I was. That feeling was heightened because I felt I had to be sad alone: apart from a handful of people, no one knew. I had to deal with high-intensity work situations without anyone around me knowing what was really going on inside my head. Although maybe that made it easier to deal with – because I wasn't actually dealing with it.

I poured myself a large glass of wine that didn't taste as good as I thought it would and I kept on moving forward. Realising now that I do want children and knowing that so many women battle things in silence. That the open highway is fun – but going down the side streets and pulling in and parking, and recognising the stillness, is important too. Feel the moment, live it, then get back in the car and keep driving, Also, when you feel sad, may I recommend reaching back to 1985 and blasting a bit of 'Chain Reaction' by Diana Ross.

Heartbreak is a strange thing, besides the obvious hurt. You also have to deal with the shame. The embarrassment of feeling sad over losing a baby you never planned.

But then also people expecting you to be sad all the time when in fact I had so many joyous experiences during that time too. There is no right or wrong way to feel.

In broken relationships, it's the same. When I found out an ex had cheated on me, I was so overwhelmed by my emotions – anger, loss, but also shame. We blame ourselves even if the cause is out of our control. Having your heart broken is shit. But it does give you life membership to a quite special club.

## The Heartbreak Club

To feel really sad meant that I'd had the privilege of feeling very happy. To be heartbroken meant that I had allowed my heart to love.

I've been in love three times. And it is both a blessing and a curse. I like to look at them as the First Love, the Tragic Love and the Grown-up Love.

## The first love

It may not be your first relationship but it's definitely the first time you've opened your heart to someone. It's hard to tell between love and lust. I was eighteen and it felt like Marianne and Connell in *Normal People* (long before Sally

Rooney put pen to paper). That same attraction, youthful naivety and awkwardness – except far fewer dramatic pauses, a lack of good lighting and my mother's not a bitch (thank God). But there WAS a chain around his neck. Why are we women obsessed about men wearing chains? Why is it so sexy? Apparently, men wearing meaningful jewellery can signify the commitment they've made and values they place on family and purpose. But I reckon it's the basic link to it touching the naked skin – the bare-naked skin. Ah, young love, young naked love.

Sometimes people end up with their first love. Good for them. But I learned just as much about myself getting out of the relationship as I did in it. First love hurts. It hurts just as much as Hollywood depicts. Because you've never had those feelings before, you are unprepared to deal with all of those turbulent emotions. You've got no armour on, no defences. *Romeo and Juliet* was so powerful because the lovers were young – the dramatic gestures and over-the-top monologues would be different if they had lived a full life, had a few kids and a mortgage to pay.

## The tragic love

Supposed to be 'the one'. You've had the First Love – the trial and error. You've opened your heart again. This

time is different, you think. You have grown-up feelings. You've given them your heart in a bag – exposed,
no padding. Oh-so-fragile. And they drop it. Splat on
the ground. Ouch.

This one took me longer to get over. People make
mistakes in life but I had underestimated how much
those wrong turns could affect me. It took me many
years to build back trust with a partner. I held myself
back for a long time. But, just as with the First Love,
you learn it does get better. What's that saying – things
don't get better; you get better at handling them? We
are all so much stronger than we give ourselves credit
for. We can't control how other people behave. But as
I've said many times before, we can control how we
choose to respond.

Torn between – do I fight for love, or throw it away?
There is no right or wrong. Everyone is different, and
you and only you can decide what you can live with,
and live without.

For me, when trust is broken I know I will never look
at that person the same way again. And so deciding
to end that relationship was never about him, it was
about me and what I can deal with. Every single person
you meet – even if they cause you heartache – is there
for a reason. Maybe in another lifetime, or if you'd
crossed paths at a different stage, things might be
different. But be thankful for the missteps and the

mistakes and the wrong turnings because they let you delve into your capacity to love and feel things you didn't know you could.

## The grown-up love

The more you learn about what you don't want, the more you accidentally compile a spreadsheet of what you do. All those mistakes in the past, all that heartache, aren't for nothing. The experience shapes you, it makes you.

Grown-up Love can be fun but it's also realistic. It's not perfect, it's flawed, but it's finding your teammate, your best friend – the person who simply brings out the best in you, rather than being your 'missing half'. Because nothing was ever missing. You are born whole and you die whole, but if you're lucky you find someone to ride along on the journey with you.

Some people will fall in love much more than others, while some may never feel that connection in a romantic or grown-up way, but love has so many shapes and forms. No one gets through life without love, be it short-term or long-term, and, because of that, heartache will never be far away.

## Feeling Sad Is OK

No one emotion is bigger than you. And no emotion should ever be ignored. There are things you can do to take back control or ease the pain of heartache.

## Laugh

Laughter really is the best medicine. You can be sad and laugh. It doesn't make you crazy or insincere to laugh while you are still feeling sad. When my friend passed away, I didn't know how to deal with it. Everyone had an opinion about the best way to go through it all. You are almost expected to be sad all the time. But being sad is exhausting; sometimes you need the light relief and escapism of finding joy, even if it feels inappropriate. At the funeral, we all shared stories about our friend. Some were hilarious and we laughed. Yes, we'd lost someone we loved but we'd also had the privilege of having that person in our lives, and having those fun memories. Nothing could take that away, not even death.

During a big break-up, I reached into my comedy stash for help. I can't tell you how many reruns of *Friends* I watched, but I knew that for twenty-two minutes I would have a giggle and forget about the prodding ache in my heart. I watched *Elf*, starring Will Ferrell, in June. Yes, it is a Christmas movie, but when needs be, whip it out. Do whatever you need to do to laugh. I'd rather hear 'Santa, I know him!' in June than the Righteous Brothers' 'Unchained Melody' on repeat, crying into my margarita on the sunlounger in my garden.

We all have those films that take you back to a place of joy and it's beneficial to revisit them when you are feeling down. I wouldn't recommend making it a regular thing to watch Christmas movies in the summer. It's almost as irritating as those people who leave their Christmas lights and decorations up all year because they are too lazy to take them down. Psychopaths. But you know those movies are there if you need them.

The day I found out I'd had a miscarriage and that the foetus I was carrying had no heartbeat, I went to a comedy gig. I had tickets to go and see my comedian friend Katherine Ryan perform her show in the West End, and the plan was to go for the scan, then have dinner and see her show. Life had other ideas for me. After I left the clinic, I considered going home and hiding under a duvet. It would have been completely understandable and fine to do so. But I felt the weight of the sadness too much and I wanted to laugh just for an hour. So I went to the gig, and it saved me a little bit. It wasn't about running away from my sadness; it was about digesting it in a way I could manage.

## Dance

I'm happiest on a dance floor. No judgement, just letting my body move impulsively to the beat of whatever music is playing. For some of my friends, this is their worst nightmare – having people look at you while your limbs sporadically flap about. But even dancing around alone in the privacy of your own home, arms doing whatever the hell they want, to your favourite upbeat song will enhance your mood.

It's been proven in research that dancing generates a bigger release of endorphins than other forms of exercise. It also connects with the emotional centres in the brain. When we dance, our brains release endorphins, hormones that can trigger neurotransmitters that create a feeling of comfort, relaxation, fun and power. Music and dance not only activate the sensory and motor circuits of our brain, but also the pleasure centres.

When we move in time with the rhythm, the positive effects of music are amplified. Therefore, a little secret to make the most of the music is to move to the beat, so we will be doubling the pleasure. Tone-deaf folk don't be disheartened, though! Even if you have absolutely no rhythm whatsoever you can still see the benefits and it shouldn't stop you from reaping them. Stop thinking about looking stupid – if a tree falls in a forest and no one is there to hear it, what sound does it make. NONE!

If the dance floor of the club isn't for you, dance around your room without people watching. Do you look stupid, if there is no one there to see you? HELL NO!

As we move to the music, our muscles relax, which allows us to free ourselves of the tension and the sadness clogging us up, our mind and our body being intrinsically linked.

## Allow yourself to rant

It's good to have a vent and let off some steam. I don't recommend doing this on social media, however, unless you're Piers Morgan and have made a career out of it. A lot of people like to blast the online world with negativity but then it stays up there forever and can have a domino effect on other people's emotions. I'd rather spread my more joyful sentiments than my ranty ones. I do, however, recommend having a good moan to your friends, so long as you return the favour – you don't want to become THAT person. No one wants to be the guy or girl who constantly brings everyone else down. But there is something freeing in getting sadness off your chest. A weight is lifted.

Venting is healthy. Although often characterised negatively as something that promotes whingeing, you have a right to complain in certain circumstances. Venting correctly is an acknowledgement of something you are not happy about, and saying it out loud can help you analyse it within your own head. There's little more satisfying than setting the world to rights with a good and trusted friend. It reduces stress and helps resolve issues when done in the right environment and with the right person or people you trust.

## The Break-up

Break-ups are shit. But you are not alone in the situation – just think of the number of songs, books, films, poems, podcasts all dedicated to telling the story of a break-up.

When you're in it you feel different, though. Alone. No one feels as you do.

I still feel protective when I talk about my own break-ups as they are so personal.

A few years ago I found out a boyfriend had been texting someone else. Well, more than just one person. Multiple. How did I become that girl? For me, I might as well have found out he'd murdered someone.

We had the perfect relationship. Yes, I had been busy with work and travelling, but had also made time for the important people in my life. My boyfriend was besotted with me, so I had thought. He got jealous but never had a need to be.

One day, I was running late for a work meeting (I'm always running late for something). With my tooth-brush hanging from my jaw and one hand clasping mascara, I whacked three licks on to my lashes, then turned to spit out the toothpaste remnants from my mouth. When I looked up, I saw his face, tears streaming down his cheeks, and he fell to his knees. This visual is ingrained in my memory forever, and every now and then it flashes back. I can't recall where I left the car keys an hour ago, but I remember this as clearly as if it just happened. Memories are strange like that.

'Please promise me you won't leave me.' Why would I leave him? I couldn't imagine him ever doing anything that would make me not want to spend forever with him. But life can surprise us all.

I've had a weird relationship with lies. I think getting over something is easier when you have the truth, all of the truth. You can't get over something if it's a lie. It wasn't a clean break, but I think at that moment he knew I would never look at him the same way again. And to be honest I never did.

The same day I had an email from my agent saying someone had contacted them with information about my boyfriend. I was living an episode of *EastEnders*, albeit a really badly written one. I was mortified. This can't be my life. A few days later I flew abroad to work on a TV show and I honestly felt I would never be happy again.

All of the things I would usually do to ease the sadness – go out and dance, hang out with friends and vent, go to a comedy gig and laugh – were taken away from me. I was on the other side of the world, staying alone in a sleepy fishing village on the Gold Coast, and working night shifts. The beach was Paradise but it may as well have been Hell. Even watching *Elf*, *Home Alone* and *National Lampoon's Christmas Vacation* didn't help.

So I wrote.

I wrote down how I felt. My anger, my loss, my frustration. It wasn't for anyone else but was my own way of venting. I recently found one of my notebooks full of vents and poems and ramblings. Sometimes it's nice to look back; at other times these things are best left in the past because you have moved on from that place and looking back is not helpful. Sometimes, you cringe at how dramatic something was in hindsight, but those feelings were real and we must always value them for what they were, and recognise how expressing them ultimately helped us.

Laura Whitmore

## A Sad Poem

*Why did you say you loved me?*
*I inhaled you in, no filter, naively*
*Let you in, absorbed you on to my skin*
*We were one.*
*Keeping each other above water when the polluted*
*    dreads of everyday existence tried to drag us down*
*The freckles on your back, the creases in your frown*
*The imperfections you had and hated, I loved*
*As they were mine from toe to crown.*
*Against the tide, didn't seem such a fight*
*But lust can tangle our eyes, smudge the lines*
*I was trapped, slowly suffocating your insecurities*
*I thought we had a bubble, a shield*
*My buoy holding me up*
*I clasped your hand in mine and never wanted to*
*    release*
*But when the waves broke, I was stranded, unable*
*    to breathe.*
*Torn gills, lungs gasping to be filled*
*Desperately searching for a relief from the sadness*
*But you weren't keeping me afloat*
*you were holding me down, I just didn't know.*
*And then I finally made the choice*
*to release the grip and let you go.*

My teenage self would be proud of some of the navel-gazing scribblings I conjured up. I was smiling on television but dead on the inside. My future with my dream guy no longer existed and I grieved for it. To the outside world, I had moved on and left him. He was the victim. And I was too embarrassed to say otherwise. Again, I felt ashamed to feel sad. So I wrote about it.

As much as we might want to avoid it, the emotion of sadness is essential to our survival. It has been a part of human experience since the beginning of time. Sadness is our body's way of telling us that an event or external experience has hurt or upset us. Escapism is OK for relief but you can't run away from sadness forever, it will catch up with you sooner or later.

During our childhood, sadness is there to communicate our distress and our parents respond by providing help or comfort while we cry. As we grow up, we learn of grief and betrayal and devastation, and very quickly sadness can morph into unbearable pain. Our parents can't make everything better. The way those around us cope with sorrow will influence our willingness to let our sadness in. I felt weak for letting a boy upset me that much. The world teaches women to be independent, to 'get over the boy', 'you can do it all on your own'.

'Get over it.' I fear that our society is becoming intolerant of sadness, which is only reinforced through throwaway labels such as 'weak', 'silly' and 'depressed'.

This social perception needs to change. No matter how long we try to avoid, criticise or hide our sadness, it will always find a way to 'connect' and force us to listen. In the end, we need to feel sad.

Sadness has two functions: to let us know that we need to grieve and to seek out those who love and support us. If you feel sad, then you feel sad. Sadness is there to help us. Own it, embrace it, and trust it. Trust in your sad emotion's ability to guide you through your pain and grief. Believe me, you'll be stronger for it. Make space for sadness to be a part of you and your experience.

Write down your feelings, keep a diary, write a letter to those who have pissed you off or hurt you, or speak with a mate to help explore and validate your sadness. If you feel it . . . those feelings are valid.

Sadness is arguably one of the more difficult emotions to express to others because it requires vulnerability (we'll chat about this later in the book). To let our internal world be seen, with the risk that someone won't support it, is bloody hard.

When we see someone else crying or in distress, most of us instinctually feel a pull towards that person – unless you sense they are uncomfortable and you try to overlook it, pretend you didn't notice. But truly connecting with that person isn't about having all the answers; often it is about listening and just being there for them. That's the most important thing you can offer. If you can't find someone to listen to you when you are sad, then listen to yourself. You have the ability to listen, so use it to your own advantage. I like to believe that most of us would willingly support someone through their sadness if we only knew what to do or how to help.

Sadness doesn't stand alone. It interweaves with so many other emotions – anger, shame, helplessness. Sadness guides us through multiple emotional and influential journeys in the course of our lives.

A broken heart will never be the same afterwards. But we aren't born to stay the same. We are in a constant state of evolution. The sadness may come back in another form but after you've tackled it once, it becomes easier to tackle it again. We need to train ourselves to deal with sadness, in a similar way to training our body if we were playing a sport. We can only tackle an opponent and win the ball in a game of football by practising our skill, by understanding their position on the field and learning from our mistakes. Just so, we train our mind to tackle the emotional obstacles we face.

When you envisage a certain future and it is taken away, as happened with my ex, it's very hard to be excited about the possibilities that might lie ahead. But there are ALWAYS possibilities. Anything can happen in life. Haven't we all experienced that? For every pandemic, there's a story of resilience and empowerment. For every tale of betrayal, there's one of strength and new love.

## A Note on TRIGGERS

Please don't pull the trigger.

I have trust issues.

It goes back to broken relationships and, even before that, to childhood experiences. When growing up, we've all inevitably experienced pain or suffering that we could not acknowledge or deal with sufficiently at the time. So, as adults, we typically become triggered by experiences that remind us of these old painful feelings. As a result, we generally turn to habitual or addictive behaviours to try to manage the painful feelings.

There are certain things people say that may have no malicious intent but they trigger me. I sometimes feel my abilities are underestimated. Tired of being told 'you are pretty' as a compliment because a childhood part of me feared it was an underhanded way of someone saying you're not smart or good enough.

I was not 'cool' growing up. I was a bit of a loner, and it took me a while to find my tribe. I remember a girl at school saying that I'd be pretty when I grew up. I was awkward, pale and a massive nerd. It was like, Oh, it will all be OK because when I grow into my body, I'll be pretty. My greatest accomplishment would be to look a certain way and fit into the popular group. FUCK OFF.

She meant it as a compliment but it triggered me and has stuck with me. At a school dance at the local youth club, the guy I liked asked me to dance – the song was Celine Dion's 'My Heart Will Go On'. I was eleven and this was a HUGE moment. A few weeks later another girl in the class – she had lovely tanned skin against my alabaster, snow-white complexion – revealed that someone had asked him to dance with me as a favour. I was devastated. I didn't want to be danced with as a favour. I felt pathetic.

For me it's important to achieve things because of who I am, rather than how I look, and I feel sad or useless if a comment triggers otherwise. It's not about anyone else. It's my trigger. It's my issue.

Once you know your triggers, the first step towards healing them is considering their origins. Ask yourself which of your triggers might relate to your childhood experiences. Only you can heal your triggers, so take a little time to look inside and make sure to be patient, kind and empathetic with yourself.

I'm still dealing with lots of triggers and the pain doesn't go away, but I can work out that not all these triggers deserve the sadness they evoke. Thinking honestly about your triggers is the only way to eventually heal them.

So what are your triggers? What do you do to manage the painful feelings that are sparked?

No sadness is too small to talk about. The only way to make our pain disappear is to feel it and process it, but giving it time is necessary too. You can't just stop feeling sad. You must understand it and work through it, just as you would with an arithmetical or algebraic problem. You can't just pluck the answer from thin air. You must go through each stage, step by step.

It takes A LOT of time to move forward. But you may be surprised to discover that wherever there is sadness, it will make you appreciate the joy to come.

## Open Your Heart

'Open Your Heart', as Madonna sang. I miss eighties Madonna. She was my favourite of all her many incarnations. When we get hurt it's very easy to retreat inwards and cut ourselves off from the world, but it's so important to keep your heart open even after it's been hurt.

It's OK to be guarded, but closing your heart is not good. Be hopeful. Be authentic. Let sadness help you find happiness. Life is full of juxtapositions for a reason. That doesn't mean you substitute the loss of one relationship with another. You won't find 'Keep Yourself Warm', in the words of the band Frightened Rabbit, by sleeping with someone else you don't care about. Although most of us will have probably tried. It will usually make you feel worse.

Sometimes it can be quite addictive to give in to self-pity and self-loathing in your sadness. Enjoying the drama of despair.

You can't control what thoughts pop into your head, but it is up to you how long you dwell on those thoughts. You can't control how certain thoughts make you feel, but you can control how long you decide you'll drown in those emotions.

And, when your heart starts to change, then you'll be one step closer to forgiving those who've broken your heart. Forgiveness is a journey and journeys take time. It took me years to forgive someone for breaking my heart. I would've healed faster if I'd known then what I know now. Hindsight is a wonderful thing. But my heart had to evolve before I could find the forgiveness I yearned for. I had to feel the sadness and go through it all to get out the other side. And you *will* get out the other side.

I still have triggers that tap into my trust and self-worth issues, and I'm continuously working through them.

I sometimes watch my dog Mick run around the park and he's just happy to be alive. For a split second I wonder what he's thinking . . . probably which one of Laura's nice shoes he wants to chew next, or 'I'd like to sniff that dog's arse', but there is also a lot I can learn from him. The art of possibility, adventure, curiosity. This is something we all possess, even when we feel hopeless. Feeling sad is temporary. It WILL get better. Trust me.

My dog doesn't dwell on sadness or feel sorry for himself for longer than about five minutes. He's present, enjoying what he's doing now. He doesn't hold grudges – he might snap at you if you take his ball, but he'll get over it quickly.

Each time you hold feelings of resentment and anger towards others, you accumulate large amounts of cortisol. Cortisol is the 'stress hormone'. It weakens the body's immune system, accelerating the ageing process and increasing the risk of heart disease, chronic pain and depression. So let's try not to hold grudges, or harbour sadness, as we are just hurting ourselves.

Equally as important as cleansing and moisturising your body is taking a mental and emotional wash to help you rebalance your hormonal system. You do this by forgiving or letting go of past hurts, resentments and grievances that you've been unnecessarily holding in your heart. You forgive others, not just because you're a good person who doesn't hold on to toxic thoughts, but because not doing so can cost you your physical, mental or emotional health.

Every time you practise forgiveness, what you're actually doing is performing your own heart management. You're being kind to yourself, not to those who hurt you. Forgiving others so that you can experience greater health and happiness is ultimately what makes forgiveness one of the most important practices you will ever learn.

Think about the people in your life you'd like to forgive, but you didn't know how to go about it. Are you one of the people you need to forgive?

Forgiveness releases so much sadness that we hold on to needlessly. Forgiving isn't saying that what happened was OK. It's about caring enough about your mental health to allow yourself to move on. I'm also almost positive it reduces crow's feet too. If I'd forgiven a few people sooner I'd definitely have fewer wrinkles!

**REFLECTION:** Before going to sleep forgive everyone and sleep with a clean heart.

**AFFIRMATION:** Sadness is only a temporary emotion. My heart is open to love.

# chapter four

## She is polished: expectations

'Expectation is the root of all heartache.'
**ANONYMOUS**

I do not have my shit together. At all. For a lot of my career I probably have portrayed the lie that I have my shit together. And I'd like to apologise. Polished hair and make-up (not even done by me). Carefully thought-through Instagram and Twitter posts. Rehearsed scripts and seamless links. It's all about a certain perception to meet a certain expectation.

The Cambridge Dictionary defines expectation as 'the feeling that good things are going to happen in the future'. What a lovely sentence. The feeling that good things are going to happen. Reading this actually surprises me because, to tell you the truth, I associate negative connotations with the word 'expectation'.

Expectations, for me, mean pressure. When did it all get so polluted? When you put the word 'cultural' in front of it.

## Cultural Expectations

Consider these two sentences:

- The cultural expectation is that men should provide for themselves and women should be provided for.
- How clothing operates in relation to age is thus significant for our understanding of how cultural expectations concerning age act upon and present the body.

Our society wants us to fit into a box. In order to function, certain expectations have to be met. For example, social and cultural expectation is why we don't shit in the street. This is an expectation I wholeheartedly support. We need a certain level of decorum, to live in a supportive functioning community and not fear treading in our neighbours' shit every time we leave the house. Literally.

But there are many other cultural expectations.

Every society has a gender structure: distinct from thinking about how men and women are different, it has to do with what you expect from each other. We raise boys with guns and girls with Barbies. Girls are taught to be empathetic and nurturing, boys are taught to tough it out and be aggressive. An opinionated male boss is a strong leader, while a confident, headstrong woman is seen as a bitch.

Women are expected to do emotional work, and men to be the financial providers. And, in fact, in many circumstances, expectations can lead to reality. You think, 'Oh, maybe I should be like that because that's what the cultural expectation is.' Expectations are ingrained in our decision-making.

Why do you do something? A: I want to do it. Or B: I am expected to do it. In the future when faced with a decision, think about whether you have chosen what to do based on A or B.

Consider this (I find food is always a good reference for us all to relate to). You're at a posh dinner. The maitre d' informs you the best dish is the raw dry-aged steak tartare. EVERYONE orders it and insists you should too. So you do what is expected (the B answer). You don't want to offend anyone and, sure, maybe they know better than you – although you have a pretty good sense of your own tastebuds. Then you sit there not enjoying your meal because all you actually wanted was the bloody fish and chips.

But what if you ordered what you actually wanted? Would everyone really think less of you? Think you didn't respect their opinion, or that you just have bad taste? Or would they even notice?

With all decisions, think about how and why you answer. If you answer A, think: how will it affect those around me? A lot of times in life we are drawn to B – the response of expectation ahead of our own actual wants or needs. You are the decision-maker in your own life. B shouldn't be your first concern – a factor to be considered, yes, but not the priority.

## Not Reaching Expectations

The biggest disappointments in our lives are often the result of misplaced expectations. Tempering your expectations of other people will greatly reduce unnecessary frustration and suffering, in both your life and theirs, and help you refocus on the things that truly matter – your own expectations. People have different expectations, of themselves and of others, and that is OK!

It's bloody hard to be yourself when everything around you says otherwise. We are told to tick a box and conform to what others want. It is so important to follow your own intuition and not get discouraged by others' progress or success if you don't match their achievements. Follow your own path. Success is ultimately about spending your life happily in your own way. Finding your own expectations.

Having faith and trust in who you are is important, but you also need a willingness to act upon your self-trust. Decide this minute to never again beg anyone for the love, respect and attention that you should be showing yourself. Reaching your own expectations is far more exciting than achieving those of someone else. In fact, in my life, by ignoring other people's expectations and pursuing what I want, I've tended to surpass what has been expected of me. What I've realised is that many people have in fact underestimated me, and if I had kept to their low expectations I would never have enjoyed the life experiences I have now. I'd probably still be in my hometown eating beef and being very unhappy. 'Oh, I didn't know you were so into music.' 'Oh, I didn't know you studied journalism.' 'Oh, I didn't know you act.' Nobody knows what you are capable of except you. Some people will see your potential, others won't.

You might feel unwanted and unworthy in the eyes of one person, but you are priceless to another. Don't ever forget your worth. Spend time with those who value you. No matter how good you are to people, there will always be someone who criticises you. And that is OK. You aren't here to please everyone.

In this crazy world that tries to make you like everyone else, the toughest battle you'll ever have to fight is the battle to be yourself. And, as you're fighting back, not everyone will like you. Sometimes people will call you names because you're 'different'. But that's OK. The things that make you different are the things that make YOU, and the right people will love you for exactly who you are.

And, of course, the reverse is also true. Stop expecting others to fit YOUR expectations. Loving and respecting others means allowing them to be themselves, just as you should be allowed. When you stop expecting people to be a certain way, you can begin to appreciate them for who they are.

Sylvia Plath once wrote that the only way to ensure you are never disappointed by someone is to expect nothing from them. This is an extreme way to look at things and I wouldn't always recommend such a dark attitude to life. But there is some truth in Plath's advice. Pay close attention, and respect people as they are and not what you want them to be. We don't know most people half as well as we believe we do. Every human being is remarkable in their own way; it just takes a patient set of eyes to see it. The more you get to know someone, the more you will be able to look beyond their appearance and see the beauty of who they truly are.

People can't read minds. They will never know how you feel unless you tell them. And even then it's impossible to comprehend the entirety of someone else's feelings. The only person you will ever truly know is YOU.

I remember being really upset on a weekend away with my boyfriend when I was younger. His intentions were good but I had put so much expectation on the trip that he was never going to live up to it. We were in Paris. I wanted to recreate the romantic vision I had pictured and there were elements that I had built up in my imagination of how it should be.

We had flown with Ryanair so we were actually about eighty kilometres outside of the capital, in Paris Beauvais. It's like saying Brighton is in London! But there we were, somewhere near Paris. Love's young dream. I think it was my first trip away with a boy and my expectations were HIGH. God love him, he hadn't a chance. I remember it was the summer of that big heatwave, and loads of old folk were dying in mainland Europe. It was really bad. The little guest house didn't have air conditioning and our lovers' embrace ended up with him stark naked sprawled across the tiled floor by the open window. I lay on top of a sweat-drenched off-white sheet on a bed in the opposite corner. We spent quite a lot of that trip in the *supermarché* chilled-goods section trying to stay cool.

But all of that didn't matter to me because, in my head, it was the date we had planned for the last night that I was looking forward to most. He had once again nipped to the chilled aisle to pick up our feast for the night (and more than likely to cool down). And we met on Avenue des Champs-Élysées just before sunset.

The picnic by the Eiffel Tower, the fresh baguettes, the local cheese and the wine. This was my movie moment, one that I would look back on later in life. A pivotal memory that hadn't even happened yet, but all the expectation was there.

So there we were, sitting on the grass in the sweltering heat, cheese melting under the last rays of the unforgiving golden sun, and I waited for the wine to come out of the cool bag he had packed.

But no wine came. He'd forgotten it.

DATE RUINED!

Not the first time an argument has revolved around a bottle of wine, but, looking back, such a needless tiff. I had worked myself up so much that the date wouldn't be a success unless the image in my head was replicated to the exact detail. That expectation had been dashed and therefore the whole thing was ruined. He ran to a nearby merchant and returned with a bottle of wine. Red wine. I don't drink red wine. Does he even know me?? (Oh, to have such nonsensical problems as this later in life.)

Unless it's sangria and chilled so cold it hurts my teeth, red wine is not for me. Also, did I mention it was the hottest day of the year and old people were dying? Red wine was as bad a choice as warm milk. Rather than say anything I held on to my glass of red with contempt, barely sipping the surface. It went downhill from there.

Looking back, I wish I could slap myself and tell nineteen-year-old Laura to get a grip. I had put all these expectations on him and he had no idea. He just thought we were having a nice chilled time. I was as chilled as that unwanted bottle of red wine.

Misplaced expectations can pop up in all sorts of places. Your boss? Perhaps he doesn't know you're hoping for a promotion because you haven't told him yet. That hot lad you haven't talked to because you're too shy? Yeah, you got it, he hasn't given you the time of day simply because you haven't given him the time of day either.

In life, you have to communicate with others regularly and purposefully. And, often, you have to open your mouth and speak first. You have to tell people what you're thinking, what you were hoping for. When you write it down, it's common sense, isn't it? And yet so many of us want others to be mind-readers, and simply know exactly what we want and need.

If there's a specific behaviour someone you care about has that you're hoping will disappear over time, it probably won't. If you really need them to change something, be honest and put all your cards on the table so this person knows how you feel and what you need them to do. When I think of that Parisian picnic, I should have just bought the bottle of white wine I wanted myself. No one can change your wine except for you. (Catchy next book title?)

Putting stupid expectations on people will just lead to your own disappointment. For the most part, you can't change people and you shouldn't try. Either you accept who they are or you choose to live without them. It might sound harsh, but it's not. When you try to change people they often remain the same, but when you don't try to change them – when you support them and communicate clearly – they gradually make the decision for themselves, if their expectation matches yours. That can be anything from getting the wrong bottle of wine to cheating on a partner. And in the end what really changes is the way you see them.

People rarely behave exactly the way you want them to. And remember what I said before: the magnitude of your happiness will be directly proportional to your thoughts and how you choose to see things – your perspective. Even if a situation or relationship doesn't work out at all, it's still worth it if it made you feel something new, and if it taught you something different. And it's OK if your expectations change and someone no longer fulfils them. You will also evolve – make sure what you do is for the right reasons.

I've followed many expectations because I wanted to fit in, some I've actively resisted. But a lot of things I've done because they were expected of me – from the insignificant to the life-altering.

## Expectation Myths

Despite how much I ought to resist, most of my life is ruled by 'shoulds'. As I get older, I'm beginning to question more and more why we do things simply because we feel we *should* do them.

In my late teens I went Interrailing around Europe with some school friends, staying in questionable and at times unsanitary places. But that's what we SHOULD do when we're young. Share a non-flushing toilet with thirty other hostel guests. It shapes us and is a sort of rite of passage. I probably could have spent what little money I had the summer before university doing something more relaxing and enjoyable, but that's not what one should do when one is young. Also, usually privileged people got to backpack around Europe and I longed to fit in back then, to be seen as belonging to that group rather than as the product of a broken home. I thought I was seeing the world, breaking out of the norm; but I was in fact just following in the footsteps of so many people before.

Don't get me wrong. I have some great memories of that trip, including what you might call 'character-building' moments. I didn't wash for a week because I didn't want to use public showers and, when I eventually did, was greeted by a spider the size of my head. I know it was this size because when I turned on the shower it fell from the nozzle head on to MY FACE.

We also accidentally got on the wrong train. We boarded one for Ostrava instead of Bratislava and ended up in the wrong country with the wrong train ticket. When the ticket collector eventually kicked us off, we tried to explain that we hadn't checked the platform and weren't trying to travel between countries without paying the full amount. 'We just didn't CHECK!'

All he heard was 'CZECH!'

'What you say about CZECH???' he screamed.

Turns out we were in the Czech Republic, not Slovakia, and he thought we were insulting his people. The conversation got quite heated until we realised the confusion. We apologised profusely and called my mate's dad because we couldn't take money out and we were stranded. Not exactly my finest moment of independence but definitely 'a life lesson'.

My twenties were full of lots of similar expectations. Feeling I wasn't as cool as the other girls who had dated more than one guy by the time they were twenty-three. How could I have got through my twenties without a one-night stand? ESPECIALLY in Catholic Ireland! I should be rebelling against the system. Trying to go against expectations when growing up has as much pressure as the original expectation. That's because it's SO expected, I'm expected to go against it to fit in as expected. A minefield of expectations.

I thought if I didn't sleep with more guys, I'd regret it. I'm not saying I had pressure from my peers; a lot of it came from this internal compass guiding me through life telling me what direction I should be going in. Have I truly lived life if I haven't slipped out quietly from under the crumpled sheets of an unknown man's bed and never seen him again? I tried to have a one-night stand after my first relationship, but it turned out I rather liked him and saw him again. I FAILED the one-night stand thing! I definitely did the sex thing, just was graced with an odd desire to see the person again.

In my early twenties I desperately tried to increase 'my number' (how many men I slept with). Then spent my late twenties desperately trying to keep the number down.

## What is our expected number?

Before I carry on with the 'how many sexual partners' chat I want to put it in writing: IT DOESN'T MATTER HOW MANY PEOPLE YOU SLEEP WITH. It doesn't matter if you don't fit in with everyone else's quota. The most important expectation is the one you put on yourself.

However, every few years a new survey comes out keeping track of our sexual shenanigans. At the time of writing this one was produced by euroClinix. So here you go:

The baby boomers – aged fifty-four to seventy-two – have had the smallest number of sexual partners, averaging 10.7 throughout their lifetimes. Boomer women have had an average of 7.4 partners, while boomer males have enjoyed 12.9. Think of my Irish female relatives who came before me and would be judged for the double figures; but for the men that's average!

Millennials – usually thought of as those aged between twenty-three and thirty-seven (I'm hanging on in there by my millennial-manicured fingernails) – have slightly higher numbers, already clocking up an average of 11.6. This equates to 10.8 partners for women and 13.4 for men. Hoorah, double figures!

Whereas Generation X – aged between thirty-eight and fifty-three – seem to be more liberated than those younger and older than them, racking up an average of 13.1 lovers. Men have had 16.1 partners, and women of this age average 10.1. I'm guessing a lot of men in this age group must be sleeping with younger women.

Meanwhile, 14 per cent of all respondents said they've

only ever had sex with one person; 2 per cent of respondents had had a total of 91 sexual partners.

This is a survey and NOT a fact sheet of how many sexual partners you should have. But our brain automatically sees these figures as expectations. Because that's what the majority of people are doing, I should be doing it too! Imagine giving yourself the cap of ten men/women to sleep with, then realising lover number ten was a waste of space; but you stuck with them because . . . you couldn't break that number barrier!

I definitely toyed with my numbers. I was at one for so long that I was scared to break my own expectations. Let's be honest. No one gives a fuck about how many people I've slept with except for me. If your partner does care, I'm sure they'll get over it if you have a healthy and understanding relationship. But why are we so judgemental of other people's numbers, whether low or high?

Because we are creatures of conformity. Sleeping with just one person may be realistic when you come from a small town. But imagine what it's like when you move to a big multicultural city. Beautiful, smart, lascivious people EVERYWHERE!

When I moved from the seaside town of Bray to Camden Town in London my eyes were opened. But I put so much expectation on myself. I was so scared of going down the unwinding dark path to sexual deviance. I was still a small-town girl and I had my small-town expectations of myself and how I should be. That meant I was hard on myself when I felt those desires to date, sleep with other men . . . Because it showed I had changed.

But looking back, I didn't change. I just had more choice. And what a wonderful selection there was. More choice, more opportunity.

## Evolving expectations

Sex isn't the only expectation that changes as you age. Yes, it gets easier. You learn that sex doesn't have to be the 'be-all and end-all'; but getting older doesn't mean that expectations become easier or you grow immune to them. Ageing just comes with its own new barrage of myths.

You're single and childless – get a cat?

I didn't get a cat.

I got a dog. Doh!

Now don't get me wrong, I bloody love my dog, Mick. He's a sassy 2.4-kilo, white Maltipoo fluffball. To the vet he can be 'savage', especially since they removed his balls. (Don't freak. It was a health essential because they didn't drop, and could have become cancerous.) But he's also great for cuddles and makes me come home at a reasonable time after a night out.

He's also chewed and damaged beyond repair about two thousand quid's worth of my shoes/clothes. So I do have to keep reminding myself of all the positives. But the love from your dog is like no other. Yes, I have moved from sexual partners to dog chat quicker than Mick destroyed my Jimmy Choos. But this is how rapidly expectations flip about in our heads.

Ahead of my thirtieth birthday, career going well but single, I bought myself a dog. I was worried I was becoming the eternal Carrie Bradshaw (I can think of a lot worse people, and her shoe collection would be very much welcomed, but I also felt I needed to stop living my twenty-year-old lifestyle). I needed a change, so for the next stage of my life I chose the challenge of a dog.

'How the hell are you going to cope with a dog!?' My mother didn't agree with what I thought was a societal expectation (a reaction to pressures in society to show you are a responsible adult). 'You are never home; you're always flying around the world and I just don't think you can manage.'

Nothing like someone telling you you can't do something – especially if it's your mother – to make you want to do it even more. Perhaps the expectation came from the outside world, but my mother expected failure.

Mick is now five and very much part of my life and has, if anything, made it better, made me better. However, I still acknowledge that the reasoning behind getting him in the first place was probably not the most thought-through. It was nudged on by the juxtaposition of wanting to conform to society and rebelling against my mother.

Doing something because it goes against a parental expectation seems to be a recurring trigger for me. One of my biggest relationships besides the one with my dog is with my hair. Not to be confused with 'hair of the dog', which is another relationship for another book. When I entered my thirties all my friends started cutting their hair. It gave them an air of class and sophistication. A new sense of maturity.

Now, I really like my long hair. Mainly because, speaking as someone with thick, hard-to-manage Irish hair, when it's long it is actually easier to control. I only have to wash it three times a week, and when I wake up with a wild mane it can be tamed into a ponytail. The heaviness of the length makes it more achievable to leave the house in a somewhat presentable manner – all thanks to a scrunchie (I'm delighted scrunchies are back in fashion). But last year I thought: 'No, I'm in my thirties, I can't be having long hair.' So I cut it off.

Now the problem is, short hair doesn't really suit me. People say it does, but I believe them to be liars who want me to struggle with the anxiety of my uncontrollable hair and live a life of misery. I'm up for someone proving me wrong. Hairstylists can talk about the right kind of layering until the cows come home but, thus far, these ideas haven't transferred successfully on to my head. No amount of layering helps. My hair just goes triangular like Helga's from *Hey Arnold!*

This didn't come as a surprise to me as I've always had this type of hair, but I still went for the chop. It was as if I had created this societal pressure to cut my hair and show a sign of evolution within myself. 'I am now ready to take on the next stage of my life because my hair barely touches my shoulders and I can't fit all my mane into one scrunchie without the use of twenty bobby pins.'

(Also, side note: I bought a pack of 100 bobby pins and I swear I only have three left. Where do they go??)

Since last year, I have handwritten and signed a letter to myself that my hairdresser Ricky guards in his salon in case I get the notion to cut my hair again to prove I'm a grown-up. I like to think Ricky has it laminated and locked away in a tiny safe. Realistically, he probably binned it the next day. But I need to remind myself that short hair doesn't make me look mature; it makes me look like a nineties cartoon character.

When I reflect on my life, there are so many things I have done because I felt there was some sort of unspoken expectation – from career decisions to friendship choices, to sex to hairstyles. Things no one explicitly asked me to do, but I felt a pressure to acquiesce because the expectations were created inside my own head.

My hair is thankfully back long again (three months of no haircuts during the Covid-19 pandemic helped with that), but I know it won't be long before I see a picture of Margot Robbie with a lob (long bob) or Lena Dunham with a fresh, edgy cut and think I can pull that off too. I can't.

## Quiz: What Box Are You In?

In society, there are many boxes we can fit in . . . So here's a really simple ten-question quiz to see where you belong. Be honest with your answers!

### QUESTION 1

You see your mate's boyfriend kissing another girl. What do you do?

A: Tell your mate
B: Punch him
C: Nothing

### QUESTION 2

How do you take your coffee?

A: Double shot
B: Milky
C: Decaffeinated

**QUESTION 3**

You stumble across a £100 note in the park. What do you do?

A: Ask everyone in the park if they've lost money
B: Give it to charity
C: Keep it

**QUESTION 4**

What type of sandwich are you?

A: Club sandwich
B: Cucumber, cut into triangles with crusts removed
C: Cheese toasty

**QUESTION 5**

Where do you sit on a plane?

A: Window seat
B: Middle seat
C: Aisle seat

**QUESTION 6**

What's your go-to breakfast?

A: Cereal
B: Poached eggs, avocado, sourdough
C: Who has time for breakfast!

**QUESTION 7**

How do you wipe your bum?

A: Front to back
B: Back to front
C: Swirly/circular

**QUESTION 8**

Which relationship in the TV show *Friends* do you connect with the most?

A: Rachel and Ross
B: Monica and Chandler
C: Phoebe and Joey

## QUESTION 9

Your go-to swimming stroke?

A: Front crawl
B: Backstroke
C: Doggy paddle

## QUESTION 10

You've just been offered tickets to your favourite gig but it's also the same evening as your in-laws' anniversary. What do you do?

A: Miss out on the once-in-a-lifetime gig
B: Explain to your partner and in-laws how important this gig is and hope they understand
C: Tell them you have to work late and sneak to the gig

## RESULTS

Add up your score. Are you *mostly* A, B or C?
(Turn page)

## YOU CAN'T FIGURE OUT WHO YOU ARE FROM A FUCKING QUIZ!!

Dare to be yourself in a society that is not set up to support anyone who doesn't fit in a box. It's one of the most heroic things you can do.

We glorify heroes with integrity, determination, grit and the ability to stand up for what they believe in – in movies. We glorify failure and innovation. Yet in my experience, I have been put down repeatedly because I don't fit into the box people want me to be in. I have been faced with:

You can't do that.

What exactly do you even do?

Who do you want to be like?

You're too . . .

strong/soft;

loud/quiet;

powerful/weak;

young/old.

I have spoken up, spoken out and been shut down. I have been judged, criticised, condemned, yelled at and told to just 'fit in a box'.

It's important to approach criticism from a place of grace and humility, truly looking to learn something from it and improve yourself. However, you do not have to fit in nicely with society's expectations. We are so much more than three categories, A, B or C. There is a whole alphabet. And beyond that. There are so many languages and interpretations of languages. This means there is an infinite number of possibilities for what we can be. Exciting, isn't it?

## I Don't Fit into Your Box

That doesn't mean I'm wrong or you're wrong. And the box may be anything – your social circle, your workplace, your city, your society, your religion or your culture. There is nothing wrong with you. We don't belong in boxes.

We are meant for unique greatness in many forms and we know when we feel it in our hearts, no matter how wrong or crazy the world tells us we are. Many of us with good intentions feel like outsiders when the whole world seems to exclude us, when the whole world points and says: 'You're the one who is wrong. Because you don't fit into a box.'

People around you may think you're wrong, but actually they just don't understand you. Society isn't built in congruence with nature and it doesn't serve you, so you are here to build a new one.

Life has a funny way of trying to define you. I get it, because that is how our brains mostly work. We need to put things in a box, to give them neat labels, so that our brains can impose order and reference them easily.

My career has shifted from model to newsroom researcher, to MTV presenter, to actor, to writer, to radio broadcaster, to *Love Island* host. And it will continue to evolve and jump from box to box.

When I won the MTV competition a lot of the people I grew up with were surprised. I wasn't the cool girl; I was the nerd who stayed after school to participate in debating. Guys didn't ask me out, and yet somehow I ended up in the *FHM* 100. It's fun to do what's not expected. But then, from being the 'blonde on telly', suddenly I had managed to jump boxes and I was stuck in a different one with all sorts of new expectations and discriminations.

Can you be on the cover of *FHM* and speak and write about feminist issues?

YES YOU FUCKING CAN.

People will try to write you off as one thing. Don't waste your energy trying to convince them otherwise.

SHOW them.

Be your authentic self and, if that means you annoy people, so be it. Annoy the hell out of them. Most of their doubts will come from their own insecurity about leaving whatever box they have trapped themselves in.

When I left MTV and got cast in a theatre production, one of my old bosses asked me, 'So what are you now – an actor?' I felt I'd burned my bridges because I had

tried out a different box for a bit. I was due to interview Ed Sheeran as a one-off during theatre rehearsals
and the day before the interview they decided to use
someone else.

'Don't confuse your audience' was a concern raised.
But surely all you can be is your authentic self even if it
moves you from the path that's expected of you? Since
then, I've juggled many different things – I've gone back
to presenting while working on lots of other projects,
including writing and starring in an award-winning
short film. Do whatever makes you fucking happy!!
You may lose out on some work but other things will
manifest from it.

I'm inspired by so many people who have broken
free of their boxes. When I was on a trip in Kenya a
few years ago I picked up a copy of *Eat, Pray, Love* by
Elizabeth Gilbert, from the bookshelf of used books at
the camp I was staying in. I had spent the previous week
working with WE, a charity close to my heart. And I
love their mantra. 'The world is full of things people
say are "not doable". But there's a whole movement of
individuals creating good in the world in ways we never
imagined. Each and every one of us is entirely capable
of changing the world. Because WE makes doing good
doable.'

They work in some of the poorest and most under-
funded communities in the world, and I had spent time

talking about this message. But I needed to live by it too. After that trip I stayed in the beautiful Masai Mara by myself. I had befriended a couple the week before and I tagged on to their safaris like a child they never knew they had . . . or particularly wanted. I learned a lot about myself camping at night in the wilderness. And it's the first time I read anything by Elizabeth Gilbert.

I felt a connection to the journey she was on in *Eat, Pray, Love*. Instead of the sexy Italian man, however, I had a maternal American couple – but the basics were there. A few years later I watched the film and, although I love Julia Roberts, I'd recommend just sticking to the book.

Then, in *The Last American Man*, Elizabeth Gilbert opened my eyes once again to expectations and living our life in boxes.

She speaks about how we are all trapped in boxes. We wake up every morning in a box – our bedroom – and then most of us eat our breakfast out of a box and then we throw that box away into another bigger box. Then leave the box where we live and get into another box with wheels and commute to work, which is really another big box divided into little cubicle boxes where a lots of people spend their days looking at computer boxes. When the day is over, everyone gets into the box with wheels again and goes home to our big box (our house) and spends the evening staring at the telly boxes for fun. We get our music from a box, food from a box, keep our clothing in a box. We are compartmentalised. We are living in a big box of smaller boxes.

Break out of the box!

We stay within the lines, follow the crowds and chase the dream. But – whose dream? Don't take advice or criticism from someone who hasn't achieved what you want to achieve. Many people talk a lot without knowing what they are talking about. They are just reflecting their current state of being, not yours. Trusting something because everyone else is doing it doesn't mean it's right. Trust yourself and go with that.

Tick as many boxes as possible rather than just the one that people expect from you. You will be all the happier for it. And you deserve to be happy.

You are not in this world to live up to what someone else thinks you should be, nor should you feel that others are here to live up to your expectation. In fact, the more you approve of your own decisions in life, the less approval you need from everyone else. You deserve to live the life you want and that excites you. Don't let the opinions of others make you forget that.

**REFLECTION:** With every decision, think: am I doing this for me or because I'm expected to?

**AFFIRMATION:** I let go of all expectations others set for me.

# chapter five

## She is vulnerable:
## open your heart

'Vulnerability is not weakness; it's our
greatest measure of courage.'
**BRENÉ BROWN**

I hate being vulnerable. HATE it. I was raised by a
strong single mother and learned over the years to
protect myself. I felt that showing a vulnerability, or
what I saw as a 'weakness', would open me up for
easy attack.

Even writing this book has been hugely challenging
– I have contradictory desires to be both protective of
myself as a person and open as a writer. I want to be a
strong, independent woman in a man's world. When I
chose to be vulnerable in the past, I exposed myself to

attack. I have felt extremely fragile. It's OK to protect yourself, to wait until you're ready to be vulnerable.

But there is power in your vulnerability.

I was introduced to Brené Brown's podcast 'Unlocking US' through a mate and, after a subsequent late-night Google search, I stumbled across her TED talk on vulnerability. If you haven't seen it, watch it.

Brené is an excellent storyteller, or, as she likes to call herself, a qualitative researcher/storyteller. A story is just data with a soul. We can collect data from our own life and relationships to help understand how we work and why we work. That's why therapists are so helpful; they don't tell you anything you don't already know, they just present it to you in a constructive way.

What makes Brené's talk especially powerful is that she doesn't simply lecture. She delves inside herself to share something personal, perhaps shameful and uncomfortable but genuine, with a group of strangers. She demonstrates being vulnerable. She argues that vulnerability is not a sign of weakness, but of strength. Anyone can boast about their accomplishments, but to share one's shortcomings honestly for the purposes of self-improvement demands true courage. Only when we acknowledge that we can be deeply hurt can we open ourselves to meaningful interaction. Each of us must suffer alone at some stage. You can't have someone else feel your pain. You must suffer it. And it is out of that solitude and place of deep pain that we come to understand the value of human bonds and the worth of our relationships.

If I wish to talk about vulnerability and the power of you, I must truly understand on a personal level my own vulnerability and how it has affected me. It's a challenge. It's easy to write a detached analysis. It's easy to preach, and throw out terms and concepts and examples from my friends or famous people I've read about, or watch a really good TED talk. It's a lot more difficult to reach deep inside myself and expose what I find to the light of criticism and judgement. But here we go . . .

I get scared. I can hide my insecurities behind helping other people through tough times. But I have come to realise that to wear my heart on my sleeve, especially after challenging experiences, is really a badge of honour. Living with vulnerability doesn't stop you from being pragmatic or exercising critical thinking; it is rather a rejection of cynicism, that dangerous trap any of us can fall into.

To survive disappointment and heartache, to emerge hopeful on the other side, is the greatest demonstration of resilience.

All well and good to say, but hard to practise when failure, defeat, pain and darkness come knocking. And so I rely once in a while on this imaginary guide to help me through my vulnerability, to remind me to practise empathy, compassion and courage with myself and others.

It's important to learn from my experiences to become better and not bitter.

There are three things I need to be truly vulnerable:

If the situation is right.

If I feel I'm in a good mental space.

If I'm speaking to someone I feel safe with.

When I think back on my life's vulnerability there are many things that make me vulnerable just by thinking about them. Simply reflecting on bad situations makes me queasy and sends me reaching for the tub of chocolate ice cream in the freezer. (Speaking of which, there's a tub in there now calling my name and perfect for writing this chapter.)

When I think of being vulnerable, I don't look back to my childhood as some may expect but rather to my adult life. My innocence as a kid shielded me at times from seeing the darkness in others. As an adult, you have more experience of the world and know life isn't the fairy tale we are led to believe. We may have seen, and been subjected to, some pretty horrific stuff. And sometimes it's hindsight that makes us realise our past vulnerability.

I remember working on a television job several years ago. I had a fucking shit time, but if you asked me about it, until recently, I would smile and claim it was a good and positive experience. Everyone else who worked on this show had always said that it was wonderful, and so I was embarrassed to feel differently. I've since learned this wasn't the case, and I was not the only one to hide my true feelings about the job behind a happy exterior. We all wear masks to keep face (metaphorically speaking; I'm aware we all wear actual masks a hell of a lot more since Covid-19). At that time I didn't want to be any different from all those others having a great time, because that would mean MAYBE the problem was me. Looking back, I realise I wasn't the problem, but the fact I didn't say anything was.

I came away from the situation feeling weak, and when I've previously attempted to open up about it, I've told myself the past is the past and I've moved on. So it was easier to be positive and put a block on that time.

Most of us face an ongoing struggle around whether to choose to be vulnerable or not. A battle around deciding to be seen only for our light, or for all our darkness – errors, flaws and all.

Up until this job, I had lived a relatively privileged working life hanging out with people of the same ilk who I connected to, who I liked. In life you'll meet people who just aren't for you; usually you can make your excuses to keep your distance. What if you can't walk away, though? I talk about choice, but what happens when you are forced into a corner, feeling trapped with no way out? Being blonde and on TV, I was used to being sexualised, even at work; but I can remove myself from most situations, or speak up, or choose not to be around those people. But what if that's not possible?

When we live in shame and fear of expressing our true feelings, we are standing in the way of our growth. At times, we lack courage and are unable to tell the original stories as they are because it brings us back to a bad place. I can still feel hurt by that specific experience even after all these years. But if I can recognise that I have learned from it, and appreciate the fact that I have worked with incredible, smart and good people, I overcome it. I have spoken in depth with friends, therapists and colleagues about what I had to deal with at that time. But it took me a long time to get there. I have been advised not to speak out publicly for my own protection and fear of bringing me back to my vulnerable state. But that doesn't mean I haven't dealt with it in my own way. I reclaimed my power for myself. There are many ways you can find strength if you can't find your voice at the time.

You can put the blame on others, but at the end of the day I had to take back control of the situation. My vulnerability came from losing control.

It takes a while to get the hang of being vulnerable. The more experience you've had with being hurt (a little or a lot) – which you can play with, seeing it from different perspectives in your mind – the easier it is to gain confidence.

Opening up and telling your truth doesn't always get your desired reaction. But, do you know what? There is nothing wrong with saying things that are difficult and questioning existing structures. Going against a system is hard. I found pretending to be strong a necessary survival mechanism. I had to make out that the situation didn't affect me. But, above all, MY thoughts were the most important. And they went to dark places. Maybe I should just do as everyone else expects?

It is OK *not* to want to be vulnerable.

There are lots of ways to be vulnerable and you don't have to bare every part of your soul to strangers. It's OK to keep something for yourself.

'Vulnerable' itself is a difficult word to grasp. During the Covid-19 pandemic vulnerable people were told to shield. And the term 'shielding' is relevant to all sorts of vulnerability outside of our medical health. Shielding yourself from situations is OK – to wait until you are fit and ready mentally as well as physically.

Becoming insecure and powerless doesn't happen in a single dramatic stroke. It's a process over time. For most people, the process is so gradual they don't notice it. They are more than happy, in fact, to give away their power by degrees. More often than not, being powerless seems like an easy way to be popular and protected.

But you are giving away your power when you please others in order to fit in. Or when you follow the opinions of the crowd. Or when you decide that others matter more than you do. Or when you let someone who seems to have more power take charge of you.

It can often seem right to sit modestly in the background, holding accepted opinions, or letting a controlling colleague hold you down in order to keep the peace. In small and large ways these kinds of decisions reduce your sense of self-worth; and without self-worth, you lose your power.

I have been in this situation so many times, but I refuse to ever think of myself as a victim. I don't want to play that role. Perhaps it was this stubbornness that made it difficult to get help. I felt victims in many situations are deliberately bringing suffering upon themselves, which not only confirms their powerlessness but encourages it to grow. The victim is always being acted upon. There are enough abusers, addicts and control freaks to drain the power from anyone who volunteers to play the role of victim. So I refused to give away too much of myself.

Holding resentment or anger is OK for a short time, but don't let it infect your core self. To have a core self is to be the author of your own story; it is the exact opposite of being a victim, who must live a life authored by others.

## You Don't Have to Grow a Thick Skin!

'Ah would ya just harden up and stop being so sensitive!'
We hear this all the time – being told not to take things
personally or let things get to us. But we shouldn't encase
ourselves in impenetrable armour. To be empathetic and
have feelings is human nature. Protect yourself and be
guarded when required, but don't stop yourself from
being vulnerable. It is a necessary state for growth and
understanding. You can find resilience through your
own vulnerability. Resilience does not eliminate stress
or erase life's difficulties.

People who are resilient don't see life through rose-
tinted glasses. They understand that setbacks happen
and that sometimes life is hard and painful. They still
experience the emotional pain, grief and sense of loss
that comes after a tragedy, but their mental outlook
allows them to work through such feelings and recover.

Resilient people are able to look at tough situations
realistically, but in a way that doesn't centre on blame
over what cannot be changed. Instead of viewing adversity as insurmountable, focus on looking for small ways
in which you can tackle the problem and make changes
that will help you overcome it.

I was asked recently if a decade in front of the camera
has meant I've 'built up a thick skin?'. If being judged

constantly by how I look or who I date has made me harden? I don't think I've built up a thicker skin over the years, it's more that my resilience has strengthened. You pay too high a price when you shut yourself off completely. The 'armour' holds on to your own personal negative thoughts, trapping them internally and not necessarily protecting you from the incoming negativity.

A 'thick skin' is not as important as being resilient. We can transmit an air of toughness, a sort of 'bull in a china shop' mentality. We can plough through life all vigour and strength and yet inflict damage. So 'thick skin' can mean being insensitive, and subsequently causing harm. That is not something we should ever strive for just to protect ourselves.

What I want, instead, is to be able to pick myself up off the floor from difficulty. To nourish myself as I need. That is resilience. The flexibility to rebound back from injury – however long it may take. Resilience gives us the emotional ability to bounce back and move forward after experiencing hardship. It leads to positive thinking, taking action, and adapting to difficulties in life. I don't think we, as sensitive, brave, vulnerable people, need a thick skin. Your delicately thin skin (my skin is so thin you can almost see right through it, all veins, bones and tendons squished underneath) helps you to sense more than other people do. It's an incredible asset, not a weakness.

So, maybe forget the thick skin routine. Maybe there's something else better to strive for. We need to learn to value ourselves. Your motivation and intention are bigger than the obstacle in front of you. Whenever you are faced with something that or someone who blocks your need, bring it back to YOU. Go for long-term gain. Value yourself and love yourself unconditionally. To be truly vulnerable you will face pain. It's horrible, it hurts, it burns, it makes you want to flush yourself down the loo. You may doubt your offerings and worth. And most of all: yourself. But you are resilient and you can get through anything!

*That's all well and good Laura, but what about when my creepy boss in the office is too handsy or my big presentation falls flat on its face??* Yes, it's easy for me to say 'things can only get better' (remember that nineties D:REAM hit?). But think about it – the shitter the situation, the more likely it is to improve. It can be hard to control our intrusive and obsessive thoughts because the voices go round and round in our heads telling us things that are just not good for us. The mind is a powerful thing and can trick you into all sorts of feelings and thoughts.

The important thing to realise is that they are YOUR thoughts and you can control them. Everyone says that time is the best healer, right? But that doesn't help you because you want the thoughts and the feelings to stop now. The only way you can do this is to really move your thought processes on to something else, but there are consequences to holding them back. They might return and bite you on the bum if you haven't dealt with those emotions.

## Acceptance

Once you have accepted that the situation has occurred and that everything really does happen for a reason and you cannot do anything about it, your thoughts will be able to move on. However, if you can do something about the situation, you will need to address it in the right way until you can resolve it with a positive action.

## Move forward

When something leaves your life, this will transfer the thoughts on to a more joyful feeling which will replace the negative thoughts. I know this isn't easily done in some situations, but it will help. Keep your mind focused on new things – it is time to be the best person you can be. This is your life and you need to think about how you feel about things and not how you should act based on other people's ideas.

## Learn to communicate

Part of life is accepting that things do go wrong and that we get hurt. If we want to make things better then we have to deal with the situation at hand. Recognise it and learn from it and don't make the same mistake again in the future. This will allow us to accept that if a similar situation arises, we will actively deal with it better. There's no use beating ourselves up about things we can't change.

## Find yourself

Life is all about finding ourselves. Life is a test of our strengths and weaknesses and will throw so much at us that sometimes it is hard to take. Our ability to just jump straight back on the horse or not will dictate whether things get better quickly or over time. Every emotion we have is triggered by our own thought processes; when we learn to control our thoughts we can decide what upsets us and what doesn't. There are billions of people on the planet who will love us for who we are; there are billions of people in worse situations than we are; there are billions of opportunities to make life better. We just have to recognise that we either live a life in grief or we accept that we have to move on. No matter what anyone tells you, things will get better and you have control. Make every day of your life count no matter what happens.

## ATTN MEN: A side note on vulnerability

*Women walking alone can often feel threatened*
*– please don't make their day harder.*

Earlier today I took my dog Mick for a walk. On the opposite side of the road leading to the park was a guy in his twenties with a large Alsatian. Now, my dog is a bit of a dick and barks at big dogs (a fight he's never going to win, but he clearly suffers from small-dog syndrome). As I pulled him away, the owner of the dog started talking to me, but I could barely hear over the incessant yelping. 'I would like to chat with you' is what I could faintly make out from his direction. Maybe he recognised me, maybe he was being too familiar, but there was something sinister that made me uncomfortable. I smiled and nodded towards Mick pulling me along and kept on walking. The young man then turned round and started following me . . . through the park and over the bridge. My pace quickened. Forty minutes later I saw him again, standing watching me. Whether this man was harmless or not, I felt scared and fragile. I ended up jumping into a cab on the main road at the opposite side of the park, as I thought he may follow me home. Now, maybe I was over-reacting, but I felt exposed and vulnerable and wanted to remove myself safely and quickly from the situation. GUYS, for the love of god, DO NOT follow a woman walking by herself – even if it's for a 'friendly' chat. Be aware that we all have the ability to make someone feel vulnerable. And, women, be aware that we also have the ability to get out of the situation.

## Dharma and Adharma

Thanks to free will, you can help guide your own evolution. The fact is that we all desire more and better things for ourselves. If those more and better things are good for our growth, then we are guiding our own positive and powerful evolution.

In India they make a distinction between dharma and adharma. Dharma includes whatever naturally upholds life: happiness, truth, duty, virtue, beauty, wonder, reverence, appreciation, non-violence, understanding, love and self-respect. Adharma, on the other hand, denotes choices that do not support life naturally: anger, violence, fear, control, dogmatism, scepticism, unvirtuous acts, prejudice, addiction, intolerance and unconsciousness in general.

Dharma is the ultimate power. It easily supports YOU, a single individual. What is asked of you is that you honestly look at your everyday life and the choices you are making. Ask yourself how to increase the dharmic choices and decrease the adharmic ones. Look at the power you have to allow light into your life.

Here's how:

• Be creative. Go beyond, through discovery and exploration.
• Challenge your thoughts. Read more, educate yourself. Learn from your own life data as well as other people's stories. You'll start having newer, more exciting thoughts than the old habitual ones you've been following. New points of view are important.
• Love and compassion. Discover that you can forgive yourself and others. Fantasies of hurt and revenge are replaced with emotional softening. You'll see that there is untapped love around you, so you move towards it.

These escape routes to light all lead back to the person you really are. The path out of feeling vulnerable, reaching for the goal of invulnerability, is opened inside yourself.

## Taking Risks

I am grateful for the risk-taker in my life, the person who had the guts to take a leap – my past self.

Risk-taking was not my thing for a long time; it's only in the last five years that I've been doing it. Not the bungy-jumping, adrenaline-junkie type of risks – I've always been like that! I mean the everyday risks that we all come up against in life. The risk of not being a people-pleaser. Pissing people off.

Risks such as moving somewhere new, standing up for myself against toxic people, travelling solo somewhere, trying something different, sharing my new talents despite the self-doubt, going out to meet new people, or applying for jobs I believed I'd have no chance of getting – the more risks I took, the less I found I was being rejected or feeling down about my life.

Don't get me wrong, there was plenty of loneliness, pessimism and nervousness. There were plenty of rejections. Risks are incredibly scary and difficult to take. It's just that the feelings of joy, fulfilment and contentment outweighed everything else. What I've now found out was that all the risks I took had something in common: it's about being completely open to opportunities, despite your fears.

I reflect, and I feel proud of myself for taking certain risks, so that I could end up where I am and who I am in this moment.

Think about this question: What makes you vulnerable? How would you answer?

I surveyed 15,000 people – an audience of 70 per cent women and 30 per cent men predominantly aged twenty-four to thirty-five. Five answers occurred frequently:

- Being the ultimate people-pleaser
- Feeling like losing my job, and my purpose
- The fear I won't be liked
- Not being loved
- Trying something new and failing

All responses involve situations that you can't control and how others see you.

The #vulnerabilitychallenge @thevulnerabilitychallenge popped up on my feed online and it made me think. What if we BY CHOICE put ourselves in a position of vulnerability?

This challenge asks us to do one thing that scares us because of the possible judgement that may follow.

This was super-hard for me! I'm typically not open to experiencing negative emotion, so I don't purposefully make myself vulnerable very often. However, I really wanted to 'show up' for this challenge.

The Vulnerability Challenge is a movement that encourages people to open up and be vulnerable. The idea is, if we can have the courage to remove our masks and reveal our truth, it will not only help us become more authentic; it will also help others feel they are not alone, and perhaps inspire them to do the same. This in turn could create a world where we feel safe to be ourselves.

In order to process our own pain, we need to acknowledge that without that pain we wouldn't be the person we are today. We are all a work in progress, and always will be, but being on the path of growth feels damn good.
ASK YOURSELF:

What are you hiding from the world?

What is holding you back?

What is your biggest fear?

What about yourself are you most proud of?

Make a conscious decision to share your vulnerability – either online or with friends. Have an awkward conversation that perhaps you have been avoiding.

The online challenge lasts thirty days and encourages us to be vulnerable every day during that period. Sounds scary. But putting yourself in a vulnerable situation does not make you a victim.

The Vulnerability Challenge is a place for love. If you see someone brave enough to share parts of themselves on social media or to you privately, please show them love and support. That being said, doing this challenge is not meant to be for other people. It is meant to help you become more whole and comfortable in your skin. Therefore, although it is nice to receive likes and positive comments, this is not supposed to be the reason for doing the challenge, and you really have no control over how people might react to your posts or vulnerability. It is not their responsibility to make you feel better.

I also think it is important to listen to yourself and know your limits. You don't have to share your dark secrets to the world if you are not ready. Perhaps your platform is just speaking to one other person.

I felt upset recently because I'd been left out of a big party. It wouldn't have been so bad if I hadn't known, but another friend mentioned it to me assuming I'd been there. Then we were both mortified by the situation. She hadn't realised I wasn't there, while I knew the truth: there was a party I wasn't invited to.

It didn't take me long to find evidence on Instagram. I went on my friend's account. No incriminating images. Then I hit the tagged button and three different posts confirmed it all. I'm a modern-day Jessica Fletcher. Without the murdered bodies.

I didn't want to make a big deal out of it. So I said, 'Oh yes, I forgot, she DID invite me, I just had plans that day. Can't believe I totally forgot.'

That lasted about two minutes. I can't lie. 'Actually, that's bullshit. She didn't invite me. I can't believe it! What a bitch.'

Now, I was never going to mention it to the culprit. That would be even more embarrassing than not being asked in the first place. I put it into a little safe in my brain, locked it up, meaning to hang on to that resentment indefinitely. But then I remembered the Vulnerability Challenge. I was hurt and I wanted to acknowledge it. I didn't want to attack her; in fact, I didn't want to say anything at all. It all felt so CRINGEY. But I messaged her.

Old stubborn Laura would probably have cut her out of her life for good. If I'm not good enough for her party, then she doesn't deserve to have me in her life. I should also probably stress, the party looked shit and more than likely I would have hated it, but that's NOT the point. So I met up with her. We made small talk about work and she was even more awkward than I was. (I may have intentionally liked the photo she was tagged in on, knowing she'd see it. I'm a right manipulative cow.)

Then I asked what she got up to last weekend. She froze.

'Oh, not much.'

So I swallowed my pride. 'Mary mentioned you had a bit of a do the other night. Was it fun?'

'Er . . . yeah. AH, GAD. I know, I wanted to ask you but then I was pissed off you didn't invite me to the cinema with the girls last month. I know it's childish but . . .'

FUCK. She's right. It wasn't intentional. I just had four freebies so I picked a different group of friends and the other girls are closer. But still. I had felt vulnerable and left out and she had felt the EXACT same thing. All the resentment was needless and just making us feel worse.

How many times have you asked somebody how they were doing and their answer quickly came back as 'I'm good'? How many times when people have asked you the same question have you said the exact same thing, knowing full well that you were not good. In fact, there are times when you are not good at all, yet you give the same response. What if we had to tell the truth every time that question was asked? How would that change our lives?

Recent leadership studies have shown that one of the most important traits of a leader is their courage to be vulnerable. Without it, how can we grow in self-awareness, learn from others, or get the help we truly need in difficult times?

I must stay strong, and confident, especially during the toughest times! When friends and family asked how I was doing, of course my response was often 'I'm good', knowing that was the furthest thing from the truth. I've been in situations that were spiralling out of control and I was just trying to get through each day. No, I was not good, and I am not sure I would have made it out of the abyss had it not been for my friends, my close support circle, with whom I could talk openly and honestly.

So, who are you vulnerable with? Next time you hear yourself responding to somebody asking how you are doing with an 'I'm good', sit back and reflect for a moment. Are you really good?

I do pretend to be better than I actually am, but by trying things like the Vulnerability Challenge, by opening up when I'm ready and questioning myself, I am in turn empowering myself. Don't get caught up in your vulnerabilities, or resent them. Learn from them and be free.

**REFLECTION:** I have the courage to be vulnerable. I open up my mind and heart. I reveal my authentic self. Vulnerability makes me powerful.

**AFFIRMATION:** Do one thing this week that makes you vulnerable – the mini Vulnerability Challenge. Take a risk by revealing a truth even if it means rejection. Don't reject yourself, even if others choose to reject you.

# chapter six

## She is insecure: stop comparing

'No one can make you feel
inferior without your consent.'
**ELEANOR ROOSEVELT**

Would we feel as insecure if we didn't know what
someone else was doing?

Hell no.

Growing up pre-Facebook, Instagram, Twitter, TikTok,
Snapchat *insert latest social media platform here*, I lived
in a state of ignorant bliss. If I wasn't invited to a party,
I didn't know. But today we can see in detail every insignificant social gathering we haven't been invited to.

I have enough insecurities without the world high-
lighting even more of my downfalls. Or someone else's
success reminding me what I haven't achieved.

It's normal to have 'down days' when you feel you can't seem to do anything right. But feeling insecure about yourself all the time can take a toll on every aspect of your life, from your physical health and emotional wellbeing to how you perform in your job or your relationships with friends and loved ones.

When I won the MTV competition in 2008 to be the face of MTV News, I felt like such a fraud. Yes, I was eager and ready to work hard to do the job as best I could (and hoped to keep the contract), but I didn't think I was the natural fit for the channel. A bit of naivety in my youth probably helped me skim over my insecurities, but they were always there, bubbling away under the surface.

I remember being in a field at V Festival, waiting to interview the singer Robyn. I had no make-up artist, and was wearing the same vintage Levi's denim skirt I wore at EVERY music festival and leopard-print leggings (I hated my legs). I had topped up my lippy in a backstage Portaloo and used some powder and loo roll to soak up the sweat on my forehead and top lip.

The MTV team consisted of me, my cameraman and producer. Far from what the outside perception was of my glamorous life, we all multitasked, carrying equipment and helping each other. Backstage, the presenters of *T4* (Channel 4's cool morning pop-culture show) had an impressive outdoor studio set-up.

Alexa Chung was interviewing Robyn for her live show, and this was before the singer came to us for a pre-record. Tanned, long-limbed, no leggings needed to cover those legs, and a make-up artist doing checks, Alexa was immaculate. I felt so insecure. Pretending to be a presenter in the presence of this cool, slick goddess was fucking brutal. God bless Robyn going from her to me – talk about a downgrade.

But I wish I could tell my past self to stop comparing, to only worry about what I had to do. And to bin those pink leopard-print leggings.

Whatever was happening before my slot was out of my control, not a knock on me as a presenter. I could just be me, and do my own thing. So what was the point in getting bogged down by everything else?

Television at this stage was still heavily male-dominated, and the women who were succeeding were constantly compared to one another. As if working in a man's world wasn't hard enough, many women who did make it felt threatened by their peers, when it should have been the opposite – women paving the way for other women.

When I first started out, I remember seeing myself in a fashion magazine. Fearne Cotton was wearing the same dress. They put a picture of each of us side by side and asked 'Who wore it best?' Underneath were comments from stylists and vox pops from the street about who looked best. Every inch of our bodies and our accessory choices were talked about, and judged.

But can I tell you a secret? We BOTH looked fucking great!

Why couldn't that be the narrative? Why did it have to be a comparison? Two women with different-shaped bodies and their own mind and sense of style wear a dress differently – shouldn't that be celebrated? The uniqueness of wearing the same dress differently is a positive, but society has long embedded a mentality of competition. One person must be knocked or diminished for the other to thrive.

You can only control one life, yours. But when we constantly compare ourselves to others, we waste precious energy focusing on other people's lives rather than our own. Comparisons often result in resentment: resentment towards others, and towards ourselves.

The problem for those perceived to be or who are a minority – be it women or people from the LGBTQIA and BAME communities – is that a lot of industries will, wrongly, allow only one 'diversity' space. I've worked on TV panel shows where I am the only female. With less space, you learn to be competitive. One of my friends, a comedian called Stephen Bailey, was told he wasn't going to be booked on another show because they already had a gay comedian. Rather than celebrating the person 'like' you, you can end up resenting your peers as you have been pitted against them. They have become an obstacle to your goal.

It's made me feel at times threatened by women like me (although no one is ever you, remember that). I have discovered there are an infinite number of categories for how we can compare ourselves, not just how we wear a dress. We are flooded by social media, and now it's easier than ever to find someone to compare ourselves to who is supposedly 'better than us'. We don't have to buy a magazine to feel bad about ourselves; we can get comparison 24/7 just by scrolling through our smart-phones. We typically compare the worst we know of ourselves to the best we presume about others, so it's never a fair competition from the get-go.

Comparisons, by definition, require metrics. The researcher Brené Brown said, and I'm paraphrasing, that when studying science you need measurements for some-thing to have worth; but as she got older she realised real worth is NOT being able to measure something. It's impossible to measure two people against one another.

You are just too unique to begin to compare fairly. Your talents and successes and contributions and value are unique to you and your purpose in this world. They can never be properly compared with anyone else's, because no one is you except YOU. I've learned that my life is the only life I can control. When I constantly compare myself to others, I waste precious energy focusing on other people's lives rather than my own, and inhibit my own growth.

Comparisons are a distraction from the unique beauty you possess. We each get 86,400 seconds every day, and wasting even one of them comparing yourself or your accomplishments with another's is one second too many. We are robbing ourselves of whatever precious little time we have in this world.

## How to Stop Comparing Yourself to Others

I wish I could say I've found the solution, but I haven't; and when others aren't doing the comparing, I'm still constantly judging myself. I don't have the secret for how to stop my brain going to that place of constant comparison. What I do try to do, however, is look at other people's success as a positive, as a form of inspiration, rather than it taking away from my own achievements. I also try to stop my mind wandering down the road of comparison and into self-loathing. That is a dangerous path. If we spoke to others as we speak to ourselves we'd be locked up for emotional abuse.

Take notice of your feelings. Be aware of the harmful effects comparing yourself to others has on your life. Intentionally change your perspective and free yourself from the damage this mindset has had on you. As soon as you see someone's Instagram pic pop up announcing a new job, a new baby, a wedding, connect to how it makes you feel. Does it make you feel bad? You're not a bad person if it does. But instead of judging yourself for feeling that way, ask why it makes you feel bad. What might be lacking in your own life that you need to develop? If they have the perfect job, perhaps it's inspiration for your own job search. Find the hope in someone else's news rather than resenting the person for their triumph.

Acknowledge your own successes. Whether you are a teacher, student, doctor, nurse, musician or still working it out, you have a unique perspective backed by unique experiences and unique gifts. You have the capacity to contribute to the world. You have everything you need to accomplish important things in your life. With that opportunity vividly in front of you, become intimately aware of your past successes. And find motivation in them to pursue more.

Your higher pursuit and your definition of success are different to anyone else's. People will have their opinions on what you should be doing, but only you know what makes you happy. Desire your happiness above everything else and, as much as possible, remove yourself entirely from the outside world's definition of success.

## Competition Is OK (Sometimes)

Unless you're the one who comes out on top every time, competition can be a bit shit. And sorry, I hate to break it to you, but no one ever comes out on top every single time. Someone will always be better than you at something. Fact.

BUT you can at times use competition as a resource. The bottom line is that, without competition, you might lose the necessary drive to accomplish great things in your life. If you pay attention, it is through competition that you can learn the biggest lessons.

People will copy you. Imitation is the sincerest form of flattery, as they say (not sure who 'they' are exactly, but they seem to have cred). If someone is copying things that you worked your ass off on, it can be super-annoying. I've been there. I once house-shared with a girl who wanted to get into TV. The whole time we lived together I was unaware that she was gathering information from me.

I remember once I had an email from Meg Matthews (she of Oasis's 'Wonderwall' muse fame and, just as important, a spokesperson for women's issues). I didn't know Meg at the time, but she was asking me if I wanted to try out veganism and write an article about it. She herself was a vegan and wanted to share the benefits of the lifestyle. I remember thinking out loud, 'Jaysus, I just got an email from Meg Matthews about writing an article about becoming a vegan. That's mad.' I had a little laugh about the randomness of it with my housemate, and the next day I emailed Meg back saying it could be a really interesting piece and thanks for thinking of me. She replied saying, 'Oh, one of your housemates emailed me saying she was interested in writing something.' My jaw dropped. I had only mentioned it because she was sitting beside me as the email popped up in my inbox. I didn't even think. Turns out that, after our giggle, my housemate had sourced a contact for Meg and, without telling me, tried to pitch the idea of herself writing it.

I get the competitive nature of the workplace, but know your own morals. Being competitive doesn't mean stepping on someone else to fulfil your own potential. When I confronted my housemate, she brushed it off. 'Oh, I needed some ideas for a column I'm pitching and thought it was a good idea.' No shit Sherlock. It's a great idea, that's why I was asked.

If I'm honest, if she'd asked me for the email address, I probably would have given it to her. A few other things like that happened and it all made me uneasy. It was only sometime afterwards that other friends in the industry opened up – they had had similar incidents involving the same girl. And, to be fair to her, her thirsty ambition served her well. But away from the obvious, she was learning from me, as perhaps maybe I should have been learning from her during that time. It goes both ways. And I've taken a lot of positives from her. Every situation is a chance to learn.

Competition takes us out of our comfort zone and forces us to do better. It is good to hustle. Rather than seeing those competing with you as a threat, see them as people just like you and perhaps even, at times, as allies. Imitation is going to happen, like it or not, so embrace it, learn to protect yourself. At the end of the day, the only one looking out for you is YOU. Competition can drive us to be the best we can be but, if we take it too far, it can also make us do things that we may regret. All you can do is work within the guidelines you set yourself.

There are times when competition is appropriate and needed but, remember, your mental wellbeing is more important than any competition. You can create your own path without inhibiting someone else's. We have all been thrown together at this moment on this crazy planet. The sooner we stop competing against others to 'win', or to be better than someone else, the faster we can start working together to figure it out. The first and most important step in overcoming the habit of unnecessary competition is to routinely appreciate and compliment the contribution of others. Always be thankful for what you are doing. Gratitude forces us to recognise the good things we already have in our world. Find inspiration without comparison.

Comparing our lives with other people's is a bit silly. As I said earlier, no one is you. But finding inspiration in and learning from others is very wise. Work hard to learn the difference. Humbly ask questions of the people you admire, or read biographies as inspiration. I read Audrey Hepburn's biography when I was younger; ballet was her dream but she fell into acting because it didn't work out. She described her childhood in Nazi-occupied Holland and the struggles behind Hollywood's glam facade. But she always had an outlook of hope. She didn't have the sexy curves of Bardot or Monroe, but still broke into an industry she was told she couldn't.

## Compare with Yourself

We should strive to be the best possible versions of ourselves. Not only for ourselves but for the benefit and contribution we can offer to others. Work hard to take care of yourself physically and emotionally and commit to growing a little bit each day. Learn to celebrate the small advancements you are making without comparing them to those of others. If you have to compare yourself to anyone, compare yourself to what you've achieved already.

However, that doesn't mean you should look back at your teenage body or young skin and make yourself feel bad for growing old. Growing old is a privilege not everyone is lucky enough to get to experience. Try to look back at the person you are growing into, with joy and satisfaction. Continue to evolve.

In Jordan Peterson's brilliant book (give it a read if you can) *12 Rules for Life*, rule number four is: 'Compare Yourself to Who You Were Yesterday, Not to Who Someone Else Is Today.' Instead, think about who *you* can be today. You have no idea how much time and effort someone else has put into achieving the results you envy. Channel your envy and jealousy into purpose.

Peterson says, 'The only person you should try to be better than is who you were yesterday.' Constantly challenge yourself to make incremental positive changes in your life. The idea is not only measurable but also fulfilling, when you see the small, gradual improvements in your life.

We need to stop comparing our progress with other people's, and instead weigh it against where we previously have been. It's a much better way to live life. The human brain has a natural tendency to make comparisons as a system of developing logic and reasoning. You can't stop comparing. It's inevitable. But you CAN channel your brain to make a better comparison, in your long-term interest, for growth and happiness.

Once you truly understand how to let go of your comparison mindset, you will see the world from an entirely different perspective. The dangers of pinning our happiness and achievements on how we measure up to others are too great to ignore. The more we desperately want to be like someone else, the more unworthy we feel. The more we desperately want to be happier, the lonelier we become.

You are here to live your own story. Don't focus on the actions of other people, but on your own. Aiming at the wrong thing has serious adverse consequences. It causes us to miss other important things in life like love, growth and happiness. Living in constant envy of others is not wisdom. Wisdom is facing the world exactly as it is and opening our eyes to opportunities to improve. The idea is to start using the 'yesterday you' as a foundation, so you can at least notice the direction and magnitude of the changes you can make today.

With enough information about who you were yesterday, you can use this knowledge to influence your future actions, so that on average you are improving over time. You don't need a radical process to grow or become your best self. The small choices you make daily matter. Create a career development plan with goals and objectives; and then work towards accomplishing these at a comfortable pace. Take charge of your life. If you're unsatisfied with the present, do something different that will improve your odds of success.

Stop giving a fuck about everything you are not and start living what you are!

## Impostor Syndrome

I have spent a lot of my life in situations I felt I didn't belong in. Waiting for the day someone would walk in and say, 'Laura, you shouldn't be here. Please leave, now.' I wouldn't even have to be dragged from the premises kicking and screaming. I would simply say, 'Fair enough. Surprised I lasted this long,' and would promptly throw myself out.

I have worked with and interviewed some of my heroes. I have travelled to places doing jobs I could only have dreamed of. I have ended up in some ridiculous situations, and at the sort of parties you can only read about in an F. Scott Fitzgerald novel.

I have spent a lot of my life feeling like THE IMPOSTOR. That nagging feeling that I'm not good enough, that I don't belong, that I don't deserve to be here; that I'm going to be found out!

The term 'impostor syndrome', or 'impostor phenom-enon', coined by two American female psychologists, didn't appear until the late seventies, but it's safe to assume that most of us, especially women, have always felt it. In the 1978 study, 'The Impostor Phenomenon in High Achieving Women: Dynamics and Therapeutic Intervention', the authors Pauline Clance and Suzanne Imes use the term to describe an individual experience of self-perceived intellectual phoniness. It appeared to be particularly prevalent among a select sample of high-achieving women. Despite their outstanding academic and professional accomplishments, many of these women experienced the impostor phenomenon and believed that they were really not bright and had fooled anyone who thought otherwise. Their numerous achievements, which we would take as evidence of superior intellect, do not appear to mitigate the impostor belief.

Clance and Imes found that the impostor phenom-enon occurs among high achievers who are unable to internalise and accept their success. Those with impostor syndrome often attribute their accomplishments to luck rather than to ability, and fear that others will eventu-ally unmask them as frauds.

Although the impostor phenomenon isn't an official medical diagnosis, psychologists and others seem to acknowledge that it is a very real and specific form of self-doubt. Impostor feelings are generally accompanied by anxiety and other negative effects on mental health. Most people with impostor feelings suffer in silence, too embarrassed to talk about them. After all, part of the experience is that they're afraid they're going to be found out.

When the two women who conducted the study first described the impostor phenomenon they thought it was unique to women. Since then, further research on the topic has revealed that men, too, can have the undesirable experience of feeling like frauds. However, the experience does seem to be more common among minorities in a workplace. Most of us will experience these impostor feelings at some point in our lives. I know I feel like I'm not pretty enough, smart enough, thin enough, well-spoken enough, cool enough, relatable enough and, well, basically good enough on a daily basis.

I put the question to a sample of my followers online: Have you ever suffered from impostor syndrome? Seventy-nine per cent (7,446) ticked 'yes', and 21 per cent (1,921) said 'no'. Impostor syndrome affects all kinds of people from all walks of life. It can apply to anyone who isn't able to see their own success, and who might be hesitant to ask a question in class or speak up in a meeting at work because they're afraid of looking stupid should the answer turn out to be obvious.

As I get older, I realise there are no stupid questions. Honestly. True stupidity is when you don't ask a question and therefore you won't find the answer. That's why I think kids are such a great influence; they can ask questions without societal pressure and expectation pushed on them.

Most of us will have to manage impostor syndrome because we all experience a type of shame that surrounds not being good enough. There's a great TED talk from 2017 led by Valerie Young. It's only about ten minutes long and examines what causes impostor syndrome and shares ways in which we can reframe our own thoughts to stop thinking like an impostor. She talks about shame and how it keeps a lot of people from 'fessing up' about their fraudulent feelings. Knowing there's a name for these feelings and that you are not alone can be liberating, but it doesn't make them go away. There are times when you'll feel stupid. It happens to everyone from time to time. Just because you may feel stupid doesn't mean you are. If you're one of the first or the few women or a minority in your field or workplace, it's only natural if you sometimes feel like you don't totally fit in. Instead of taking your self-doubt as a sign of ineptness, recognise that it might be a normal response to being an outsider and even a leader.

Henry Ford once said, 'Failure is only the opportunity to begin again more intelligently.' Instead of beating yourself up for being human and blowing the big project, recognise the value from the mistake and move on. You have just as much right as the next person to be wrong, to have an off-day, or to ask for help.

## Visualise success instead of failure

Do what professional athletes do. Before you tackle that big project, or job interview, or important pitch, spend time picturing yourself accomplishing and succeeding. It's better than picturing impending disaster. I know being modest is important, but it's OK to strive for success even if it feels out of your reach. I have a visualisation chalkboard over my desk where I write things I want to achieve. I set myself goals and imagine the possibility of getting what I want. I put EVERYTHING up there – from the dream job and the perfect trip away to what I want for dinner. Write down anything that creates a positive response when you look up and see it.

## Don't get stuck in a moment

As my fellow Irishmen U2 sang, you're just 'Stuck in a Moment You Can't Get Out Of'. Rather than having an impostor life, think of it as an impostor moment. Something that passes and doesn't engulf your whole being. You may feel stuck and that you can't get out, but, just like all moments, this too shall pass. It is not a lifestyle choice.

When I first started working for BBC Radio 5 Live, I felt like a fraud. I was covering for the presenter Nihal Arthanayake, a brilliant broadcaster who trusted me to keep his seat warm. I had spent ten years working in music and entertainment (and even felt a fraud doing that) and hadn't been in a radio newsroom for over a decade. Now I was covering a daytime breaking news chat show. Was I out of my depth? I sure felt it. But trust that you are not where you are just because of luck. You are there because of hard work too and someone seeing your potential, even if you don't. All you can do is try and learn to be better. All experiences help you gather information that you can use in whatever situation you are thrown into.

Back when I was hosting for MTV, I once was invited to a P. Diddy Party (yeah, it's an actual thing). The rapper popped open a champagne bottle and poured me a glass. I definitely didn't belong in that situation. Irish girl who just got lucky and found herself in these surreal surroundings. Everyone around me was wearing diamond bling and I had layers of those cheap plastic friendship bracelets around my wrist that I'd bought in Camden Market. And one was from a mate years ago who got it from Claire's Accessories. Could I stand out any more?? Both situations were very different, but both equally out of my comfort zone. I usually feel like a complete outsider – not clever enough, not cool enough – but looking back at those situations, I had every reason to be there (if only to share the memories). I just didn't know it. Most people who look down at you do so because of their own insecurities. Yourself included.

Of the many things you will hear in your life, the most important of all is what you say to yourself. When that well-known beauty brand came up with the 'you're worth it' slogan, it's relevant to so much more than just good hair. (Although you are also entitled to good hair if you should so choose.) You are worth your place at the table. You are worth that space you occupy in your family. You are worth your existence. Don't feel like you are ever in someone's way; you are where you are for a reason.

It takes a lot to show yourself, warts and all; and it's only natural to want to put your best foot forward. Remember, EVERYONE is doing the same thing. Even those showing their warts. There's usually a reason those warts are on display in such a constructed manner – perhaps it's an attempt to highlight their authenticity and realness for personal gain. So stop comparing yourself to everyone else's highlight reels. Social media can be a brilliant tool for connecting to a new community, informing yourself or promoting your work, BUT when you're feeling shit about yourself, it can be a minefield of contention.

It's easy to lose control down that spiral of wishing you had the body of your ex-boyfriend's third cousin's friend who just posted pics of her post-baby body posing in a skimpy outfit. And, actually, how did you even end up on this page?? You were just having a quick harmless peek at what your ex was up to! Suddenly you're not even comparing yourself to his new girlfriend (and you TOTALLY don't care, by the way, as you're in a healthy new relationship; you were just passing through his page out of natural curiosity). Now you are on some girl's page you hadn't even heard of five seconds ago yet want every inch of her life (including those tiles in her hallway from her profile picture). So what do you do? Remove yourself from the online world? Well, maybe for a bit, but you don't have to completely if you can control certain things.

Three tips to help you stop comparing yourself to others on social media:

## 1. It's YOU not them

It's never about the other person. It's about your own self-confidence. What's being triggered inside you, and why are you feeling that way? Were you feeling shitty already? Were you feeling sad?

It's usually that you're imagining the person has whatever it is you want. Whether that's confidence, radiance, comfort in your body, happiness, sex appeal, joy, etc. You think this person has it and YOU want it.

So, how can you get more of this in your own life? What makes you feel confident and radiant? Let go of their life and focus on yours.


## 2. Everyone is fighting their own battle

You never know what's really going on. It may look like the girl with the great tiles is living her best life, but I'll tell you right now: you will never, ever know what really goes on in someone else's world. She could be miserable in her marriage, stressed beyond belief as a working mum and insecure about her own body. On Instagram, it looks like everyone is having an amazing time *all* the time, from the seductive thirst traps to the heart-warming baby snaps. But is anyone really as lucky as their feed suggests? Everyone has their own issues and things that they are dealing with away from the public eye of judgement.

You can never compare what's going on inside you to the front put up by someone else. Because you'll never get the full picture. At the height of my darkest days, I was the image of a smiling, happy, everything-is-perfect-on-the-outside kind of gal. Yet inside I was so sad. And no one knew.

I'm not saying everyone you see on social media is a fake. But some are. Everyone has their own demons.

Whether it's a career problem, relationship struggle, infertility issues, body hang-ups – we've all got something. So be easy on everyone. And that includes you too.


## 3. It's your story to tell

I saw someone on Instagram announce a new project this week and I was chuffed for them. Then it made me feel sad.

'Should I have been up for that?'

'Why am I not doing it?'

'I'm just not good enough!'

How did my head move so fast to that outcome? I had to remind myself of all the great things I have already accomplished. And the fact I'm writing a book!! (That takes up a lot of time, ya know.)

At the end of the day it's about your own journey and being grateful for the steps you are taking to love yourself and be OK with yourself. Next time you find yourself triggered by someone's Facebook or Instagram pics, make it about your story not theirs. I will never have Alexa Chung's long tanned legs, but my pale Irish legs have served me well and I'm grateful for them. They are also great for a jig on a night out.

## Online Love

I had been in a love-hate relationship with social media for a long time. I'd tried to take a step back, but it was really tough. I'm fully aware how much it's affected the way I have behaved around other people in the past. It's caused me to dislike myself and feel detached. But now I've taken back control. I am creating my own community.

I'd even go so far as to say: AT TIMES, and on SOME occasions, social media feels like my safe place. There, I said it!! What a relief. I may end up eating those words but we've come to an agreement, social media and I.

I take a step back when I need space in the relationship. But when we're good we are great. A place to express myself, use my voice and scroll Gemma Collins memes.

Last year, I had had enough of my smartphone. I told my boyfriend, 'No phones in the bedroom.' I woke up regularly with the symbol of a bitten apple glaring back at me instead of his face. The phone was getting between us, literally.

I'd go for dinner in a restaurant and see people, heads down over their devices, devouring their scrolling screens and not noticing the world go by. Their fellow diners? Nothing more than a side dish of bread rolls, never touched. It made me sad.

I've worked in television for more than ten years, so I've always been aware of the negativity online – people disliking my Irish accent, saying I'm too thin, I'm too fat. But you learn to grow a thick skin. Magazines had been doing much the same thing for years so it was only natural it would evolve online. The problem with online is that too many people have a platform without realising the privilege and responsibility it brings. Too many remain nameless, hiding behind their overused keyboard, compiling words of hate and hurt.

When I first joined Twitter, it was just for fun; but it suddenly became a stressful place. The love affair that began with no pressure suddenly brought on anxiety. When should I post, what will people say? Anything you don't like about yourself is magnified a thousand times.

'She's had so much work done.' 'Bad nose job.'

Inside I'd be screaming, 'This is how I look. I was born like this. Now FUCK OFF.' Of course, I would never respond like that online. My mother follows me, and she would not be impressed. Worse still, she'd be disappointed. So, I'd feel bad about myself and how I looked AND anger my mother. I couldn't deal with all that.

Like any relationship, we had good days and bad days. The good days on my phone were great. Putting up a picture on Instagram of me on set, or after a big interview, or posting about a new, shiny job I'd landed. All the likes boosting my ego like the pings of a winning fruit machine in a casino. But the bad days were . . . shit (sorry, Mum).

I'd watch people in the public eye be torn apart and think, 'Well, everyone gets it so it's just normal and must be OK.' But it's not OK. When Caroline Flack took her own life, I remember thinking back over what she'd had to put up with. All the comments I had seen online, and savage headlines sprawled across the papers. Caroline always seemed like nothing bothered her. She was feisty and strong-willed. I had been jealous that she was able to not let it all get to her, whereas I knew that in a similar situation I would have crumbled. But it *did* get to her. Whatever happened in her personal life, or the bad decisions she may have made, she didn't deserve the attention she had to deal with daily. It was not the business or duty of the keyboard warriors to publicly shame her.

When I was asked to host *Love Island* – although I LOVE the show – a part of me thought, 'Do I want to put myself on that platform and be held up to public scrutiny?' I had intentionally been working on other very different projects and finding my voice. Getting away from the 'blonde girl dressed up on the telly' after hosting MTV for years. I'm tired of the energy it takes to correct people who misquote you, or say untrue things, when I could be doing so much more worthwhile things with my resources. But I'm good at my job and I love doing live telly. My decision should be based on my opinion, not those who haven't even formed one yet. I needed to follow my own advice and take heed of my opinion, my expectations and not others'; not let other people's opinions control me.

So I made a decision: Twitter would be for work-related posts moving forward, and Instagram was merely a space to put up controlled images and publicise my work, not somewhere to express my whole self. I was angry and fed up with this culture I had seen manifest itself around me and become acceptable, the norm. I felt disconnected from real people and I wanted to reclaim my real-life connections.

Then something none of us expected happened. The outside world was taken away from us. The eating out at restaurants, the bread rolls all on lockdown. Suddenly, self-isolating in our homes was not the wild plot of some apocalyptic B-movie but our daily life. The only way I survived the 2020 lockdown was using my smartphone. The outside world became social media. FUCK. (Sorry again, Mum.)

But as our real world got scarier, the internet got, well, a little bit nicer. There will always be trolls and shaming, but in large part the space felt safe and inclusive. We were checking in and we were talking TO each other. I felt part of a community that was bringing us together, not dividing.

I had been trying to get my mother to join FaceTime for years and, during the pandemic, she finally signed up.

The first attempt was a conversation with her perfectly groomed eyebrows (thankfully, done just in time for lockdown), but as the weeks grew into months I saw her smiley face every morning, just for a check-in before she got on with her day, doing the gardening or bingeing the next box set on my Netflix account. She was savvy enough to set herself up a separate profile so as not to mess up my viewing recommendations. And I'll be eternally grateful to her for that, more than she knows.

Living in London, neighbours don't really talk to each other; but our 'Neighbourhood' app was bouncing and we helped one another. This was not usual London protocol. I joined EVERY platform out there to stay connected with people. Zoom, House Party . . . TikTok. I was ON it all.

And I kinda fell in love with online. We both grew up. (Although me joining TikTok reminds me of when my mother got on Instagram. I'm a millennial trying to be part of Gen Z and I don't care.) I didn't feel lonely as there was a whole community out there that I found, my tribe. And I wanted to be part of it.

Life works in mysterious ways. The one thing that has previously made me feel disconnected connected me more than I ever imagined was possible. A catalyst for permanent change, to be nicer to each other. I still would like to wake up and see my boyfriend's face in front of me and not his phone. One day, sure, anything is possible.

REFLECTION: What are you most insecure about, and is comparing yourself to others enabling negative thoughts about your self-worth? You control what you see. Curate your online news-feed to accounts that benefit you.

AFFIRMATION: I am not led by others. I am a leader and I am worth it.

# chapter seven

## She doesn't always know what to do: faking it

'To conquer oneself is a greater
task than conquering others.'

**BUDDHA**

'Where do you see yourself in ten years?'

Eughhh! I HATE this question. I get asked it ALL the time. Please, for the love of God, if we bump into each other, do not ask me this. My usual response is: 'Who fucking knows?!!'

That's a lie. I usually respond with the safer and less aggressive comeback of 'Being happy'. That's one of the few things I know I won't change my mind about, I'll always want to be happy. If I'm truly honest, I'm not sure where I see myself tomorrow, let alone in a decade. I can't even decide what I want for dinner tonight. Right now, I'm feeling something healthy, like goat's cheese salad, but after a day in front of my laptop and depending on how that goes, I'll probably want pizza. I'm not very good at planning because I've learned that plans don't always go to . . . er, plan. You have to be flexible and open to change, grow and move forward. This doesn't mean I'm not ambitious or don't have life goals.

I'm going to say something that no guidance counsellor will ever tell you: you don't have to have a plan.

The idea of a ten-year plan is popular because it promises the certainty that, if we follow a pre-made path to success, fulfilment will inevitably follow. But trying to predict the future is a losing battle. It's impossible to know what your priorities will be a few years from now, let alone the opportunities you'll be presented with.

Yes, it is great to be goal-oriented, but if you are so preoccupied with trying to execute every last detail of your life plan to perfection, you can get trapped in 'analysis paralysis', missing new possibilities. You can still be successful without pushing and forcing it.

I have tried to make plans and they've rarely worked out. Sometimes I've ended up in a better situation, sometimes worse. Everything you do in life is a risk, even when it's planned. It may not be obvious from the outside looking in that things haven't worked out as expected. But most of us, myself included, end up adapting. As soon as you think you know where you are heading, life has a tendency to throw a spanner in the works, doesn't it?

If you are so fixated on structure and following the plan set out ahead of you you may miss so many opportunities occurring on the periphery, where you haven't noticed them. Alternatively, if you follow a plan that doesn't work out, you may feel like a failure. Even if you have accomplished so much, you are never going to live up to an unrealistic expectation. You are not a failure. You are where you are meant to be at that particular time.

Here comes the important bit: you don't have to have a step-by-step plan BUT what you do need is a PURPOSE. (If I could have jazz hands around this word and fireworks exploding off the page I would. But my publisher informs me it's both expensive and impractical. There's probably a safety element too.)

You need purpose. You need a sense of motivation. Otherwise why bother getting up in the morning? Your purpose consists of the aims of your life. Your 'why'. The reason you do what you do. Purpose can guide life decisions, influence behaviour, shape goals, offer a sense of direction and create meaning; but it also allows for flexibility.

## Finding Your Path/Your Purpose

My path is always changing, but my purpose is something I'm constantly striving towards.

When reflecting on your purpose, you must justify it to yourself; because by doing so, you make it your own – and, once you make it your own, you ignite an inner drive. A drive that's immune to the thoughts and opinions of people around you. That nagging feeling of 'what will other people think?' quietens, trust me. Approval from others becomes less important.

But what if you haven't found your purpose? Well make it your purpose to find it! Go on a journey. What are you passionate about? Engage in deep introspection. See where it takes you. Look at where it leads you.

Purpose will vary from person to person simply because we were raised in different circumstances, different cultures, and have different beliefs. Your purpose is of your own volition and ONLY your own and therefore it can never be taken from you. It becomes something real, something tangible that you can hold on to for the rest of your life.

One thing I want to point out is that we can never judge another person for the purpose they choose to follow. Some people may choose money. Some fame. Some charity. Some parenthood. Some a life of solitude.

That's fine. That's their purpose and their purpose alone. Not yours.

When you find your purpose and make it your own, you begin to see exactly what you're made of, because when purpose is activated it naturally drives success. Life has a habit of working itself out when you know what it is you truly want.

When you have purpose, you'll find yourself spending time pursuing it, discovering and interacting with people of similar mindset and purpose – your community or tribe – and encouraging one another to go for it. The people you hang around with, your choice of books and entertainment, your diet, your lifestyle, all of it will start to revolve around your purpose, feeding it and helping you reach for it. It may SEEM like a plan is coming into effect but you haven't actually planned anything.

John 'Hannibal' Smith in the iconic TV show *The A-Team* used to say, 'I love it when a plan comes together', but think about it – they never really spent a lot of time planning, did they? Most of the time it didn't look as though they had a plan at all (the magic of television, maybe). But it does reinforce the power of drive over everything else, and of having goals.

Your purpose is not the same as your goal, however. Goals are there to serve your purpose, not to *be* your purpose. The A-Team had a goal such as 'to rescue the kidnapped rich girl from the bad guys', but that's not the same as purpose. The purpose is to live in a world that is peaceful, safe and not controlled by the bad guys. Oh, and money. They got paid handsomely, let's not forget.

Purpose is the driving force behind setting the goals you want to achieve. Goals are simply a reflection and minor subset of your overall purpose.

When I look at people I admire – Mary Robinson, Brené Brown, Tom Hanks, my parents (now there's a dinner party I want to be at) – beyond a shadow of a doubt having purpose in their lives played a central role in their success. The one common factor they all had within them is that their purpose was something much greater than themselves and that they genuinely loved pursuing it.

YOU must find out what your purpose is. Only you can figure it out and undertake the journey to find it (and you eventually will find it). My friend Britt, who lives in LA, always says 'Hustle in purpose', and I love this phrase. Nothing worthwhile comes easy. It's all a hustle, but as you're hustling keep reflecting back to that purpose. Even though your purpose may change, life constantly has struggles, so make sure what you are hustling for has worth in your heart.

## It's OK to Change Your Mind

I am a contradiction of indecisiveness and knowing exactly what I want. I guess what that reflects is having purpose but not an actual plan.

If you're someone who always changes their thoughts, that is OK. If you're the opposite, that's OK too. The risk of changing your thoughts is that you allow others to influence your thinking, but not being open to other people's ideas leaves you with a very narrow-minded view of the world.

The world changes fast. Especially right now. That means we need to be able to adapt all the time. So it's completely normal to change your thoughts. I've probably thought differently over the last year than I ever have before. Scrap that – I've had conflicting views just this past week.

Think about this. YOU also change all the time, not just your situation. If you meet new people and are constantly educating yourself, you're probably not the same person you were a year, month, week or even a day ago. So if you think about it more deeply, it would be weird if you never had new thoughts or ideas.

Changing your mind doesn't mean you don't know what you want. It's a sign that you're learning, and that you in fact know your purpose.

When you're a kid it's all so simple, or at least appears to be. You are told things as fact. As you get older, you learn to question people and even yourself. It's OK to be questioned by others too. I've had my own opinions challenged and changed through educating myself.

I've written tweets, made comments that were intended to be positive. However, others may be offended by optimism at a time of sadness. It's important to listen to others, but at the end of the day go back to: what was the purpose of what I put out? If it didn't fulfil your purpose, maybe you need to rethink. But if it did, if it brought a little bit of light into the world, maybe others need to consider again. It's all a learning game.

One thing I've been thinking a lot about recently is my faith. On Christmas Eve, you'll find me in the same place as last year, and the year before that: at Midnight Mass with my mother in Ireland (which isn't even on at midnight, by the way, but leaves enough time for one last drink catching up with mates in the local pub). It's a tradition that I've been following since I was a kid (not the pub bit) and one I rather like. It's the only time, except for weddings and funerals, I go to church now. What was once a weekly tradition is now an annual one.

I don't remember exactly when I stopped going to Mass. It reminds me of one of those lost friendships from school. You'd see that person every day because they were in your class – friends through convenience and lack of choice. You got on fine and it was someone to hang out with and stopped you being the dreaded loner (though being the loner does have its benefits too). When you left school, you might have tried to meet up for a coffee now and then – mainly out of guilt. Then one day you realise you've lost contact; and you don't actually miss them.

That's how I feel about the Church now. I didn't turn around one day and say I'm not going to Mass. It just fizzled out, like a relationship that has run its course.

I was born in Dublin, a Roman Catholic like the majority of people in the Republic of Ireland. I went to a convent secondary school and had sex education taught by a nun (looking back, probably not the best person to learn this specific part of education from). And I went to Mass every Sunday – because I had to. I didn't hate it; all my mates went and sometimes I got to give a reading at the altar (good practice for what was to come, just minus the autocue).

As I got older and travelled more, I began to question all those things I learned in RE class – how did Noah fit all those animals on one ark? Eve was made from Adam's rib?

What really made me question my whole religion was the feeling of betrayal, when allegations of sexual abuse of children in Ireland emerged. If there is a God, why would He let this happen, and why by the hands of people using His (I'm using the masculine form for convenience but could easily say 'Her' here) good name? These people were trusted by communities and used their power to take advantage of those who were vulnerable. And as I got older, the Catholic Church's views on gay marriage and female reproductive rights continued to push me away.

That said, I can't give it up completely. In fact, I still classify myself as Catholic, but it's more to do with cultural heritage than what I actually believe. I like the comfort and belonging and nostalgia but don't want to sign up for the whole shebang. Does that make me a hypocrite? Maybe. But open my kitchen cupboard and you'll find a bottle of holy water. Actually, you'll find several scattered around my home – from Lourdes, from Fatima, from Jerusalem, even Knock in Ireland where in 1879 the Virgin Mary apparently appeared.

Now in my thirties and living in cosmopolitan London, I'm jealous of people who believe without question. My brain won't allow it – I'm constantly asking 'why?'. Yet I still feel the need to believe in something. I celebrate Christmas, and have a handmade nativity set on my mantelpiece. I will go to Midnight Mass and sing along to the carols and shake hands and say, 'Peace be with you', and even receive the Eucharist. I like flying back from the hustle and bustle of London and listening to the priest relay a homily – even if it's not relevant to me in the slightest. I will pray and it will make me feel all lovely and warm inside and full of love, and give me a sense of community.

I'm not ready to give up on Christianity completely. But can I be a Catholic if I don't agree with so many of the Church's views? I know that at its core religion says to be kind and good to one another, yet why is it the cause of so much war and conflict? I'm constantly struggling with what to believe – so can I take what I want, and what I need, from multiple sources?

My mother still classifies herself as Catholic. In 1979 she queued for four hours to get into Phoenix Park along with a million other folk to see Pope John Paul II. In the summer of 2018 Pope Francis had less than 200,000 fans show up. I asked my mother why she didn't go this time and she simply replied: 'I'm not bothered.'

My grandfather was born a Protestant and my granny a Catholic, and at the time my grandfather converted and became Catholic to marry her. My partner Iain was born into the Church of Scotland and I'm 'Catholic-ish', but it's not something we have even talked about or need to discuss really.

I have Jewish friends who put up a Christmas tree and Muslim mates who drink. Their religion is their heritage, but can they define themselves by their faith? I asked my followers on Twitter if they were religious. Approximately 90 per cent said 'NO' but with the caveat of a massive 'BUT'. If something bad happens most of us will say a prayer, even though we're not sure who exactly we're praying to.

With technology and a busy life, I find myself looking elsewhere for comfort, filling the gap that traditional religion once held. From meditation, to yoga to reiki to sound baths – I've dipped my toe in it all. And I'm not the only one. Most of us seem to be searching for something.

For my granny, Sunday Mass was where she found out the latest gossip, wore her fanciest clothes and looked for words of wisdom. Now we've got social media for that. And today my granny would be that yummy mummy in her latest Sweaty Betty or Fabletics activewear, heading to hot yoga with her soya matcha latte. Instagram and Twitter are full of 'thoughts for the day' and 'inspiring quotes' – who needs a passage from the Bible (especially if it's in Latin) when you can have a perfectly illustrated Grid Post telling you how to 'live your best life'?

As part of my searching I've gone on retreats, met with shamans, chatted to Muslim pop stars and Orthodox Jewish journalists – people who have lost religion, people who have found it and people who have never had it at all. I looked at a recent study that, unsurprisingly, showed the proportion of young adults professing a Christian faith in the UK is among the lowest in Europe. Stephen Bullivant, a professor of theology and the sociology of religion at St Mary's University in London, told me that 22 per cent of those aged between sixteen and twenty-nine said they identified as Christian, while 70 per cent described themselves as non-religious. Stephen, who wasn't born into a devout family, has found that since studying theology he has become religious. Religion in this country is 'moribund', he says. 'With some notable exceptions, young adults increasingly are not identifying with or practising religion.'

So what does all this mean? Should traditional faiths re-evaluate the scriptures that are thousands of years old? Or should we just be able to practise what works for us individually?

When I publicly campaigned to repeal the Eighth Amendment of the Irish Constitution recognising the equal right to life of the pregnant woman and the unborn, I had mixed responses online to my views. My opinion went against my Catholic upbringing, but we are no longer living in the Dark Ages – shouldn't we evolve with the times? Everything around us evolves – science, technology, Madonna's fashion sense. Can't our religious values too?

I'm still searching for what to believe in. I like the idea of karma, of a protective energy guiding us, of guardian angels and of kindness. I have crystals in my pockets, meditate when I'm stressed, wear a cross around my neck and bless myself before I fly. In a world where we don't have to choose a gender and can have numerous jobs (Hi, I'm Laura and I'm a presenter/writer/actor/DJ/chancer) why do we have to choose a religion?

I'm still negotiating my view on religion and I respect, and at times envy, people with devout views. But it's OK not to know what you believe in. You need to suss it out for yourself.

## Your Path Will Change

When I was younger the assumed plan was to be married in a church, but now that doesn't serve my purpose. So much has happened since then, my path has changed. The dream wedding of the eight-year-old me is not the same as the thirty-year-old me.

Finding your path in life is not an act of searching. It is an act of allowing and taking each step as it comes. This is my first time living this life. No one has lived my life before. There isn't a predesigned path to help me. This isn't a hike up the Wicklow mountains, following a pre-walked path trodden by lots of other folk. You can only judge each step as you see the condition it's currently in. Should I go left or right? Well, what's the weather like today? It's different from yesterday. Is the ground hard or soft today? Will I slip if I take a shortcut? There are always so many changeable factors to consider, just as in life.

Also, for all you hikers, just an fyi: the Wicklow mountains in Ireland (near my hometown) can be challenging even with pathways. Fair dues to the first person who navigated them before there were footpaths. It's so much easier to follow someone else's footsteps but I can tell you one thing – it's not half as much fun!

When you do let go of what you think should be, who you should follow, you allow what is meant to be. While this may sound a load of tripe, it is simply the act of following your heart moment by moment, step by step. Your purpose is already built into your being.

When you follow your heart, your inner GPS, you are nudged in the right direction. Because what finding your path comes down to is living life to the fullest. It comes down to following what feels alive to you, and doing your best, in this moment.

I've tried to be a planner. Many, MANY times, beset by anxiety and constantly thinking about what I needed to do to get to where I wanted to be. Even though I didn't actually know where that was. The thought of not having a plan sounded insane. Everything we are taught is based on having some sort of structure to prevent potential future failure. What if I haven't packed enough? What if my flight crashes and I die before I get to cross everything off my bucket list? What if I die before I even make a bucket list?

Enter, snowball of emotions. One worry turns into

ten million worries. When we're growing up, an easy-to-follow guide on how to live a supposedly happy life is pushed upon us:

- Don't hang out with the bad kids.
- Go to a good school.
- Go to a better university.
- Find a good job.
- Find a better job.
- Get married.
- Buy a house.
- Get good house insurance.
- Have kids.
- Get better life assurance.
- Die having ticked off the bucket list you made in your twenties.

What they don't tell you about is how many unplanned events can happen and completely disrupt everything. What if you don't get into the right college? What if the dream guy turns out to be a dick? Are you going to have more children? Are you going to have ANY children? What if your old bucket list doesn't interest you any more? What if you want a new bucket list?

If we just spend all of our lives waiting for our life plan to come together, then are we really living? Life isn't just about the big things; it's all the little things in the everyday too. You don't always have to have a plan for EVERYTHING. You're allowed not to know what you want to do with your life. You're allowed to ditch the plan and go travelling for a year – universities and jobs aren't going anywhere; they'll still be there when you come back.

As you know by now, I love live music. Glastonbury is my happy place. But it can be incredibly overwhelming. So many people, so many stages, so many bands on the schedule. You can't possibly see them all. Apart from a few exceptions, I don't plan who to see at Glastonbury. I kind of go with the flow. See who I bump into. Stumble across a small tent with an act I didn't know was playing and the serendipity of it all usually ends up adding to what is my favourite weekend of the summer. I once ended up in a secret ceilidh attempting *Riverdance* with a Michael Flatley lookalike (I mean, it could have been him). Don't overplan and miss having fun in the moment.

We all make 'bad' decisions. But I question if there's such a thing as a bad decision (the fifth tequila shot on my first night after the Covid-19 lockdown was probably a bad choice, but I'd probably do it again). We may make decisions we feel we regret, but learning from them is how we better ourselves.

If you don't even attempt to do something you really want to do, then you will regret not having done so all the more. You can't really make a bad decision if it's something you have your heart set on and something you're going to enjoy. I want to be clear before I'm bombarded with messages about my grasp on reality. Life is also about responsibility, but don't spend the rest of your life being miserable because you felt forced into a career you didn't want. I have friends whose parents decided their future for them. My dad wanted me to be an actuary, because it paid well and was stable, and his father had put pressure on him to go to a certain school and get a good, solid job in business. His ambitions for me came from a place of love, but I can tell you I am far happier (and, as it turns out, wealthier) for having made my own choices.

It's your life. Don't let someone else decide how you're going to live it.

## 'Spontaneity Is the Spice of Life'

**Definition: Spontaneous** (adj.)
Happening or done in a natural, often sudden way, *without any planning* or without being forced.

Being spontaneous is about being fully present, not living in the past or future. There are no regrets about what's happened, no worries about imagined future scenarios. Preconceived notions always leave you disappointed.

Only plan when you need to. Spontaneity is harnessing the power of now and turning the present moment into a party.

Some of the best memories I have were of when I made the conscious decision to just 'go with the flow' and 'see where life takes me'. Those moments in which I felt wonderfully alive were when I was purely spontaneous, heeding love-based, intuitive inclinations.

If there was a spontaneity chart, I would probably be off it!

I remember, when I was single, just meeting a guy who asked me if I fancied going to Barcelona with him; and I went. I'd had a shit break-up the year before, and had never been to Barcelona. I had met him the day before through a mate at a film screening and he was great fun. Like SO much fun. I was lucky to be in a position where I could jump on a plane and head off for two days, and afford to pay for myself – just so there was no imbalance of power. (People with money can use it as a hold over you, so always try to be self-sufficient.) And I just went. Two days on the back of his Vespa in the Spanish city; whizzing around galleries and food markets like I was in some noughties indie romcom. He also looked like 'the guy' from those films (probably because he was), so that helped. I was back before I had even told people I had gone. And, you know what? It was fucking great! I've crossed paths with him a few times and he's lovely, but to be honest that weekend wasn't about him, it was about me. Just going with the flow, no pressure, no expectations. Re-establishing my purpose and taking back free will. 'What would people think?' Who bloody cares!

Let go of fear and trust in the universe. Have faith – be it in yourself, life, love, the universe or whatever god you may or may not believe in.

Follow your intuition. It has served me well – most of the time. Follow your heart, even when it gets you in trouble. Follow your excitement, wherever it may lead – arms around a cute guy driving through a new city soaking up life's surprises.

Do some crazy shit, as long as you're not harming yourself or others. Don't be afraid to experience life from any and every perspective. It will make you a better person. Be impeccably dynamic. Be masterfully flexible.

Why are we always in such a rush to have it all figured out? We think we should know where we're going, or even who we are. We look for concrete things to grab on to, such as a plan, an identity, or confirmation that we're good enough. But none of those things is relevant. What's relevant is the willingness to take one step at a time towards what makes us feel most alive. Spontaneity can give you some relaxed and uninhibited qualities, because no matter what happens next, YOU can deal with it.

This is an incredible trait to have in life. When you let go of trying to know what's going on, you become truly free.

Whether you believe in a religion, in a god or goddess, a higher being or just the divinity you feel within, to trust that if you jump all will stay OK is the best thing you can do. Set intentions, create the space to be open, and it's amazing how quickly that space will fill with the things you want and the things you need to take you where you are meant to go. Your worth is never predetermined; you determine it and, once you do, the rest of the world will respond to it.

Where to start? Write down what is important to you. Don't make your list in just one sitting. Take your time. I have notebooks all over my house; all shapes and sizes stashed in different handbags, pockets of jackets, so I can jot down things as they come to me. My notepad on my smartphone is bursting with ramblings too. A lot are incoherent, but when I write something by hand or on my phone, I'm putting it out there. It's not just locked away in the back of my subconscious any more.

My advice is to start with simpler examples of what you'd like; for instance, work out regularly, spend quality time with friends and family, learn to play an instrument, etc. From there you can progress to more sophisticated ideas: become more assertive, discover little things that make you happy, learn to enjoy the moment, become open to different ideas, become more tolerant and accepting.

In my notepad I have everything from 'call that friend I haven't talked to in months' to 'finish this book'!

Keep this list of precious thoughts close to you. My cosmic chalkboard over my desk at home is constantly within my range of vision, reminding me of my goals, how I intend to achieve my purpose.

## Say 'yes' more!

As important as it is to say 'no', open yourself up to 'yes'. Imagine being completely open. Imagine a life in which we accept every single chance, offer or challenge; where we take every single risk. Danny Wallace did just that in his book *Yes Man* and it turned out pretty good for him – he got a movie deal out of it.

Danny may have been a bit extreme taking on a challenge from a lady he met on a bus who said to him, 'Say yes more.' So he said 'yes' to everything for a year. He said 'yes' to pamphleteers on the street, the credit card offers stuffing his mailbox and solicitations on the internet. He attended meetings with a group that believes aliens built the pyramids in Egypt, said 'yes' to every invitation to go out on the town and furthered his career by saying 'yes' in meetings with executives. I'm not telling you to say yes to EVERYTHING. But to give yourself more credit than you do. Say yes to yourself.

Sometimes the biggest obstacle you must overcome is yourself. A lot of the time, people are stuck in old routines, entrenched notions of how they believe things should be done, but sometimes you just have to step outside your comfort zone. Say yes to something you don't think you can achieve. Think differently to ignite a spark. Say yes to being spontaneous.

## Be Self-aware

In order to be comfortable with walking down the path of life we must be more aware both of our feelings and thoughts and of the way we influence others. Know that minor missteps are totally normal and OK.

Try to get an insight into how you feel and how you think in different situations. Think about what you've found out. It is very important to get rid of that autopilot.

Consider this common belief: 'You'll never get anywhere unless you know where you're going.' This seems like common sense, and yet it's not true if you stop to think about it. Conduct a simple experiment: go outside and walk in any direction, and feel free to change course randomly. After twenty minutes, an hour . . . you'll be somewhere! It's just that you didn't know you were going to end up there.

You have to open your mind to going places you never expected to go. If you live without set plans, you'll explore new territory. You'll learn some unexpected things. You'll end up in surprising places – some good, some bad. But you will have allowed possibility into your life.

When you don't feel like doing something, you have to force yourself to do it. Your path is chosen, so you don't have room to explore new territory. You have to follow the plan, even when you're passionate about something else.

The biggest misconception in life is that everyone knows what they are doing. They don't. No one knows what lies ahead. But not all uncertainty is bad news. While it can at times make you feel anxious, uncertainty also makes positive events more exciting.

Ponder this scenario: you sort of fancy a mate's friend and know they have seen your profile. Your friend says they may or may not like you; it's uncertain. Now look at the same situation, but this time you're told the person definitely likes you. In most circumstances you will be more attracted to the person when you don't know for sure how much they like you.

The excitement of not knowing for sure is thrilling. Think about it. I'm convinced I'm not the only one who has been put off by an eager beaver (yes, I just said that). A bit of uncertainty makes life all the more interesting. There have been thousands of studies on human behaviour and why we react like this. We are beautiful creatures, designed to be uncertain; we have the tools to work out problems. The more we try to avoid the distress uncertainty brings, the less we're able to develop the ability to effectively handle uncertain situations. We better ourselves by stretching to try out new activities and meet new people.

As life is never perfect, we need to be at ease with making mistakes, learning from them and changing our goals when they are thwarted. When we are flexible, we are more willing to reflect on disappointments, access appropriate emotional support and be less self-critical.

Now at this stage you know having purpose is mandatory, but it's OK not to win every race. It is OK to enjoy life and be in a state of flow. It's OK to be average. Average feels like a dirty word, doesn't it? When it comes to the number of people we've slept with, we want to be average, as I've discussed in chapter 4, but what about in other areas of achievement? We are fed lies and told we need to be the best, but what if someone else's average is our best?!

**Definition: Average** (n.)
Not the best, not the worst.

It doesn't take a lot to be average, apparently; in fact, the very definition of average means that there is a pretty good chance that you are average. Congratulations.

The problem is, we are told that average isn't really good enough. We need to be better. Let's just take a moment and let this concept sink in. The average person IS average. You are where you are expected to be. You are a safe 'OK'.

Now, I am by no means saying let's not be arsed to motivate ourselves. I mean, I am writing this book to help show you the potential you have. The power we all individually possess. I am an ambitious person and I like a sense of challenge. But can we give ourselves a break?

What's hard is this feeling that we have to be good at EVERYTHING. From the moment we're born, we are compared: what's the weight of your baby? Oh, that's a big baby, but average for a Western baby. Actually, even before that, when you are floating around in the foetal position in your mother's womb you are already being talked about. 'The first child is usually the most difficult.'

Back to you minus umbilical cord. If you are the best you can be, you are doing your best. You are only average compared to other people. So don't compare.

Years ago, we didn't really know what everyone else was accomplishing. We read stuff in newspapers and gossiped about the neighbours, but our sphere of comparison was small. Now we are bombarded with the successes of someone else the minute we unlock our phones. We constantly compare our lives to someone we may never have met.

I feel bad about myself when I see a random influencer Instagram her new retro pink fridge, while the light on mine blew a year ago and I have no idea how to replace it. Would I feel jealously towards this girl and her perfect fridge if I never saw the picture in the first place??! Why can't I stop thinking about my shit fridge?

Side note: I've tried unsuccessfully numerous times to change the light in my fridge. I'm not even sure what that dark stuff wrapped in clingfilm at the back is, but it gets no light so I guess we'll never know.

I'll let you in on the worst-kept secret. There are over forty filters on Instagram for a reason (that's without downloading all the other apps to refilter that filtered picture). Most of us are average, we just choose to display that averageness in an exceptional way.

We don't have to eat the best food to survive: a basic diet will get us through. We wear clothes to stay warm and hide our modesty; they don't need to be the latest designer collection. We have to move but we don't have to do the Argentinian tango. The musician Brian Eno says, 'We have to communicate but we don't have to write epic poetry.' What I think he was actually getting at is that art is something we all can (and indeed should) inhabit every day. We can do things and not be the best. Maybe you were late to work but, by God, at least you got to work. You may not have had the most productive day, but well bloody done for getting out. Sometimes we feel like a failure, like we don't know what to do. But maybe, just maybe, you do know what's best for you. You are exactly where you should be.

> **REFLECTION:** Get yourself a chalkboard or notepad, which you can regularly go back to, and write down your purpose. Remind yourself regularly of what you have written.
>
> Go for a walk and don't plan your route, and see where you end up. Find new places in your neighbourhood you've never really seen before.
>
> **AFFIRMATION:** I was put on this earth to achieve my greatest self and to live out my purpose. I have purpose.

# chapter eight

## She learns: we're in a constant state of evolution

'You Learn'
**ALANIS MORISSETTE**

Never stop learning. Everything you do — be it good or bad — is adding pages to your inner, ever-expanding encyclopaedia. One of the best things about life is that we never have to stop moving forward until we die (sorry if that's a bit morbid). The good news away from inevitable death is there are always new skills to learn and techniques for us to adopt. It makes living fucking interesting, doesn't it?

For us to live life to the fullest, we must continually look for ways to improve and grow. As kids we are constantly like sponges, learning and absorbing. As we navigate the process of 'adulting', we must continue to inform ourselves, so we can make educated decisions.

I was clearing out some shelves in my childhood bedroom recently. Lots of old school notes and school books, old photographs and almost completed copy-books. I found a dented protractor case with my initials etched by a compass needle that had somehow survived being binned decades ago. Among the school books were my geography book and maps of the world from 1990. I distinctly remember thinking this book will be a good thing to hang on to for reference and some-thing that might come in useful as the years go by (not sure about the reasoning behind that protractor case, though).

Flipping through the maps of the world, I realised this book hadn't aged well. The world has changed so much. New borders, new counties, new curren-cies. Back in 1992, if I had learned it cover to cover, I would have aced my geography exam – now, with that same information, I would most definitely flunk it. The information was relevant to the world thirty years ago and to a specific landscape, and perhaps maybe now as a piece of historic resource; but it is not really very useful today.

But even in the few years after publication SO much changed. German unification didn't happen until October 1990, after the book went to print. In 1997 the Republic of Zaire changed its name back to the Democratic Republic of the Congo. And in 1991, the Federal Republic of Nigeria moved its capital from Lagos to Abuja. And that's just a handful among so many more.

The irony is, the dented protractor case that had a working compass in it (the protractor sadly smashed years ago, in case you're wondering) was far more useful now than the book. The world is changing and what we learn has to change too. How we see the world and our perspective must adapt and be open. We are in a state of constant flux and our brains must constantly gather new information to keep up.

In an ever-expanding world, it is not possible for a person to know everything about everything, but understanding the constant changes and the need to continue learning about the world around us will take us a step in the right direction. What we believed we knew as fact, as in that geography book, is no longer true.

From technological advances to environmental concerns, societal issues to political developments, the basics of geography, history, mathematics and English, the information out there is never-ending and changing, our learning opportunities are infinite. We should not stop learning after compulsory education ends.

## Self-development

The skills that come with learning as an adult are invaluable for all areas of life. Life can fluctuate between feeling like you have it all figured out and feeling like you know nothing at all. There are always challenges, whether it's trying to build a good career, a happy home or a better you. Fortunately, every experience (whether good or bad) ends up teaching you something. The beauty of life is that the opportunities for learning arise just when you need them the most.

If you never stop learning, you will remember that the journey and each chapter of life makes you wiser, a better version of you.

When George Floyd died needlessly and the Black Lives Matter movement took on much-needed momentum, the one thing I knew I had to do was adopt a new perspective. Re-educate myself. Information was more powerful than any weapon.

'I can't breathe' were the words George Floyd uttered with his hands handcuffed and held behind his back, as a white police officer knelt heavily on his neck, refusing to move for more than seven minutes. When the police officer finally removed his knee from George's neck, George's body was unresponsive. He was taken to a hospital where he was pronounced dead.

George Floyd was an unarmed black man. Earlier, a grocery clerk had called the police thinking George had tried to use forged currency in the store. That phone call proved to be fatal. If the police hadn't used force unlawfully, George would still be alive today.

George's death comes in the wake of a series of acts of racist violence against black Americans that illustrates astounding levels of brutality and discrimination in the USA. This includes the killing of Ahmaud Arbery, a black man who was out jogging; the killing of Breonna Taylor, a black woman who was sleeping when the police raided her apartment and opened fire on her, and so many more. The police commit human rights violations with shocking frequency, particularly against racial and ethnic minorities, and especially black Americans. In 2019 alone, the police were involved in the deaths of over a thousand people in the USA. Those aren't just numbers, but a person's life: someone's parent, sibling, cousin, nephew, spouse, child.

The officers involved in George's death have been fired from their jobs, but this cannot be considered justice. If George was white, would he still be alive? I believe yes.

But racism isn't black and white. And it's not just prevalent in one country and in one form. It's everywhere. Perhaps discrimination may be less lethal here in the UK where I am currently, but it still exists. This is not just an American issue; I'm simply using these examples because they are so extreme.

When he was president, Trump tweeted that four elected representatives, all women of colour, should 'go back' to where they came from. Despite their American citizenship, the American president stated that they should 'go back and help fix' the 'places from which they came', even though they all came from the United States.

While some news outlets called out the president as a racist, most chose not to explicitly label the comments as such, instead saying that the tweet was 'widely denounced as racist'. Once again, we were asked to consider, in hundreds of headlines and essays all over the world, 'Is the president being a racist?' It's the same debate we often have whenever anyone of importance does something or says something that demonstrates a racist idea. Coming from a journalism background it is instilled into you that you must be impartial. But you can't be impartial when it comes to racism. There is a long-standing racist idea: that people of colour are not or cannot be American or British or Irish (insert any Western country here) in the same way as white people and so should return to their 'own country'. Let's be frank, unless they are indigenous, even Americans aren't originally from America. Most white Americans came, generations back, from Germany, Britain and Ireland.

Despite this, Trump and his supporters were quick to claim that he does not 'have a racist bone in his body', another long-standing American idea: that to be racist is to have some unseen and essential character defect. Racism is not like an on or off switch. It's not something that a person either has or doesn't have that can come popping out to reveal a person's true character, a previously well-hidden flaw.

No white person wants to be revealed as racist. As a result, many of us are reluctant to label someone 'racist', preferring instead to say that we cannot truly know what is in a person's heart or mind. But when we teach ourselves to see racism for what it is – an idea that can be expressed through behaviours and cultures – we free ourselves and others to see things more accurately and with more openness to change.

There is a brilliant author called Ibram X. Kendi, who defines a racist idea as any concept that regards one racial group as inferior or superior to another racial group in any way. Racism, then, is easily defined as supporting or upholding racist ideas. Most people at some stage in their life have held a racist idea, without even realising it. You don't have to tweet like Trump or commit horrors as those police officers did to harbour racist notions yourself. Part of understanding the racism in our society as a whole is recognising how we have internalised racism without realising.

Kendi's simple definition shows a powerful way of thinking about a complicated problem, allowing us to fold multiple types of racism into a single understanding.

For example: you think a black friend might not be comfortable at a mostly white party, so you don't invite them – this is a racist idea expressing itself through a discriminatory behaviour. It might not be a racist idea that you implicitly hold, but it is still an idea that is being expressed and one that will have consequences. Scaling up and out, we can see how racist ideas are built into the rules and policies and culture we create, ensuring that white people are elevated and that other racial groups are deemed inferior.

## Rethinking What We Think We Know

Rethinking our views has a number of advantages. We need to break down institutionalised racism by learning and questioning our own beliefs. 'Everyone's a Little Bit Racist,' the song goes from the Broadway musical *Avenue Q*. We have to constantly examine what we think, how we think and WHY we think as we do.

We learn, we grow, we change. People can hold a variety of ideas about race all at the same time. We may sometimes express both racist and antiracist sentiments in the same conversation or even the same sentence. 'I'm not racist but . . .'

We can all make conflicting comments and we need to constantly better ourselves. The world is not a level playing field. Labelling someone 'racist' may not necessarily be helpful or fully accurate, but in a moment a thought can express both an antiracist ideal and a racist assumption.

To get a more accurate understanding of racism, let's look at it as an idea rather than as a trait or personality flaw. Most ideas are learned from a young age at home and in the classroom. We need to teach children about racism in school just as much as we use our protractors to show there are 180 degrees in a straight line.

Kids are pretty malleable. In just a couple of years they learn how to move, crawl, walk, run, feed themselves, speak. They even learn about the culture they live in, what's expected of them, and how to manipulate some situations to their benefit. They are like sponges for information, and they are anxious to learn how to do whatever new activities they can find. Looking through all my school notes and books my mother had kept – science books, my maps, my mathematical compass – I couldn't help but wonder (who do I think I am? Carrie Bradshaw?): maybe we learned the wrong stuff.

Continuing to learn as we get older is bloody hard. In adulthood we feel we should know everything, or maybe we think we already know enough. Sometimes we feel embarrassed that we don't know things we should. When I moved from Ireland to England, I had a wake-up call. We didn't learn the same history. And because of a seeming ignorance or a different perspective on what happened in history, bitterness and resentment can fester between nations.

'What if you ended up with an Englishman?' This was a genuine concern from an older relative before I moved to London. Ireland and England have had a tumultuous relationship considering they are such close neighbours.

In 2018 there was research commissioned by the TV channel History for the comedian Al Murray's show *Why Does Everyone Hate the English?* Murray travelled to England's nearest neighbours to try to find out why everyone seems to hate them so much. A lot was thrown up by the research, including Irish people considering the English to be arrogant, rude, that they think they know it all and they go on about the war. AND also in the top ten reasons why the Irish don't like the English – they wear socks with sandals! Yep, that one really tickled me and, personally, when it comes to footwear I'm OK with this. Don't judge me.

I'm not going to dare pretend I can speak for all 6.5-plus million Irish people, but I can give you an insight into how this one Irish person sees things. English history books miss out vital parts of Ireland's past and most Brits are unaware why the underlying resentment remains. When I lived in a house share in Camden, one of my housemates, a lawyer from Surrey, didn't know about the 1916 Easter Rising in Ireland

– I mean, why should she? She had a different history book from mine.

On 24 April 1916, Easter Monday, a group of Irish nationalists proclaimed the establishment of the Irish Republic and, along with some 1,600 followers, staged a rebellion against the British government in Ireland. The rebels seized prominent buildings in Dublin and clashed with British troops. Within a week, the insurrection had been suppressed and more than 2,000 people were dead or injured. The leaders of the rebellion were soon executed. Initially, there was little support from the Irish people for the Easter Rising; however, public opinion later shifted and the executed leaders were hailed as martyrs.

In 1921, a treaty was signed that in 1922 established the Irish Free State, which eventually became the modern-day Republic of Ireland. This accomplishment is hugely significant and celebrated by Irish people. To a lot of English folk – sorry to generalise – the Irish idea of celebration is to get intoxicated beyond function. Rather than understanding us as an oppressed country for so many years, the sense of community and partying can be seen as wasteful and frivolous instead of the uniting of a nation.

I like many English people a lot. They have welcomed me to live here. I can walk through Soho and nobody cares if I dress or sound different. As Mayor Sadiq

Khan says, 'London is open.' It's a place full of interesting people with a great sense of humour, plenty of self-deprecation and, undoubtedly, a high regard for learning. It's defined by its relative tolerance and acceptance of different views and cultures. As an Irish person, I was able to see England as a mature country fully engaged in a changing world (well, until the Brexit vote happened, although I have still to meet anyone who voted for it). A country that, despite some deeply questionable moments in its past, has become a place I admire, with an NHS system full of hard-working staff.

The problem arises when people forget about the colonies, war and dominance; people of any country who think they are exceptional and superior, because of an accident of geography, class, accent or skin colour; people who choose to remember the good bits of their country's past and whitewash the rest.

To accomplish great things in life, we have to keep learning, to see the good and bad. Keep educating each other about our past from all perspectives. Can I be angry with my housemate for not knowing something that her schoolbooks left out? Not really. As I'm sure mine left out lots of important facts too. But as adults we have the responsibility to pass on the knowledge that has been handed on to us. I have had a huge backlash for talking to a British Army soldier – a twenty-three-year-old female who I admire – about working in a male-dominated sphere. I have friends who are doctors and nurses in the army, but that doesn't mean I accept the atrocities the British Army has inflicted on many countries in the past.

It doesn't matter how smart you are or how knowledgeable you are in certain areas. You can always learn more. To assume you already know enough is to become stagnant.

If you were to interview the most successful people in the world today, there is a common denominator. They say they are always learning, always curious. Successful people seek and find people who know what they're talking about, so they can make sure to learn from them. They read books and magazines. They watch what others are doing and they ask questions. And they never assume they know everything.

READ: the internet is great, but books and magazines have fact-checkers, not to mention more legal responsibility if they print something that's incorrect. We are bombarded by fake news. Traditionally, we got our news from trusted sources, journalists and media outlets that are required to follow strict codes of practice. But the internet has enabled a whole new way to publish, share and consume information and news with very little in the way of regulation or editorial standards.

Many people now get their news from social media sites and networks and often it can be difficult to tell whether stories are true or not. Information overload and a general lack of understanding about how the internet works lead to an increase in hoax stories, misinformation and conspiracy theories.

It is your job to make sure you get your information from credible and numerous sources. Ask yourself where the information has come from, and who is behind it. Question what the intentions might be behind their words. Don't just assume what you scroll through is valid.

LISTEN: when you're with other people, especially those with skills you want to acquire, use them. Listen to them. Ask them about themselves. Ask them about their ideas. We often feel a need to broadcast information about ourselves, especially if we want to impress the other person. But if you really want to impress the person across from you, you'll do so with your ability to ask questions and listen.

Older people in the room have lived longer than you, so take advantage of their experience. Younger people tend to have a naive view of the world, which can bring a hopeful perspective. Use them too.

I love the medium of podcasts as storytelling. It feels as if you have eavesdropped on someone else's conversation. It's another learning approach. When everyone was sharing books to read during the Black Lives Matter protest, I turned to podcasts and changed my listening habits. I pushed myself to listen to new voices, to things

I didn't know about. I asked for recommendations from people I respect. Just as a child would, I observed it all. You don't have to sit in a quiet room alone with a book if that doesn't work for you. I had friends who read twenty books in a month and I found that over-whelming. We all resonate with different learning styles and practices. Find your medium. Maybe it's watching documentaries, or TED talks, that aids your learning. There is no right or wrong way to do it. Broaden how you view learning.

## No One Knows Everything

In order to grow we need to accept that no one knows everything. Even David Attenborough has his team of researchers and is constantly discovering new things about our planet. He watches, observes and shares. A smart person has no trouble admitting what he or she doesn't know. Trying to prove you know everything only cuts you off from learning more. Instead of trying to prove yourself a know-it-all, prove yourself confident enough to admit you don't know it all. The most powerful reply can be, 'I don't know.'

Reading and listening can take you far. But you also learn by doing. You can read every book on sea-life ever written, you can admit you know very little about what lies beneath the ocean, and then you can listen to every marine biologist talk about it, but none of that will make you an expert. Along with learning, you have to see it for yourself, you have to experience it. Attenborough hasn't spent his life in a voice-over booth in central London reading a pre-written manuscript. He has travelled the world. He has seen things with his own eyes, lived his own experiences.

I'll stop with the David Attenborough references now. I just really like him.

Successful people are lifelong learners. Learning can help bring you to exactly where you want to be in life, but it is also our duty to pass on the knowledge we have gathered and inform others. When we explain some-thing to other people, we come to understand it better ourselves. The process of teaching others often helps us to recognise gaps in our own understanding and to better compute the information we already have in our head.

It's OK not to have all the answers, and it's OK to be wrong. Framing the process as 'sharing what you know' gives you more leeway to feel comfortable making mistakes, changing your mind, and sharing your know-ledge in the context of your own experiences. It's been shown that first-born children usually perform better on intelligence tests than their younger brothers and sisters. This could be due to their efforts to share knowledge and experience with younger siblings. (This is the part where I point out I'm the oldest sibling and piss off my younger brothers. Can't ignore the facts, guys!)

If nothing else, pass on what you know for your own sake. Even if you have an audience of zero, start journaling, podcasting or creating videos to share the knowledge you're learning. You'll reap the benefits in your own learning progress even if no one sees.

Abraham Lincoln said, 'I do not think much of a man who is not wiser today than he was yesterday.'

I take this literally. Learning is a daily adventure that we carry and explore throughout life. If you make a commitment to yourself to learn something new every day, you will not only enjoy what you discover, but you will be able to apply your knowledge and become a teacher to future generations.

## 'Fake It Till You Make It' versus 'There Are No Stupid Questions'

In my life, I've felt I'm making a lot of it up as I go along. I've talked about 'faking it till you make it' and pretending I know what I'm doing, even though I have no idea! Realistically I am probably being too hard on myself and not giving credit where credit is due. However, I have found myself in situations where I've blagged it, afraid to ask a stupid question.

When I started hosting the live ITV aftershow for one of the biggest programmes on the telly, *I'm a Celebrity . . . Get Me Out of Here! NOW!*, I was asked if I wanted 'talkback open or switch?'. Not a fucking clue what either of them were.

'What're Ant and Dec (the main show hosts) doing?' I confidently replied to the producer.

'Switch!'

'Yeah, I'll do that.'

Took me into the next series before I fully understood what it meant and what I had asked for. 'Open' is when you can hear EVERYTHING in the gallery (the large room with people wearing headsets and with lots of screens on the wall that looks like NASA's Houston headquarters) through your earpiece, and 'switch' is when you only hear a person when they turn on a switch to talk to you. Thank God Ant and Dec don't like unnecessary distractions. It's hard enough reading an autocue when someone is counting backwards in your earpiece without having to hear people having conversations about what they want for lunch during a live recording.

But why was I afraid to simply ask the producer what the difference was? Why did I pretend I knew when I didn't? Because I didn't want to be caught out as a fraud. I already felt that way without everyone else thinking it too. But not knowing everything doesn't make you a fraud, even if you feel like one.

Just because someone may know less than others, that person should not be afraid to ask and instead pretend they already know. In many cases multiple people may not know, but are too afraid to be the one to ask the 'stupid question'. But the one who asks the question may in fact be doing a service to those around them.

The writer Carl Sagan said that while there are many kinds of questions in the world, there is no such thing as a foolish question.

He recounted a story about an old man who used to answer all a woman's 'stupid questions'. The old man explained to her that it was better to ask questions in life and look stupid for five minutes than to remain stupid for fifty years.

Asking a question when those questions have already been answered, but the asker wasn't listening or paying attention, can be embarrassing, not to speak of frustrating. But what's even more frustrating is never knowing the right answer.

A lot of people assume others know something just because they themselves already know it. If anything, I hope that, if you're ever in the position of working in television and are given an earpiece, I have helped you know the different types of talkback without even asking.

But is assuming someone doesn't know something as bad as assuming they do? Oh, this is a tricky one.

No one likes to be mansplained to. It's everywhere these days and in various forms.

**Definition: Mansplain** (v.)
(Of a man) to explain (something) to someone, typically a woman, in a manner regarded as condescending or patronising.

Mansplaining is, at its core, what occurs when someone (usually a man) talks condescendingly to someone (especially a woman) about something he has incomplete knowledge of. It accompanies the mistaken assumption that he knows more about it than the person he's talking to does.

Although 'mansplain' originally came from a LiveJournal user (thanks, Know Your Meme), no discussion of it is complete without mention of Rebecca Solnit's 2008 essay 'Men Explain Things to Me', now also the title of her 2014 collection of essays. Although Solnit didn't use the word 'mansplain' in her essay, she described what might be the most 'mansplainiest' of experiences anyone has ever had. Solnit and a friend were at a party where the host (a wealthy and imposing older man), upon learning that Solnit had recently published a book on nineteenth-century photographer Eadweard Muybridge, proceeded to tell her all about a very important book on the same photographer that had just come out. The book, of course, was Solnit's, but the man had to be interrupted several times by Solnit's friend before he'd absorbed that knowledge and added it to the knowledge he'd absorbed from reading the *New York Times* review of the book.

The 'splain' of mansplain isn't new. More could be said on this topic, but lest I be accused of explaining 'splaining', I'll stop here.

If someone, regardless of gender, doesn't know or understand something, and a man does, then by all means he should explain it! Men can absolutely, without offence, explain things to women and to other men. And women can explain things to men, and to other women, and anyone can explain anything to anyone else. Information is important! Explanations are bloody great!

I dropped my car in for a service at the garage recently. When I came back to the garage the mechanic said my vehicle was in desperate need of another maintenance service that happened to cost £350 and a part that would take six weeks to locate. When I said that I'd like to get a second opinion before proceeding, the guy rolled his eyes and laughed along with the other male mechanics as if to say, 'Stupid woman'. I felt so deflated that I got my boyfriend to go back to collect the car. He got a second opinion in another garage, and learned that 'essential maintenance' was not, in fact, essential at all and that part took a day to get. My boyfriend had an entirely different experience.

There are certain fields that are traditionally dominated by men, and there are some women out there who know a lot about those fields, and some who don't. Whatever your level of expertise may be, you are allowed to voice your questions and concerns, without being treated like an ignorant child.

Women have their vices too. They can demonstrate the opposite, and explain nothing, to their detriment.

'How are you?'

'I'm fine.'

I've been in relationships where I've assumed my partner knew more than he did about what I was thinking. SURELY he knows I'm not fine? Sometimes we expect men to just know what in our view are a few simple things about us and how we'd like to relate, but the truth is that, unless explicitly told, most men have no clue. Why should they?

As we assume men know certain things, we get ourselves stuck in bad relationships for longer than we should. Why? Because we keep expecting men to just get it. It doesn't seem that hard to us, so they should know. Right, guys?

Except they don't. Not always. And even when they do, they might not put it into practice the way we hope they will.

Because we're so attached to the idea that men should know, we hang around for longer than we ought to, waiting for something to happen – often in vain.

If we appear to have enjoyed our first date, we want men to get that we expect to be asked out again. And soon. If we seem reticent about going out with them, we expect them to get that we're not that interested.

We expect them to read us for signs that we want to go to bed with them, or for signs that we don't want to rush into anything. We want men to know we're looking for commitment, just by noticing how quickly we answer or don't answer texts, or that we don't want anything serious just by how we occasionally mention our jerk of an ex-boyfriend, with whom we broke up a few weeks ago.

We assume men know how to time perfectly every step of our relationship so that it all flows as smoothly as possible. And when they mess up, which they inevitably will because no one is psychic, we get pissed off. Two words I want you to think about and mentally keep somewhere safe.

TELL HIM.

Tell him how you feel. What you want and what you expect. The poor fella probably hasn't a clue. Life is too short to leave important words unsaid. You never know what tomorrow may bring or when you will see that person again. It's liberating to know that you left this person saying everything you wanted to say, instead of beating yourself up for letting them go without telling them what they really meant to you.

I know, I know it's embarrassing to be that honest. What if your expectations are rejected? Fuck it. It's brave to risk getting rejected and it's brave to tell someone how you feel when you're unsure of the response. It's also brave because you're not afraid to ask for what you want and you are robust enough to handle the consequences. It shows that you are both strong and mature.

When you want to understand what's happening and where things are going, it means you have standards; and it means that you respect yourself enough to walk away instead of getting played, or staying in the friend zone when you want more.

It feels great to get it off your chest and tell someone you like them and you think they're great; it feels great for them also, to know that they are liked and appreciated. Regardless of how they feel, everyone wants to hear that they are special. Consider it your good deed of the day.

## Can I Give My Brain a Break Please?

Learning is important, but we can also overconsume news and information. It's OK to give yourself permission to step away.

Yes, you can take a break from bombarding yourself. When we have a constant stream of opinions and images coming at us, we tend to forget the value of taking time to process what we've absorbed. What I like to call 'time to dream'. We may not be sure what to do with this information, or how to put it into context, and that's why we need time to digest it. It is superhuman to think that we can take in all of these stimuli and function without regularly stepping away.

In recent times (especially during the lockdown and our close relationship with the contents of the fridge), the fortunate among us have recognised the hazards of living with an overabundance of food (obesity, diabetes) and have started to change our diets. But most of us do not yet understand that news is to the mind what sugar is to the body. The media feeds us titbits that don't really concern our lives and don't require us to engage our brains. Think of this as snacking. We become so saturated with all the news, especially the bad stuff, that we cannot digest everything correctly and safely. Unlike reading books and long magazine articles (which require thinking), we can swallow limitless quantities of newsflashes, which are bright-coloured jelly babies for the mind.

There is science to explain this. News and negative headlines can trigger your limbic system. (The limbic system is a set of structures in the brain that deals with emotions and memory. It regulates autonomic or endo-crine function in response to emotional stimuli and also is involved in reinforcing behaviour – I googled this so you wouldn't have to. You're welcome.)

Panicky stories spur the release of cascades of gluco-corticoid (cortisol). This deregulates your immune system and inhibits the release of growth hormones. In other words, your body finds itself in a state of chronic stress. High glucocorticoid levels cause impaired digestion, lack of growth (cell, hair, bone), nervousness and susceptibility to infections. The other potential side-effects include fear, aggression, tunnel vision and desensitisation.

Online news has an even worse impact. As it is constant it's very hard to step away. We don't just read the morning paper any more; we are constantly being showered with news. Society needs journalism – but in a different way. Investigative journalism is always relevant. We need reporting that polices our institutions and uncovers truth. But important findings don't have to arrive in the form of aggressive news. Long journal articles and researched books are good, too.

It's OK not to watch the news every day. Unless it's your job, of course. If you're the BBC News Editor, you really should be watching the news daily.

But if you feel exhausted, depleted, overwhelmed, anxious or depressed after watching the news, you are far from alone.

In this age of constant news, what can we do to protect ourselves? Stepping away gives you the time and space you need to process what you read and also to recharge. In the end, it'll help you make more sense of the news and information. Even knowing you should step away, it can still feel impossible to take a break from Twitter or resist spending hours on Facebook. Compelling narratives, following important stories and feeling like it's our responsibility to stay informed are a few of the many reasons that keep us constantly scrolling through our Twitter feeds. Also, it's bloody difficult to resist a funny meme!

REFLECTION: Tell someone how you are feeling, and share a new piece of information you've learned. Download a new podcast or a new book.

AFFIRMATION: I'M STILL LEARNING. I don't have all the answers, but I am curious.

# chapter nine

## She is you: the future

'What lies before us and what lies behind
us are small matters compared to what
lies within us. And when you bring what is
within out into the world, miracles happen.'
**HENRY DAVID THOREAU**

Do you remember that kids' movie *The NeverEnding
Story*? It had that big furry white dragon called Falkor
that looked a bit like a giant version of my dog Mick.
Like a cuddly hound, but it could fly and had magical
powers? Sure you do! Bear with me, I have a point
coming, I promise.

Equally as memorable from the film was its
eighties hit theme tune by Limahl, 'The never-ending
storrryyyyyyyyyyyyahhhhhhhhhhhhhhahhhhhhahah'. Once

it gets in your head, it's stuck there, so apologies in advance.

Limahl had that iconic bleached-blond mullet, loved a bit of guyliner and his face is permanently displayed on the album cover of *Now That's What I Call Music!* – the first one. I know this because I have it framed on my wall of albums in my house, sandwiched between the Rolling Stones' *Exile on Main St.* and Fleetwood Mac's *Rumours*. Thinking about those *Now* albums, God knows what number they are on now. I gave up in the early noughties when they were nearing number forty.

Years later, Limahl would be a contestant on ITV's *I'm a Celebrity . . . Get Me Out of Here!*, and my spin-off show would religiously play bursts of that song every time we mentioned his name on TV. 'The never-ending sto-o-or-y-y-y-y-y . . .'. It was probably good for everyone's sanity when he was eventually voted out of the jungle and, like in a fantasy film, skipped across the rope bridge to the waiting masters of ceremony, Ant and Dec.

Anyway, I digress. Basically what I'm saying is it's a great song and the movie is just as great (if, in hindsight, somewhat dark for a children's film; though, to be fair, more realistic that some of those old Disney films – AND it had a flying dragon, which was cool).

So, in the film there's this kid called Bastian (great name) who finds a dusty old storybook when he takes refuge in a bookshop to escape the school bullies. Bastian starts reading all the adventures of the characters in the magical land called Fantasia and becomes engrossed in their exciting lives and tales of bravery. It's only when he gets to the end of the book, and the film, that he realises the narrative is around him and he is in fact the protagonist of the tale. He is the hero of the story. Not the empress he was reading about or the prince in the plot, but him, just a regular kid. It took him the whole film to realise, as sometimes it's hard to see yourself as the hero. I like this idea. I liked it then and I like it even more now.

Most of us have no idea of our own capabilities, our potential. Think about this: anything you have ever accomplished, any change you've made to improve your life, has been because you made the effort and you took action; your achievements so far, no matter how significant or insignificant, came from you . . . not someone else; you had an idea and you made it happen; you were your own real-life hero.

In any situation where you are not happy, or where you are not feeling fulfilled, ask yourself: 'What could I do to make it better? How can I save myself? How can I be my own real-life hero?' Write down your options. You might not always have many but I promise you this: there is ALWAYS something you can do to make a situation better.

You can't change everything. Progress is acknowledging that, not dwelling on it, and moving forward
with what you CAN do. Think about that guy Aron
Ralston, an American outdoorsman, mechanical engineer and motivational speaker, who is known for
surviving a canyoneering accident. That Danny Boyle
film, *127 Hours*, with James Franco, is about him.

I'm going to be honest. I never intended to watch
that film. We all know how it ends. But just in case you
completely missed it, I'll briefly explain it in as little gory
detail as I can manage. During a solo descent of Blue
John Canyon in south-eastern Utah, Ralston dislodged
a boulder, which pinned his right wrist to the canyon
wall. After five days, or 127 hours (hence the film's
name), of waiting for help, he took matters into his own
hands . . . well, hand. Using a dull pocketknife, he cut
off his crushed forearm and then made his way through
the rest of the canyon, abseiled down a 65ft drop and
hiked seven miles to safety.

As great a story as this is, I would much rather watch
flying furry dragons or Tom Hanks play piano with his
feet in a department store.

I recently filmed that television show *Gogglebox*,
where people watch you watching TV. As mundane as
it sounds on paper, it's one of my favourite programmes
and people's reactions to what they see is bloody enter-
taining. The producers decide what you watch and after

almost ten years of avoiding a film about a real man who chops his own arm off, I was forced to watch it. You can guess it's pretty uncomfortable viewing and my reactions, now immortalised in a TV show, prove this.

It's a shocking piece of film but it did make me think. Had Aron decided that there was nothing he could do, he would have died there in Blue John Canyon without a doubt. There were things he had no control over. That boulder jammed his arm and he couldn't move it. But Aron looked at what he could do instead. And he saved himself, albeit fairly gruesomely.

Most of the situations you and I find ourselves in are not as dire, thankfully. But we can get ourselves out . . . usually without cutting off a limb, praise be.

Let's explore. Pretend you have a horrible boss who makes you hate going into work (some of you probably don't have to pretend too hard). What can you do?

- Try to talk with your boss; ask them why they are treating you so badly. Talk about how they make you feel.
- Complain to HR.
- Leave your job.

Not all of the above may be an option, but look at what you can do. There is always something you can do, some way to improve or at least change the situation. Even if all YOU do is ask someone else for help. That is YOU taking action. That is YOU taking some control.

We spend a lot of time looking for other people to accept us or treat us right. We fail to see that what we seek outside us is usually already within us. We can give ourselves validation, satisfaction, permission and love. Also, when we give these things to ourselves, we are much more likely to get them from other people.

We are constantly awaiting approval and permission to be successful from others. Artists, authors, musicians and actors wait to see what the critics and reviewers say. But we live in a world where it's also possible to give ourselves permission. There's never been a greater time in history for people who are creative. We have almost free access to tools, resources and platforms.

We make the content to our own life. We can put our voice out into the world (so be careful how you choose to do so) using so much technology at our fingertips. We can communicate our feelings quicker, and we can hear a more diverse range of other people's stories. But if you aren't willing to do something until someone gives you permission, you may be waiting a long time.

Pain or pleasure, joy or misery, it all happens inside you. The mistake we often make is to always seek joy from outside ourselves. You may use outside as a stimulus or trigger, but the real thing always comes from within.

The more I've looked outside for answers about love, happiness and fulfilment, the more it has led me inward. Everything you are searching for is already inside you.

I've learned that any issues I've had with relationships in the past are a reflection of my issues with myself. If you want your boss to respect you, then you must first respect yourself. If you want a partner who understands you, you must first understand yourself.

For example, coming from a place of emotional security and self-respect reduces any temptation to get involved in a romantic relationship simply to fill in our emotional gaps. Knowing and respecting ourselves allows us to approach potential relationships from a position of wholeness and strength, rather than from a position of neediness, loneliness or desperation.

Also, possessing this kind of self-confidence will make you dramatically more appealing to the very type of person you're hoping to attract. Isn't that always the way? You find someone who makes you happy when you find the happiness inside you. If you're seeking a partner, you'll have more luck attracting a healthy and well-balanced individual – someone interested in building a real relationship. If you're already with someone, you'll be better able to see his or her strengths, and he or she will be far more likely to share them with you.

Something I've started to do, to develop my existing relationships, is to reflect an inward focus rather than an outward one. For example, instead of saying, 'I wish my boyfriend was _____' (fill in the space), you might try saying, 'I wish that I could be more _____', and seeing if that sentiment rings true in any way, or if that sort of evolution might be possible for you.

This is vital because, unconsciously, we tend to seek out characteristics and attributes in others that are as yet undeveloped in us. Most things we desire come from a wish to reduce our own insecurities, if that makes sense. We want other people to see us in a certain way. I want my boyfriend to become more organised . . . but really that comes from my own personal wish that I was more organised.

Another way to shift perspective is to take full ownership of your issues. OWN IT! If you're in a relationship where communication is challenging, instead of asking, 'How can we understand each other better?', you might ask, 'How can I understand *myself* better – so that I can take responsibility for my own shit?' Rather than ask, 'Why can't he give more to this relationship?', you might instead ask, 'Can I give that to myself instead of just demanding it from my partner?'

It can seem a bit counterintuitive to look inside for what you so obviously want from someone else. You might think, 'But I don't want to love myself, I want someone else to love me. I want someone to meet MY needs.' To be honest, I think most of us feel this way.

From a young age Disney films and fairy tales teach us that if we can just find the right person, we won't have to do anything – we can just relax and be adored unconditionally. That would be nice, wouldn't it? But would we really find that passive mindset attractive in a good friend or potential partner? Probably not.

Even Disney has caught on to this, which is why the *Frozen* franchise has done so well. It's not about Prince Charming coming to rescue the princess any more. She's got to do it for herself.

The greatest advantage to becoming the person you want to find is that, even if you do end up flying solo for a while, you'll still have many of the components of the relationship you've always desired. To feel truly validated, the only person who can validate you is YOU. (Are you sensing a theme at this stage?)

## A Note on LOVE

Love has nothing to do with someone else. It is all about you. It is a way of being. Even if you lose a loved one before their time, you are still capable of loving that person. We don't look for anything outside of ourselves as much as we do for love. We look for it from our parents, friends, romantic partners and Instagram/Twitter followers. All of the things mentioned above are really a search for reassurance that we're loved.

As someone who works on a show called *Love Island* – however superficial some might regard it as being – I can confidently assert that the programme is not about finding someone who makes the other person in question feel complete. The islanders all go in there as whole people. In the winter series, Shaughna wanted scaffolder Callum to love her, but she needed to love herself first. He wasn't ever going to be enough for her until she learned to see herself for all her worth. When he came back from Casa Amor with Molly and subsequently dumped Shaughna, Shaughna didn't lose part of herself. In fact, I think she became even more empowered, because she was no longer trying to be validated by someone who could never validate her. It was only she who could validate herself. See? We can learn SO much from a reality dating show!

The relationships that work on that show, and which have resulted in marriage and babies, are when both individuals are equally invested. We have to love ourselves as much as we seek others to love us.

We all want to be seen, heard and, above all things, loved. But we also have an expectation of what that looks like, how that love is expressed. If we choose to give love to ourselves, we can be kinder to ourselves, more open to see love.

We can't expect other people to fill our hearts or make us feel whole and complete. It doesn't matter if it's permission, validation or love. When we expect to get those things from other people, that not only puts unrealistic pressure on the situation, it's also not stable. It's just not going to last. If you have a low opinion of yourself, you will inevitably attract people who agree with that low opinion.

Searching outside of yourself for everything that's already within you allows you to avoid responsibility. If you can see that everything you're searching for outside of you is already within you, then you'll have agency over your life in a way that you never had before. No one was put on this earth to make another person happy. (Though Ryan Gosling in *Crazy, Stupid, Love* came close.)

Sorry, I lost my train of thought there . . . Damn you, Ryan Gosling.

As much as we may want to make others happy and require that they also make us happy, it is not our or their responsibility to make anyone happy. That is a fact we must cement in our brains. When we understand that our happiness is our responsibility, no one will ever have the power to make us unhappy. If you think about it, that's fucking great, isn't it? You can't hurt me if I don't allow it.

It's your duty to make yourself happy. It's a massive responsibility so don't take it lightly.

As good as delegating work is in business, we can't delegate the responsibility of making ourselves happy to the world. It's OK to ask for help, but we can't expect happiness to just fall into our lap. In this tough world, very little comes for free. Someone usually expects a reward for making you smile, laugh or be happy. The author Roy T. Bennett said, 'If you expect other people to make you happy you will be disappointed.' He's right. No one knows how to make you happy as you do.

Letting yourself be open to creating your own happiness is scary, though. I recently interviewed a performance psychologist called Dr Pippa Grange for my BBC Radio show. She wrote a book called *Fear Less: How to Win at Life Without Losing Yourself*. She also worked with the England football team, helping them to reach the World Cup semi-finals in 2018. No mean feat. Surprisingly for a book about living without fear, she talks A LOT about fear. She talks about how to find your true voice and succeed on your terms. Sounds like vital advice on our journey to becoming the hero of our own lives.

Pippa identifies two types of fear (though I could have sworn there were about a thousand!). Firstly, 'adrenaline fear' – the immediate fear when you feel you are in danger and adrenaline kicks in. Then there's the 'not good enough' fear, which I'll talk about a bit later. The first fear is that you can't control the situation. If you are confronted by a thief, you can't change the situation but you can control your reaction to protect yourself as much as possible. If someone robs you of your handbag on the street, you should remain calm to prevent physical danger.

Consider this, though. My mother was walking home from the Wexford Inn on Aungier Street in Dublin, a pub she worked in when she was younger. A man confronted her and grabbed her handbag with such force that her adrenaline fear kicked in. Instead of freezing until out of danger, my mother, the strong and stubborn Irishwoman that she is, smacked the man across the head and he dropped the bag out of shock and ran off. Go, Carmel Whitmore! I'm not saying this is the right thing to do. In fact, it's very dangerous and could have ended badly. But there's a bit of me that loves this story.

When I first moved to London I was walking through Camden, talking on my phone, and a guy on a bike pushed into me, whacked my face with his elbow and snatched my phone. I felt so vulnerable; not to mention being phoneless in a big city I'd just moved to, which made me feel even more helpless.

A few months later, I was on the phone (a new one) to my mate Claire as I came out of King's Cross train station. I could hear the wheels of a bicycle getting louder behind me. A guy reached out and grabbed my phone. I screamed: 'NOT FUCKING TODAY, PAL!' I sprinted after him as he wobbled off with only one hand on the handlebars and the other desperately clutching my phone. I ran after him for what felt like minutes but was probably only seconds and grabbed the phone back to his utter surprise and disbelief. He quickly put both hands on the handlebars and frantically pedalled away.

'Sorry, Claire. Some lad tried to rob my phone. What was I saying again . . .?' And I continued with my day.

This is another good example of adrenaline fear. I can't describe what kicked in but I was not going through another day of having no phone/reporting lost phone/getting a new phone/transferring old contacts and all the admin shit that would follow.

But this isn't the fear that I want to look at now. I want to talk about that second type of fear – the 'not good enough' fear. In this type of fear, we create the original situation ourselves. There's no villain trying to mug us. We are visualising and creating the situation in our mindset; feeling anxiety and worry because we think we are going to fail as a person and be unlovable.

Being successful isn't about trophies or beating others; it's about winning at the very deepest level: winning from within.

Pippa says: 'When fear gets hold of you, what you need to do is press pause and turn those hazard lights off. And from there you have a range of possibilities.' Think of all the times in your life when you've been up against something terrifying, and somehow managed to survive: the first day at school; the job interview; your first time leading a presentation at work. You can do so much more than you give yourself credit for.

The fear of not being good enough is exhaustingly prevalent, but it is you and only you who can overcome it.

## Find Your Power and Feed It

When I feel sad or angry, I like to vent. For me writing is my power. Most of what I write, no one sees. Writing has always been one of my places of complete openness, without judgement, because no one but me has to see it until I choose otherwise. I turn to writing when I need to find clarity and perspective.

You may find clarity elsewhere – in playing sports, yoga, painting, nature or something else. Perspective could be in feeding the hero part of yourself, helping to give your hero purpose and meaning.

I know it can feel like you can't do it alone, that you could really do with that knight in shining armour to swoop in and save the day. But, hate to break it to you, he ain't coming! You are stronger than you think. You have more answers than you know. You have super-powers – the same ones you've always had and that have served you well previously.

There have been times in my life when I honestly believed I needed help or to be given an opportunity. Like wanting someone else to get me out of a toxic relationship or praying a bigwig would get me booked for a particular job. But when it didn't come, I knew it was up to me. If I wanted something to change, I had to create that change . . . or, I had to change. Being stuck in work situations that were toxic, vocalising my concern to no avail, was tough. Being called 'cold' because I chose to stand up and not just be 'the pretty girl' can knock your confidence and make you feel helpless. But looking back, I'm fucking proud of myself. Everything that I thought had made me weaker in fact did the opposite. I am stronger for it and I know what I will and will not put up with.

Look back at your past and remember what you tell yourself about you – the stories we tell ourselves have a lot of power. We build our identity and beliefs about what's possible on the back of the stories we take as true.

In his brilliant podcast George the Poet says everything you know is a story. An idea that you've accepted, until the day you cross it out and replace it with a better answer. If you got out of a toxic situation, don't look back at the old you with judgement. Rewrite your story. It's never too late to rewrite your story.

In her book *The Art of Showing Up*, writer Rachel Wilkerson Miller talks about how the most important person you need to show up for is yourself. I love this. I waste a lot of my time running around like a headless chicken, trying to please everyone and usually pleasing no one, least of all myself. So remember to show up for yourself, particularly when shit gets hard.

Being your own hero also means calling yourself out (kindly but fairly). Call out your own bullshit when necessary. Notice when you don't apply for that job you want or message that person you like for fear of rejection. The part of you that wants the best for you won't put up with self-defeating or soul-draining speech and habits any more. Being your own hero means showing yourself real love, by developing your own values and staying true to any commitments you've made to yourself.

Do what you say you're going to do and feel proud of yourself. In the end, heroes are all about showing intention, consistency and compassion.

Heroes have always faced pain and struggles in their past, and all have their weaknesses. Realistically, being your own hero is about being your own friend. It's about choosing to rise from experiences and live each day compassionately. If you complain about something more than twice, you're obliged to try to find a solution. Deflecting blame, shirking responsibility, won't cut it.

Sometimes we just need a metaphorical kick up the backside and to take responsibility for every single thing in our lives, regardless of who we think put us in that situation. Instead of powerless, we suddenly feel motivated.

The brilliant thinker Don Miguel Ruiz looks at the process of 'domestication' in his book, *The Four Agreements.* When you are a child, the people who take care of you teach you what they know, how they perceive the world, and most of that knowledge isn't the exact truth. Believing in lies (or a *distortion* of the truth) leads you to limitations in your life, to needless suffering and drama. In human domestication, you don't have the opportunity to choose your beliefs. All the rules and values of your family and society are imposed on you. Just like a computer, all that information is downloaded into your head. Finding your own truth, separate from what you've been 'domesticated' to believe, leads you to your authenticity, to happiness.

We form an image of what perfection is in order to fit in. We create an image of how we 'should' be in order to be accepted by everybody, but we need to determine what we should question.

There are many things in life you have zero control over. You can't force your husband to change, you can't prevent a storm from happening, and you can't control how other people feel. All you can control is your effort and your attitude and your truth. When you put your energy into the things you can control, you'll be much more effective.

You can't force things to go your way, but believe me you can have a strong influence. So while you can't make your kid be good at school, you can give him or her the tools they need to do their best. And while you can't force people to have fun at a party, you can create the best party atmosphere possible.

## Choose Your Tribe

You can't choose your family but you can choose your tribe. The people who let you be the real you.

The people who have held your hair back as you lay with your head against a toilet bowl and retched your brains out. These are the people we need to have around us. I went to Thailand with a group of girlfriends a few years ago and we all ended up with the shits. Too much curry and not enough Imodium. One unworkable toilet in Koh Samet, sleeping on a floor in a hostel and being eaten alive by mosquitoes with no mosquito net is not fun, but it is bonding. You share that experience with anyone and you can get through any shit (metaphorically speaking) together.

It's great to have a loved one, someone to share your life with, but it's our mates who've more than likely helped us cope with that 'love of our life'. My friend broke up with her boyfriend after she found out he had sent very inappropriate messages to another woman. (Who knew people sent 'dickpics' in real life?) Nevertheless, she was very sad and missed him, though the emotion was over-ridden by sheer undiluted anger and hatred. I told her she shouldn't text him. Of course, she did.

She knew she shouldn't, but sanity can go out the window for 'a woman scorned'. So what we decided was that every time she felt the urge to text him, she would text me instead. Every bit of anger or rant she felt she needed to get off her chest would be typed out, but sent to me; like the contemporary version of writing and burning a letter before you actually post it.

I did have an interesting inbox at the time, and had to be careful I didn't have my phone out in public. No one wants a notification saying, 'You don't even have a decent penis!' popping up on their screen during a very important meeting.

I have two other friends, Stephen and Denis, and we don't see each other much but we check in weekly and keep fuelling each other when we can. In order to create fire, you need oxygen, fuel and a spark, so to be empowered you must make sure you are providing your-self with what you need. Every Sunday Denis, Stephen and I do a video chat no matter where we are and talk about our purpose and goals. They fuel me.

One night I was chatting to Stephen about what I was doing in life (a recurring thought for most people,

I assume). I was thinking, perhaps 'overthinking', about the difficulties of relationships in this industry, and in everyone's life – no matter what you do. It's hard to remain constant in a world of instability. But just maybe, as Stephen said, 'we are your constant – and you are mine'.

You have the power to surround yourself with people who fuel your superpowers.

If someone, even a friend, is constantly holding you back or making you feel like you're not good enough, get rid of them.

Regardless of any situation or who you have around you, always know that you are your source of your emotions. You decide who is deserving of your time and friendship. It is your strength that will guide you to where you need to be.

Just like that young lad in *The NeverEnding Story*, we don't actually know how strong we are until we face up to challenges. Rather than wait for life to inevitably test us with hardships, we can save ourselves a lot of time and pain by learning to be our own hero, in good times as well as bad.

However mistake-riddled, dirty and stained life might feel, start by owning where you're at and acknowledging the choices that helped get you there. It's the way to begin to make better choices to help you reach your full capability.

Once you admit your weaknesses and mistakes in a kind way (I know that when admitting our failures to ourselves we can often do so in a very aggressive way, but that is never helpful), you can move on from them rather than being stuck. When you try to help another person you probably don't start by launching into a diatribe at them, citing everything they've done wrong or aren't good at. They wouldn't find that very supportive. So why would you?

We speak harshly to ourselves in our own minds, despite it being the worst thing we can do for self-growth. Being your own hero means stepping in, at the point when critical self-talk and negative spirals of thinking are starting up in your head.

It means standing up for yourself to yourself. I'm not saying you should start talking to yourself in public or have full-blown arguments with a mirror. Focus on what you *can* do, not what you can't. The hero in you isn't going to stand for any more self-bullying. What will make you a hero is not what you can't control or what has happened to you, but how you respond; and the meaning you draw from things that have happened to you in your life.

Your stories of losses and failures can become inspirational reminders to you of your resilience. Focus on the strengths and wisdom that have grown in you through the difficulties you've faced. Becoming a hero is reframing adversities you've confronted as battles you've survived.

You don't need a suit of armour to be a hero. In fact, being exposed and vulnerable takes more guts.

Everything you're searching for is within you. As a culture, we constantly look outside of ourselves for answers. We read self-help books thinking they will give us the answer. I love self-help books, not because they have the answers but because they usually trigger something inside me that 'helps' the 'self' I already am. I can't tell you what to do, but you have made the decision to read this book. It's for you to decide what to do with what I've written.

As Wilson Phillips sing in their song 'Hold On', 'No one can change your life except for you.'

Life won't stand still so neither should you. You want something, go get it. Your life is your story and you get to write it. And, while writing it, make it the best story it can be – even if it doesn't have a flying dog or an eighties theme tune. It's a great story because you have the privilege of living it. And it is your choice, and only yours, to live happily ever after.

REFLECTION: Write out the things in your life you want to change. Then brainstorm each 'problem' you've identified with solutions you can make.

AFFIRMATION: 'I am the hero of my own life.'

# acknowledgements

This book is a part of me. It's my blood, sweat and tears (but don't worry, not literally, that would be gross). To get to here, though, I've been supported by so many wonderful people.

Firstly, Mum, thanks for getting me that Wilson Phillips cassette and being the kick-ass woman you are. Dad, thanks for believing in my potential for success, even if I didn't always believe myself.

To Iain, or as I like to say, Eeeeeeennnnnnn! Thanks for always being a ray of sunshine even on my dark days. Your zest for life is infectious. Thanks for cooking dinner and supplying me with mugs of tea when I've been stuck to deadlines. Now I know how good a cook you are, there's no getting out of it. You are the best person I know. And I know a lot of great people. I love you.

# Acknowledgements

To Alex Fisher, Richard Thompson and everyone at Merlin. We bloody did it! We made this book happen. It's been a journey and I can't wait to see where the adventure leads us to next. Thanks to Jamie Scallion for reading the very first draft in its raw state, and Jakki Jones and Nikki Dupin for bringing the book to life through your art. You all rock!

To all my friends and family. I am truly blessed to have such a strong tribe around me. From the Bray lot, to the DCU lot, to the London lot and all the lots between. Your friendship, support network and constant advice will never be taken for granted. Thank you.

To Pippa Wright and everyone at Orion Spring. Considering I've written so many words, there aren't enough to express my gratitude. Thank you. Pippa, you cycled during a lockdown for a socially distanced meeting in a freezing park – your dedication and brilliance are inspiring.

To Mick, thank you for keeping me company during all of this, and for those much-needed walks to the park when I needed a break from the computer screen. I probably should also thank Gail's coffee, Ben & Jerry's, Häagen-Dazs and all the multiple brands of ice cream and treats I scoffed and ploughed my way through while writing this. I hope this book sells as I've already spent the advance on snacks.

To everyone who has messaged me and contacted me. I see you and I thank you.

# credits

The author and Orion Spring would like to thank everyone at Orion who worked on the publication of *No One Can Change Your Life Except for You.*

**Agent**
Alex Fisher, M&C
Saatchi Merlin

**Editor**
Pippa Wright

**Copy-editor**
Loz Jerram

**Proofreader**
Linden Lawson

**Editorial Management**
Rosie Pearce
Jane Hughes
Claire Boyle

**Audio**
Paul Stark
Amber Bates

# Credits

**Contracts**
Anne Goddard
Jake Alderson

**Design**
Lucie Stericker
Joanna Ridley
Debbie Holmes
Nikki Dupin
Clare Sivell
Helen Ewing
Jakki Jones

**Finance**
Jennifer Muchan
Jasdip Nandra
Rabale Mustafa
Afeera Ahmed
Ibukun Ademefun
Sue Baker
Tom Costello

**Production**
Nicole Abel
Fiona McIntosh

**Marketing**
Folayemi Adebayo

**Publicity**
Francesca Pearce

**Sales**
Jennifer Wilson
Victoria Laws
Esther Waters
Frances Doyle
Ben Goddard
Georgina Cutler
Jack Hallam
Ellie Kyrke-Smith
Inês Figuiera
Barbara Ronan
Rachael Jones
Andrew Hally
Dominic Smith
Deborah Deyong
Lauren Buck
Maggy Park
Linda McGregor
Sinead White
Jemimah James

Jack Dennison
Nigel Andrews
Ian Williamson
Julia Benson
Declan Kyle
Robert Mackenzie
Megan Smith
Charlotte Clay
Rebecca Cobbold

**Operations**
Jo Jacobs
Helen Gibbs
Sharon Willis

Lucy Brem
Sneha Wharton
Steven Dennant
Lucy Olley
Rochelle Dowden-Lord
Isobel Sheene

**Rights**
Susan Howe
Richard King
Krystyna Kujawinska
Jessica Purdue
Louise Henderson

# Help us make the next generation of readers

We – both author and publisher – hope you enjoyed this book. We believe that you can become a reader at any time in your life, but we'd love your help to give the next generation a head start.

Did you know that 9 per cent of children don't have a book of their own in their home, rising to 13 per cent in disadvantaged families*? We'd like to try to change that by asking you to consider the role you could play in helping to build readers of the future.

We'd love you to think of sharing, borrowing, reading, buying or talking about a book with a child in your life and spreading the love of reading. We want to make sure the next generation continue to have access to books, wherever they come from.

And if you would like to consider donating to charities that help fund literacy projects, find out more at **www.literacytrust.org.uk** and **www.booktrust.org.uk**.

THANK YOU

*As reported by the National Literacy Trust